THE DIARISTS and THE DIARIES

Robert Scott Yule [1906- 1982]
prior to leaving for Australia.
From family collection.

Anne Copland Yule (née Brown)
[1912-2002] in July 1931. Portrait by
Elsmore of Glasgow in Family Collection.

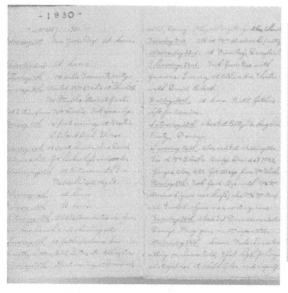

Scan of 2 pages from January 1930

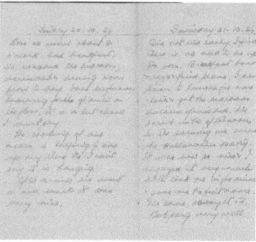

Scan of 2 pages from October 1936
Note: "Bob sang very well"

OTHER TIMES - OTHER PLACES

The travels and travails of two young Scots in the 1930's

By

Donald Yule

"All diarists, even the most humble, must somewhere along the line be convinced that their own experiences are somehow remarkable"
Ruth A Symes

First published 2019

ISBN 978 1 78723 285 3

British Library Cataloguing

A catalogue record for this book is available from the British Library

Printed and published under the auspices of CompletelyNovel
www.completelynovel.com who designed and hold the copyright for the cover based on an aquatint of TS *Duchess of Argyll.*
Typeset in Baskerville Old Face and Tahoma by the author
Maps on pp ix – xii are ©2019 JET Documentations Services www.jetdoc.co.uk

DEDICATION

This book is dedicated to the memory of Susan Elizabeth Hadfield (1950 -2018) who so loved books and inspired its preparation but did not live to see its completion.

This book has been written especially for Finlay, Oliver, Edie and Phoebe hoping that, when they read it, they will see they are part of a tradition and will keep its memory bright.

SKETCHES by R S YULE

Original sketches measure full 18cm x13cms unless otherwise noted

Ref	Title	Type	Detail
1	Harbour Entrance Tarbert 1926	Landscape	Date added later
2	The Castle Tarbert 1926	Building	Freehand
3	The Chopping Down from the Camp, Kanegarup, Kojonup, W. Australia July 1930	Landscape	With border 15.5 cm x 10cm
4	The Camp, Kanegarup, Kojonup W. Australia July 1930	Landscape	Picture of the hut. Figure in doorway. 15 cm x 10 cm
5	At Camp, Katanning W. Australia Aug 1930	Landscape	Tent + figure over camp fire. 15.5x10cm
6*	Stirling Ranges from Katanning Dam Oct 1930	Landscape	14 cm x 10 cm
7	"The Pines", Piesse St., Katanning Dec 1930	Building	Exterior of bungalow 17 cm x 12 cm
8	"Shadows of the evening" At "The Pines" Katanning West Australia Jan 1931	Interior	Shadows on veranda 15 x 11 cm
9*	War Memorial Perth West Australia Feb 1931	Exterior	Freehand
10	Freemantle from RMS Orsova 23-2-31 8 pm	Nightscape+ town lights	With border 16 x 8 cm
11*	Sighting Ceylon 4-3-31 7am	Seascape + ship's detail	With border 16 x 11cm
12	Glasgow Central Station Steeple from 175 Hope Street Aug 1931	Cityscape	With border 10.5cm x 16 cm
13	King George V Bridge GLASGOW Aug 1931	River scene	1 cm bottom margin
14	Base of Cotton Tree Masaboin Hill Marampa Sierra Leone Jan 1932	Jungle scene	With border 16.5 x 11 cm
15	Freetown Sierra Leone 1932	View from harbour	With border 15.5 x 8.5 cm
16	Moonlight on Port Loko Creek – Pepel Sierra Leone Feb 1932	Nightscape	With border 16 x 11.5 cm
17	Las Palmas – (evening) Oct 1932	Nightscape +ship detail	With border 15 cm x 10 cm
18	Constructing Loading Bank MARAMPA Nov 1932	Landscape	With border 15 cm x 11 cm
19	SS Wilston 28/5/35	Deck from bridge	With border 10.5x13cm
20	Near Frodsham 14-4-46	Landscape	Freehand

The above is the list of scanned copies of sketches by R S Yule.
*indicates not included in this book

CONTENTS

ILLUSTRATIONS

Images reproduced elsewhere

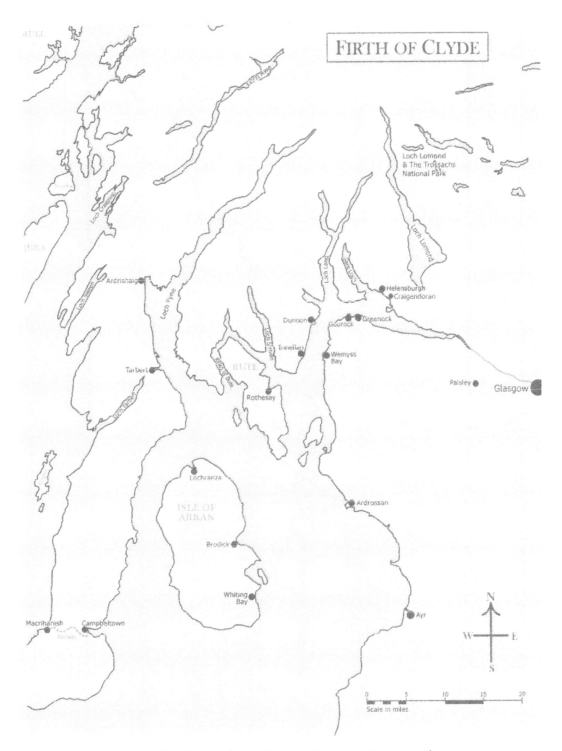

MAP 1 The Firth of Clyde showing locations in the text.
Map provided by courtesy of JET Documentation Services

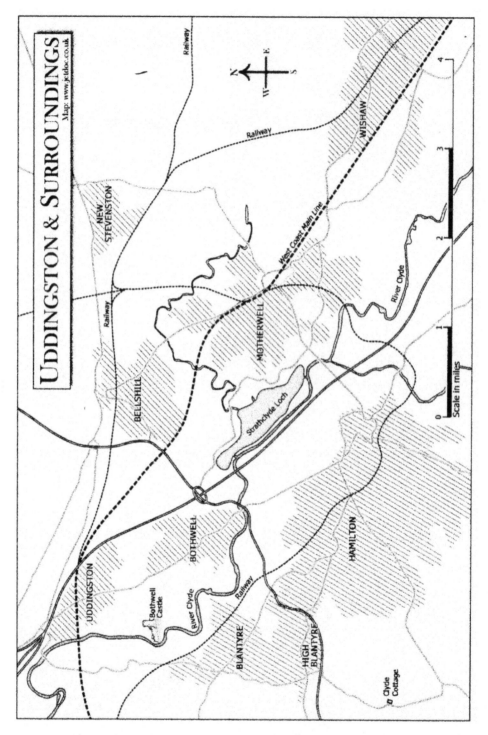

MAP 2 The region around Uddingston showing locations in the text.
Map provided by courtesy of JET Documentation Services

If you are Australian, you are probably quite familiar with MAP 3 ...

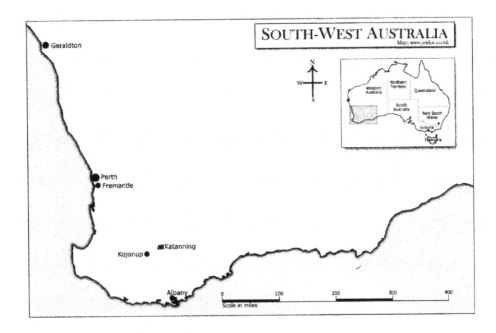

Map provided by courtesy of JET Documentation Services

.. but probably have not seen Dad's photos from November 1930 of Austral Terrace, Katanning [below left] and [below right] the busy Katanning railway sidings with a 3ft 6 in, gauge engine identified from the works of the celebrated O S Nock as a Western Australian Government Railways Class P Express Goods Locomotive. [Family Collection]

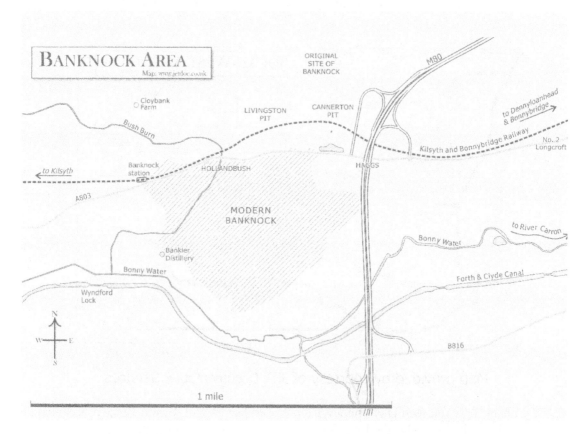

MAP 4 The Banknock area showing locations in the text.
Map provided by courtesy of JET Documentation Services

The picture below shows the Doubs Burn [in the map above called the "Bush Burn" the name by

which Mum knew it] pictured by the author from the A803 bridge in Banknock in the first decade of the 21ˢᵗ century with the former establishment of the Browns to the left. This wee burn was flowing down the brae when Charles Edward Stewart's army passed by on their way to the Battle of Falkirk Muir in January 1746; it made legal history in 1895 when a test case on the use of its water established that owners of upstream riparian rights may not prejudice the rights of those downstream; in its time its course has been a boundary between ecclesiastical and civil parishes; it flowed throughout all the years covered in this book and it seems likely that its water will gurgle on down to the Bonny Water, the Carron, the Forth and the North Sea long after this book and its author are forgotten

AUTHOR'S PREFACE

What this book is about ..

The *Other Times,* as my subtitle suggests, are the 1930's – specifically 1931 to 1937 -but, to get to the start point of the diaries, this book looks at prior years. The *Other Places* are Western Australia and Sierra Leone but the vanished industrial scenes of central Scotland in the early 20th century which feature here now seem like an "Other Place". The Young Scots – as they were then – are my Dad and my Mum: Robert Scott Yule [1906 -82] and Anne Copland Yule née Brown [1912 - 2002], a Mining Engineer and a Civil Servant respectively. This book is built around my transcription of the diaries they both kept in those Other Times recording their travels to Other Places and ensuing travails.

.. why I wrote it ..

On being entrusted with the safekeeping of the diaries, I was urged by friends and family members around the globe to transcribe them into a digital record for the benefit of succeeding generations. I am a retired Charity Accountant, not an author or historian, but, when I finally began this task in January 2016, it quickly became clear that producing mere transcriptions would be to provide merely "incomplete records" - as there was quite a tale to tell.

.. and why I set it out his way.

Accordingly, I researched the background of both stories and, bearing in mind the target readership on the "Dedication" page, have added my commentaries and some illustrative material – which includes Dad's sketches never previously published - with the aim of providing a rounded picture for the reader in the 21st century. There are, of course, two diaries: thus, the book is arranged in two Volumes with a "bridge" between the two. In the manner of all the learned tomes I have on my shelves, I have added explanations or comments in the form of footnotes. I know these are not currently fashionable, but I felt the reader would want the explanation at hand rather than flicking ahead and, also, the modern screen user is used to a multi-facet aspect. Where I felt there was too much extra information to fit in a footnote, or that the reader's curiosity might have been aroused, I have added an Appendix and make no excuse for the large number of these. I also taken this opportunity to publish some related family material and (selfishly perhaps) air my thoughts on my Great Uncle Hugh Scott and the Battle of Loos, 1915. This is *not* a "Family History", so there are no genealogical tables but, as some names of family members in the narrative are confusingly similar, I added some notes [Appendix 0] to help the reader. I have tried to maintain a narrative thread throughout but, of course, the reader is free to jump right now to the diary transcriptions and hear the authentic voice of the 1930's presenting a picture which is not blurred by fading memory or nostalgia.

The images

In building this book around transcriptions, a great deal more than just Diary entries have been included. In selecting images to illustrate people and places mentioned in the text, my policy was to prioritise items which were the work of the Diarists or their families or contemporaries. This means that much of what is included is not the work of professionals – and that includes the author! I hope that hours of scanning and enhancing faded, torn or blemished family snaps has resulted in images which are sufficiently clear to fit my purpose. Throughout, I have denoted them as part of a "Family Collection" and anyone wishing to make further use of any, may do so with the credit "From the collection of Andrew Donald Yule and Family". Scanned, professionally produced illustrations are also included and their provenance, where it has been possible to ascertain, has been cited throughout. Family, friends and contacts around the world offered illustrative contributions which have been included as space permits and I apologise to those whose offerings were precluded by the need to keep the size of this publication within reasonable bounds.

The sketches

Dad was perhaps more eloquent with the pencil and Sketch Book than with his Diary entries, so wherever appropriate, I have included his work. The 17 sketches I have scanned and reproduced are here on the grounds of their relevance rather than artistic merit. A well-qualified judge of such matters has opined that Dad "drew what he saw" and probably had not been taught the art of Composition. That would seem to reflect the fact that Dad had passed exams in Engineering Drawing and probably his most appreciated work is his line drawing where he shows the meticulous attention to detail one would expect from an engineer trained at Glasgow's Royal Technical College. Some of the sketches make pleasing framed pictures and my kinfolk and I are prepared to transmit electronically a scan of the original in return for evidence of a substantial charity donation. Please see the available list on p vi and contact me at donyule@the-pres.org.uk.

The text

What appears here then, is not a continuous narrative, it is more a of patchwork of writings of the Diarists, the author, quotations and recalled anecdotes. The framework of the story of Mum and Dad has of course been their written work but to this was added information obtained from the Statutory Certificates - Birth, Marriages, Death - freely available to the public, Valuation Rolls, Passenger Lists, newspaper archives, all now accessible through internet sites. Cladding that skeleton is my own original writing, based on educated surmise and recalled anecdote – far cry from the Report and Accounts of my professional career!

The Serious Student

This is not a learned treatise but there is plenty of previously unpublished information here which just might be of interest to a researcher and I am happy to help any project. Anyone wishing to quote my original text or use one of my images for educational or non-commercial purposes is free to do so without further ado. Anyone wanting to borrow a substantial amount of content or wishing to correct me regarding fact or challenge an assumption should contact me at donyule@the-pres.org.uk.

Now read on – as much as you choose *[but DO read pages 196 to 200]*

You will not find herein any deep insight into the human condition, first- hand accounts of world-shattering events or celebrity scandal; neither does this work reveal any skeletons in the family cupboard nor attempt to settle old scores. What you get is a guided tour of a glimpse -*and a unique one* - into the lives and the world of two quite ordinary young Scots who became my Mum and Dad.

DONALD YULE
St Leonard's on Sea
East Sussex
April 2019

AUTHOR'S THANKS

This work would never have come about without the help of many others. So, I must thank the following:

First, my kinfolk and old pals

My sister, Esther Margaret Lyons and her husband Alan of Stockton Heath Warrington, for her safekeeping of Mum's Diary and her other works and family photos and memorabilia;
My nephew, Steven Scott Dandy and his wife Jayne also of Warrington for doing likewise with Dad's Diary;
My cousin Alexander Andrew ["Sandy"] Arneil and his wife Marlyn of Laurieston, Falkirk, for looking after family snaps and postcards of the Browns and for checking that my memory of Hollandbush was not at fault;
My cousin Roberta Scott Yule of Glasgow, for filling in details of her father, Dad's younger brother, Alex Yule, and for her welcome on my research trip to Scotland in 2017
My second cousin, Beverley Scott of Palmyra WA whose monumental work on the Scott family was my inspiration. Her detailed knowledge of Bella Yule's family was of great help and her pilgrimage to Great Uncle Hugh's grave rectified a serious omission on the part of my family. Additionally, she helped with her research work in Western Australia which

included talking to the late Mary Wright, one of the very few left who remembered Dad in Katanning

My old pal Neb Peberdy of Droitwich, Worcs., co-author of *Droitwich Through Time* [Amberley 2014] whose work led me into the world of "Then and Now" photographs

My old pal John Lovesey of Kings Norton, Birmingham who ran his well-qualified critical artist's eye over Dad's sketches.

All my pals at Warrington, Rosslyn Park, Hastings & Bexhill Rugby Clubs and Middlesex County Cricket Club for putting up with my obsessive behaviour over these writing years.

A host of others

Obviously without these contributions this work would not exist! However, a great many more persons and organisations made telling contributions over the years it took to research and compile the book. I must mention:

Staff of Mitchell Library for helping me to locate 175 Hope Street

St. James Place Wealth Management Glasgow Office for access to the Hope Street scene in 2017

Katie Stewart of Falkirk Archives for helping me select illustrations and, similarly, Hannah Henthorn at North Lanark Heritage Centre

All the dedicated Archive staff at Glasgow University Archives

David Bell and his team of volunteers at the splendid National Mining Museum Scotland

Irene Doyle and Arthur Todd in Katanning WA

Joan O'Halloran and family and Angus Warburton (jun.) and other folk in Kojonup WA

Helen Ashby OBE and the Friends of the Sierra Leone National Railway Museum

Anne Larg and Linda Hendry, Church Secretary and parishioner respectively in Dunbarney and Forgandenny Parish for help with the background of Rev. David Mailler Yule.

Jim Penman at Cloybank for updating my Banknock knowledge

Jim Summers and the experts of the Caledonian Railway Association for ensuring I did not perpetuate any myths or misconceptions regarding their specialist subject

Jessica at Completely Novel for guiding a newcomer and Jane Teather of JET Documentation Services for contributing the high- quality maps

Finally, thanks to Jodie and Corinna of Carrianne Care, Hastings and their staff: Emily, Danny, Donna, Jo, Lisa, Natasha, Sarah and to Emily and Glynis and the Beaufort Court Staff who kept me safe and well during the years it took to patch this work together.

ADY

VOLUME ONE

Dad's Diary 1930-1931

Author's Note: What you will find here.

This part of the book centres on the Diary Dad kept on his travel to Western Australia, his life there and his return to Scotland and I have split the transcript into three parts which record each of those very different phases in his life. In 1931, Dad was on his travels again, to West Africa this time, and made additional entries which I have described as a "Coda".

I have written a detailed "Introduction" explaining the background of the Diarist and the illustrations selected to cover that follow before we look at the Diary.

I start with some General comments and have written a Commentary on each part of the Australian saga and the selected illustrations follow. Thereafter come the Coda with a Commentary followed by a bridging passage which takes us from the last of Dad's entries to the start of Volume Two. This latter part I have titled "Intermezzo" and the third set of illustrations covers that and the Coda.

Australia Bound: Dad and travelling companions
-probably the Fairbrother and Roach families -
Pictured at Port Said 12 II 1930.
[Family Collection]

INTRODUCTION to VOLUME ONE

To begin at the beginning ...; Yules and Scotts; Mining Folk; Uddingston; A built-up environment; Doon The Watter; Rails and Bails; A wee laddie & a wider world; A Little Learning ...; ... and other Accomplishments; Denny; The Eldest Brother; The Uncle; The first move; A plan unfolds

To begin at the beginning ...

. is not easy as the new reader of these entries cannot possibly be party to those events which led to Dad catching the Alexander's bus from Denny at 8.10 am on the morning of 31ˢᵗ January 1930. Even then, that is not the start as Dad had clearly decided that this was to be a momentous year in his life and began his recording at the start of the year when he was preparing to emigrate and, in effect, leave Scotland forever. So, let us look at Dad's family, and his background- as succinctly as suitable - and try to determine the reasons behind that momentous decision.

Yules and Scotts

Despite Dad's lifelong identification with the wee town – or "village" as its inhabitants like to call it – his parents, though Lanarkshire folk, were not Uddingston born. His father, John Crawford Yule, a Mining Engineer [but not an underground worker]and son of a Mining Engineer, was born in Lesmahagow in 1870, in 1899 married Isabella ("Bella") Scott, born in Carluke 1872, eldest daughter of John Train Scott [1847-1924] and Isabella Kay Smith [1849 -1935]. After a brief spell in Cathcart, south Glasgow, where their eldest son, David Mailler Yule, was born in 1900 and they began their married life proper at Clyde Cottage, Auchentibber, High Blantyre, Lanarkshire. This is a surprisingly rural location, [See map 2] and it was where the next two sons were born: John Train Scott Yule (1902) and William Yule (1904). They then moved – probably for logistic reasons and perhaps for Bella to be near her mother at No 11 Kyle Park -about 3 miles to the north in the Clyde Valley, to 1 Cresswell Terrace in Uddingston which is Dad's birthplace and, now much restored looks a very desirable address. [See Illustrations Set1] The 1911 Census shows them at 3 Church Street, in the centre of Uddingston and well placed for the expanding tramway network [Uddingston was to be connected to both Glasgow Corporation and Lanarkshire Tramways systems], where, in 1912, Alexander Yule [Crawford was added later] was to be the last addition the family.

Mining Folk

The 1881 Census shows the "The Scott Grandparents", John Train Scott & Isabella living at 12 Merry's Rows, Blantyre and we can find an official description of their environment from a Royal Commission Report [This one sourced from the Scottish Mining website www.scottishmining.co.uk]

We visited these two rows of miners' houses on 24th March 1913. They are situated near to the Glasgow Road, in the Parish of Blantyre, and are owned by Merry & Cunninghame, coalmasters. They consist of 46 single- and 50 double-apartment houses. They are built with brick, and were erected between thirty and forty years ago, and are a very poor type of house, low-ceilinged and mostly damp. The rent per week, including rates, is 2s. 4d. and 2s. 11d. for single and double houses respectively. Within the last five years this property has been included in a special scavenging district, and consequently the sanitation of the place has been very much improved. The water is supplied by means of stand-pipes at intervals along the front of the row. There are no sculleries or sinks about the place, and all the dirty water is emptied into an open gutter. There is a washhouse to every six tenants, and a flush-closet to every three tenants. Bins are in vogue, with a daily collection of refuse. No coal-cellars or drying-greens. A man is kept for tidying up the place. [Evidence presented to Royal Commission, 25th March 1914]

Bella was in far superior surroundings in Uddingston.

Uddingston

Uddingston in the 21st century is probably recognised as the home of Tunnock's bakery, famous today for its caramel wafers and tea cakes but a small family firm in Dad's day providing the then staples of Scottish life: pies and morning rolls. Cricket buffs might recognise the name as a venue for A-list international cricket and travellers on the West Coast Main Line might have spotted the station or speeding motorists glimpsed directional signs. Connoisseurs of the ghoulish may remember it as the site of some of mass murderer Peter Manuel's killings in the 1950's. but otherwise, it seems to be a place largely bypassed by the mainstream of Scottish history and so deserves some description here.

Readers from outside UK shores thinking of Scots place names full of guttural "ch's" might be as surprised as Dad was later horrified on finding out that it is an **ENGLISH** place name. To be accurate it is "Early English" or "Anglo Saxon"[1] marking the fact that speakers of the Germanic tongue from which the Scots language is derived, found their way to the banks of the Clyde from Northumbria sometime in the first millennium AD and found a site suitable for a farming family. As the Yules later became a farming family, this seems appropriate! [Ignore any suggestion that it is "Baile Uddin" a recent invention during the fad of giving invented Gaelic names to southern locations.]

A built- up environment

The photos in the Victorian postcards emphasise the pleasant environs and the handsome appearance of Main Street but off- screen, the picture in the years of the Yules and Scotts was somewhat different. This is not "Lochs and Glens" Scotland. Today it is a land of

1 See Sources

urban sprawl, trading estates and a network of roads and motorways. When the Yules and the Scotts were in Uddingston, it was a land of coalmines, steelworks, heavy engineering factories and a network of railways.

This might seem to be dull, drab, smoke-laden and dispiriting world to grow up in but in fact it seems to have been the opposite for Dad. An industrial community is a vibrant one, so with massive steam powered plant and machinery all around, the novelty of the street tramways and the expresses of the Caledonian Railway thundering through the village this was a stimulating environment.

But one is never far from the countryside in central Scotland and having a river, the Clyde still in moorland stream mode, running by the village and the ivy-clad ruins of Bothwell Castle [See Illustrations Set 1] nearby for youngsters in that unsupervised era meant that adventure was part of Dad's young life. Fishing for minnows, wild swimming and, when in his teens, he met up with a pal, Alan Blanner, even canoeing, suggest that this was in no way a deprived childhood. For an adventurous boy, the presence of the local Boy Scout troop was just the thing and the annual Scout Camp in the Campsie Fells – hills that on a clear day could be seen from Uddingston - or in Tarbert, Loch Fyne - gave him all the experience of living an open-air life which was to prove so valuable later in Australia.

Doon The Watter

Acres of prose have been written about "The Clyde" and the propensity of Glaswegians to enjoy to the full their neighbouring coastal resorts - "Doon the Watter" is still the local expression for such a trip. This is not the place to make significant additions, to the literature, but the river and its estuary played an important in Dad's life, so some note must be made about both. Any reference work or website will provide data, so this is a summary: The Clyde's headwaters are in the Lowther Hills from whence it commences an easterly course before swinging northwards as an upland stream. Rejuvenating over falls near Lanark but not significantly gaining in size, the river follows a north-westerly course through traditional Lanarkshire towards Glasgow. There it enters a westerly- flowing second phase, having been canalized, spawning industrial communities on both banks as far as its v-shaped estuary which brings it to its third phase – the Firth. "Firth" is a word of Scandinavian origin which has not really travelled beyond Scotland and may be taken to represent any stretch of water – strait, inlet or estuary – where a harbour or harbours may be found. A glance at the map will show that this is indeed true of the north-south aligned fjord system which constitutes the Firth of Clyde. With its mixture of lowland and highland scenery, open waters and long fjords, and a pattern of islands it is a holidaymakers' paradise – provided always the holidaymaker is prepared to come to terms with the weather of south west Scotland! This was all on the doorstep of the Yules, reachable directly from a wharf in central Glasgow - the Broomielaw - or by train to Gourock, Wemyss Bay or Ardrossan; local facilities they made full use of. That use was in the form both of day trips and holidays where the destinations might be the fishing village of Tarbert on Loch Fyne or the Arran villages of Whiting Bay or Lochranza. There are excellent contemporary illustrations of the island villages and their steamer services in Andrew Clark's 2015 **Steamers to Arran** [See Sources and Further Reading]

John Crawford Yule may not necessarily have been with them all the time, [though it was possible to commute by steamer and train from Arran to Glasgow Central Station in less than an hour and a half] but we know from one of Dad's many annotations that his mother took the boys a sail to Campbeltown, presumably from Lochranza. Bella Yule certainly knew what would excite her laddies: standing for'ard on the turbine steamer as she sped [literally: those ships could top 20 knots!] down the sheltered waters of the Kilbrannan Sound; alighting at a remote port then boarding a wee train [See Appendix 2] which was like the trams in Uddingston, to journey to where the Atlantic rollers crashed on the shore. Maybe they stood on that shore and dreamed of journeys on liners far beyond the horizon.

Liners they were familiar with, as any sail from central Glasgow would have taken them down Auden's "glade of cranes" representing the busy shipyards but also the docks where ships loaded and unloaded cargos for and from around the world and the star performers would the elegant ships of the Anchor Line. As laddies they had to be content with voyages on "miniature liners" – the Clyde Steamers of the day. Once again this is a well-documented world and the reader seeking more information is directed towards perhaps the definitive work: Andrew Clark's 2012 **Pleasures of the Firth.** [See Sources & Further Reading] Ships and shipping and, especially, those of the Firth of Clyde were boyhood obsessions which remained with Dad throughout his life and pinned to his walls were images of two of his favourite steamers: the lavishly appointed MacBrayne's paddle steamer *Columba (1878)[2]* and the railway-owned fast turbine steamer *Duchess of Argyll (1906).* [See Appendix 1]. When it became Dad's turn to introduce a young family to the Firth's pleasures, the paddler had long gone to the breakers and he was disappointed to note that the youngsters preferred the more modern turbine steamers, *Queen Mary II (1933)* and *Duchess of Hamilton (1932)* to his ageing favourite.

Rails and Bails

There are two other lifelong obsessions which characterise Dad's records: railways and cricket both of which can be seen to stem from the Uddingston childhood. When a wee laddie lives alongside a main railway line, the chances are that he will develop an interest in railways! "Trainspotting" had not developed as a hobby in Dad's youth but having the expresses of the Glasgow - Carlisle route hurtle past the back of the Yule's house in Kyle Park certainly made its mark on him and he was a lifelong fan of the Caledonian Railway Company. [See Appendix 3]

---

[2] For details of this remarkable steamer- see Paterson *Victorian Summer of the Clyde Steamers* pp109-114 or Clark *Pleasures of the Firth* pp67-78 [Sources & Further reading]

Having cricket fanatics in your Mother's family is also likely to affect your youth. His Uncle Hugh [See Addendum 1] played for the local club, Uddingston CC at a time when league cricket in Scotland was at the height of its popularity and matches at Bothwell Castle Policies could attract a Saturday afternoon crowd of no less than ten thousand. The Yule brothers all seem to have played at various levels with Johnny apparently the best performer. Dad may not have excelled for any Uddingston side, but he fondly remembered playing "alley cricket" in the lane between his house and the railway embankment – "The Gully" [See Illustrations Set1] and forming "The Gully Cricket Club" in tribute to the local side.

A wee laddie & a wider world

The first two decades of the twentieth century was an exciting time to be alive but to be young – to be exact, a wee laddie – probably meant that you missed the significance of great events. But the War DID affect the Yules – as it did almost every family in Scotland, so we should take time here to examine that. The civilian population of Scotland did not come under concerted attack as was the case in the later conflict, but there remained with Dad's parents and brothers lasting memories often recalled to a later generation in passing anecdotes and references.

The older Yule brothers reached working age during the conflict and would have had, with their parents, to "register" for possible service in 1915. Under the terms of the Military Service Act of the following year, apart from Mailler, they were to be under age for the duration of the War. John Yule being a mining engineer would be "exempt". Two family members, however, were victims, one fatally which we will discuss below, after trying to picture the wartime world of "Wee Bobbie".

Dad would have become familiar with the appearance of khaki clad – often kilted -soldiers on leave in the streets, have seen recruitment posters, headlines in the papers and on the newsagents' billboards, would have become aware as the war progressed of the privations of rationing and would have constantly heard adults discussing events. He would have been aware that his Uncle Hugh [see below] had joined the colours in the heady patriotic fervour of 1914 and seen the post cards [See Addendum 1] from him received by various family members in Uddingston, However, the first wartime shock was not a battle but an accident, what the Yules called the Gretna Train Disaster the site of which was always pointed out by Dad and his brothers whenever travelling by rail or road to or from England. What seemed to have disturbed Dad was not the enormous death toll but that it happened on his peerless Caledonian Railway [See Appendix 2] and that one of his favourite class of locomotive had been wrecked.

The realities of war would have come upon a small boy in July 1915 when an anti-submarine boom was installed on the Firth of Clyde – between Dunoon and the Cloch - which meant all sailings to Rothesay, Adrishaig and Campbeltown left from Wemyss Bay [see Clark "War and Peace" pp111 et seq]

A Little Learning ...

Of Dad's schooldays we know little and it seems this adventurous boy did not excel academically as did two of his brothers, John before him and Alexander after him. However, somewhere in his schooling, first in Uddingston and later in neighbouring Bellshill, someone gave a love of art and painting and drawing. A prized family possession is his sketchbook which contains over thirty pencil sketches mostly dating from 1930 to 1932 and thus cover the Diary period. Somewhere, somebody taught Dad the concept of perspective which he used in the line drawings he did in Katanning in 1930 and when he was back home in Glasgow in 1931. *"I liked Art"* he once said to the author in a rare remark about his own schooling. Certainly, a teacher had spotted a flair and encouraged him, and we are the better for that. Inculcated in him, perhaps from the technical background of his father and the rigorous environment of Scottish Elementary Education, was an attention to detail and a capacity for taking pains. The sketchbook exemplifies this especially his *"Shadows of the evening" At "The Pines" Katanning West Australia"* of January 1931, drawn at a time when he was at a low ebb. These were attributes which were his great strength in his career as a civil engineer/ surveyor, both above and below ground, where accurate measuring, setting out and drawing and careful monitoring of concrete pouring were his trademark.

... and other Accomplishments.

As Dad's teens turned to his twenties, we may envisage this active sports-mad young man enjoying life. He gravitated towards the local rugby club and the club photo of Uddingston RFC [Illustrations Set 1] shows a sturdy young man in the ranks of the 2ⁿᵈ XV during a period of some success for that club. Not having attended a rugby-playing school, he would have picked up the rudiments of the game as he went along. One skill he seems to have acquired was that of goal kicking and he was fond of relating how he had once kicked a penalty goal – with the old heavy leather ball – from the half-way line.

Working hard as a mining surveyor and, in winter, putting in the hours at night school at Royal Technical College. Here he achieved success. Having passed the preliminaries, he moved to specialist subjects and his preserved Certificates[3] show that in the 1926-27 session he gained Second Class passes in **Geology** and **Geological Drawing** with a First Class, meaning he scored over 80%, in **Mining Engineering and Mine Surveying.**[4] This last, one feels, being very practical would be more to his liking and probably involved much of what he was doing as part of his job. But the Geology also caught his fancy and the knowledge

---

[3] The original Certificates are now on permanent loan to Scotland's National Mining Museum, Newtongrange, Edinburgh

[4] For details of his syllabus and textbooks, see Appendix 3

stayed with him, not only as a help in his subsequent career but as providing the explanation why the Scottish scenery[5] differs from that of England.

Denny

All this was to come crashing down as the Great Depression hit Scotland. Although usually thought of as starting with the Wall Street Crash of October 1929, the economic decline in Scotland had steadily worsened throughout the 1920's[6] and the fortunes of the Yule family were clearly closely linked to mining[7] and heavy industry. The causes and effects have been widely analysed elsewhere so all we shall note here is that the industrious Yules found themselves out of work.

The Yules were always rather reticent about this time in the family's history. [The author remembers a childhood diversion when returning in the family car from Stirling, which went from Denny through Castlerankine to Banknock via Braeface, when Parkhill and Holehouse – pronounced "hollis" – were pointed out as though they were sites of battles!] However, there was a family link to Denny, as Dad's Uncle David, Rev. David Mailler Yule, his father's younger brother, had been Minister of Broompark United Free Church[8], Denny from 1906 to 1915. According to contemporary reports in the *Falkirk Herald*, he and his wife from the Scots Borders, Bessie[9] [Elizabeth Scott whom he married in 1901 in Galashiels,] took a very active part in the local community and were highly regarded[10]. It may be that the Yules of Uddingston were visitors to his Manse[11] or had been to hear him preach and were thus familiar with the Denny area. The Yules always seemed to the author to be rather in awe of their erudite[12] Minister relative and he may have been the "go-to man" in a family problem who came up with the solution that the family resume the semi-rural life of High Blantyre and was able to point them to a possible location in Denny.

---

[5] He was able to explain to his family such features as folded strata, faults, whin sills, volcanic plugs, as well as collecting fossils when working on open cast coal sites.

[6] At the peak of the Depression, it is estimated that 30% of Glaswegians were out of work, so the Yules were not alone in feeling hardship!

[7] The General Strike of 1926 was never spoken of but would obviously affect the family being quite violent in Scotland with striking miners derailing the Flying Scotsman express train at one point!

[8] One of several strands of the Church in Scotland, formed in 1900 by the union of the United Presbyterian Church of Scotland and the majority of the Free Church of Scotland. The majority of the United Free Church of Scotland united with the Church of Scotland in 1929.

[9] Clearly her preferred diminutive as the fly-leaf of his copy of the Revised Version of the Bible – a family heirloom and a birthday present reads: *To Davie from Bessie 11th Sept 1907*

[10] To the extent that the Provost (Mayor) of Denny in 1948 had been christened David Mailler Yule Ferguson!

[11] Equivalent to "vicarage" in the Church of England

[12] The local paper in August 1932 reported that he: *"was recently awarded by examination the Diploma of Theology of the University London"* - presumably through one of their many "Distance Learning" schemes.

So, April 1927 finds the Yules relocated, set up and advertising in the local press as being Messrs Yule who had hatching eggs for sale, (Leghorns) at Parkhill Poultry Farm, Castlerankine. This tenancy was not a lasting one as the Valuation Roll for 1930 suggests that the land had been purchased by the Local Authority but the same source shows: "John & William Yule, Poultry Farmers" as tenants at nearby Holehouse Farm. It may be just a coincidence that in the list of proprietors of the land, farm and mineral rights is a Mr Alexander Gillies who gives an Uddingston address. With John Crawford Yule now reaching his 60's and the eldest son, David Mailler Yule already departed to Australia, it is clear that John Train Scott Yule assumed the role of head of family, a position he maintained, providing a home for his parents and brothers for the next four decades.

As with Uddingston, Denny - about 25 miles NE of Glasgow - is not a site of note in Scottish history nor yet a site of natural beauty – rather the reverse. Rather bypassed by motorways today[13], when the Yules moved to its western environs, Denny was a much more frequently visited place, as it stood astride the main road from Glasgow to Stirling, the A80 which met the main road from Falkirk at Denny Cross. At the time we are concerned with, Denny would have been yet another depressed industrial town although its principal employer, Herbertshire Colliery was still working. The Yule family's rationale may well have been *"times are hard, but people still need to eat, and we are producing food".* Thus, the world of mining and engineering was left behind as far as the older Yules were concerned.

One can see Dad having another opinion. He was away from his beloved Uddingston, with its sport and proximity to Glasgow and the Clyde and living in what were undoubtedly more spartan conditions than comfortable suburban Kyle Park. Although the Alexanders' bus connected directly to Glasgow[14] and the countryside was close at hand in the Stirlingshire hills[15], it was a long bus ride and they were not "the hills of home". So, one could see Dad becoming very disillusioned with Denny, Scotland and life in general and very willing to consider an alternative to those first two.

Precisely when correspondence from Australia arrived that gave Dad the impetus is not known but it clearly was by the latter half of 1929, as his Diary implies that his decision to emigrate had crystallised and his travel arrangements put in place by the December of that year. We do know the instigators: his Uncle Bob and his elder brother David Mailler Yule. These people have a major role in the story, so this is the place for a bit of wider biography.

---

[13] Three motorways, the M9 to the north, the M876 to the east, and the M80 immediately to the west. Both Parkhill and Holehouse Farm lie close to the present M80.

[14] Glasgow -Stirling via Kilsyth or Cumbernauld.

[15] For example: Touch Hills, Gargunnock Hills, Fintry Hills and to the west, Kilsyth Hills and his beloved Campsie Fells.

The Eldest Brother

Dad's eldest brother, David Mailler Yule, (named after his uncle David, a minister in the Kirk), was born in Langside, Cathcart, Glasgow, in 1900, the first of the five Yule boys and always known as "Mailler" presumably to distinguish him from his uncle. As we have seen, ships and the Clyde were a great influence on the family, but he was the only one who set out to make the sea his career, achieving what was many a wee Scots laddie's ambition by joining the prestigious Anchor Line. He would be a "Boy Seaman" and we know he was in the crew of the SS *Elysia* [see Appendix1] a passenger cargo vessel built in 1908 as the family mementoes include his Christmas card home [See Illustrations 6] which Dad annotated perhaps inaccurately as "1917". Crews may have moved about from ship to ship at that time and he would certainly be at the bottom of the pile. However, we have another memento, a souvenir model of the passenger liner *Tuscania* [see Appendix 1] which is annotated "Mailler maiden voyage". [See Illustrations 6] This ship, a turbine driven passenger liner, the largest in the Anchor Line Fleet was launched in September 1914 and to be on its maiden voyage to New York in February 1915 would be a quite a prestigious posting. Sadly, this ship was to meet an early end. She was requisitioned by the Admiralty and became a troopship sailing under the management of Cunard and on 5th February 1918, ferrying one of the first contingents of US troops to Britain, she was almost home in the Firth of Clyde when she was torpedoed by UB-77. The Anchor Line's finest was hit amidships in the starboard boiler room and she sank off Rathlin Island where her wreck lies today. Records suggest that although she was carrying over 2,000 passengers, largely US servicemen, most of them and most crew were saved as it took some time for the ship to sink. However, there were fatalities and it seems 30 of Mailler's fellow crewmen, mostly stokers and engine room crew, lost their lives. Records suggest that about 200 US servicemen died, and this was widely reported in the USA at the time, a shock to a nation which had only been a belligerent for a few months[16].

As a crew member, one would expect that Mailler had to man one of the lifeboats which struggled in the wintry Atlantic seas but got survivors ashore on the island of Islay. On the other hand, he may have had to remain on board whilst the soldiers were disembarked and would then have probably been rescued by one of the destroyers which bravely came alongside as some of the lifeboats and rafts were destroyed by the explosion after the torpedo hit.   Whatever happened it was an incident which seems to have had a traumatic effect on the teenager. Remembered remarks from family and friends suggests that thereafter he had problems in settling to anything. Beverley Scott remembers her father,

---

[16] The American Monument on the Mull of Oa on Islay commemorates the incident and on 5th February 2018, a commemorative service was held in this rather inaccessible spot.

Robert, saying that Mailler had become "taciturn and uncommunicative"[17] in his later years in Geraldton. Casualties of hostilities are not confined to fatalities.

The Uncle

For the details of Robert Scott, I am again indebted to my second cousin Beverley Scott of Palmyra WA and her masterly family record: **Our Scott Family History** *first published privately in 1992 with subsequent revisions. Some of what follows is surmise based on memory or anecdote! ADY*

Robert Scott, whom Dad refers to as "Uncle" throughout, was born in the mining village of Auchinraith, Blantyre in 1882, sixth child of John and Isabella Scott[18] and his early life would appear typical of that industrial era. However, he broke the shackles of convention when he and a pal travelled the world in the early part of the 20th century. So, he clearly had the family adventurous streak – that which drove his younger brother Hugh to rush to the Colours in 1914 - and family anecdote has him sheep shearing in New Zealand, harvesting peanuts in Hawaii and visiting San Francisco in time for the 1906 earthquake. We know he returned to Scotland round the end of the decade and, as the Scotts were a close-knit family, would have visited his elder sister and her wee boys. One can imagine the effect the appearance of this sun-tanned figure from over the seas with his tales of his experiences would have had upon the adventurous young Yules! My surmise is that there remained with them some lasting impressions: abroad was the place for adventure, not smoky Scotland; and farming was an eminently suitable occupation for fit men who liked the open air. This would seem to be borne out by the fact that three of the Yule boys went abroad – David Mailler to stay permanently -and the other two made a career in farming. Family anecdote does not record it, but one is driven to wonder what the Yule parents, who must have had ambitions for their sons to make it into salaried professions, thought of these unsettling impressions. However, Robert clearly retained fond memories of the wee laddies who had no doubt been his rapt audience in Uddingston where a seed had been sown.

The first move

Fast forward to the 1920's.

One of Robert Scott's intentions when he made that return to Scotland must have been to tell his parents that he had met someone from Western Australia whom he intended to marry and settle down with her there[19]. Thus the 1920's finds him duly settled in Katanning WA, in the process of "founding a dynasty" - there were eventually three sons and two

[17] Email to me Feb 2018. However, he corresponded regularly with Dad & he sent us newspapers and a West Australia calendar most years. His father, John Crawford Yule, was a rather taciturn man.
[18] Three of the 8 children died in infancy. See Appendix 0
[19] For a family tree of the Scotts, please see Our Scott Family History op.cit.

daughters – a manager with the agricultural merchants Elder Smith &Co. and beginning thereby to occupy a position in society.

The nature of the man and the stature he ultimately gained in society may be best gauged from an article in the Western Mail of 20th Sept 1939 in a feature on Katanning's Jubilee, which picked him out as a prominent resident. The author is obliged to Irene Doyle of the local history group for scouring the archives of the National Library of Australia for this clip:

Mr. ROBERT SCOTT, manager of the Katanning branch of the well-known firm of Elder, Smith and Co., Ltd., is a native of Lanarkshire. Scotland. As a young man he travelled extensively in California and America and was associated with coalmining interests. Subsequently some years were devoted to farming operations in Honolulu and New Zealand.

Mr. Scott visited his homeland before coming to Fremantle in 1910, and in 1922 he opened the Katanning branch of Elder, Smith and Co., Ltd. His many commercial activities have been supplemented through the intervening years by a keen interest in public, sporting and social affairs, and practically every movement of note has had his support. He served on the committee of the agricultural society for many years; as captain of the bowling club; president of the Great Southern Cricket Association's annual competition, staged by clubs from Narrogin south to Albany; president of the Katanning Club, an institution which plays a big part in the town's social life; and he also sat, with Mr. G. L. Hardie (Broomehill), the late Mr. J. Johnson (former manager of the Katanning branch of the West Australian Bank) and Mr. E. B. Anderson on the first local Football Control Board. Mr. Scott is gifted with a fine voice, and he has used this in the cause of charity and other efforts without stint. Incidentally, the firm he represents celebrates its centenary this year.

In this picture of an active man, it should be noted that he suffered from a disability. Beverley Scott tells us [op.cit. p44] that in 1914:

".. Robert had a serious accident. He was driving a Sulky[20] when the horse bolted, he was thrown and a when ran over his left foot, which was badly crushed. He was in hospital for eighteen months, looked after by a Dr Gillespie. He was left with a bad limp due to his deformed foot and he had a special boot made at regular intervals for the rest of his life".

To get a picture of the 1920's, we can turn to the Elder Smith's house magazine, *"Teamwork",* who featured his reminiscences for the December 1968 edition[21] just before

---

[20] "Sulky" OED: A light two-wheeled carriage or chaise …. Seated for one person.
[21] A copy of the article is appended to Our Scott Family History op. cit.

his death. There he recollected, that in 1922, when he became their first branch manager in Katanning, he had two staff to help him and he used a second-hand Model T Ford as their means of transport. Transport he would certainly have needed as, in that interview, he describes his territory as "truly immense" – it eventually required 5 offices to service the business – but importantly for our purposes, it covered Kojonup.

Back in Uddingston was his nephew, the unsettled, David Mailler. Robert Scott would have been aware that Australian Government policy was to attract immigrants from UK and may well have felt he was doing his bit in developing underpopulated territory by suggesting his nephew joined him. On the other hand, Mailler, having tried his hand at making a living in Scotland at a time when the post-war economy had begun a decline [22] may have got "itchy feet" and decided to follow his uncle to Australia. We know from Beverley Scott that Robert Scott had an agency with Massey Harris the agricultural machine manufacturers and thus it would appear that farming in Western Australia was becoming mechanised at that time with the result that there would be opportunities for those who service petrol driven machines. (Perhaps that included the Model T Ford which Robert Scott used!) On landing at Freemantle from the SS *Orontes* in May 1925, Mailler gave his occupation as "motor mechanic" so one can see a good reason for his new start and for his feeling, perhaps, that he had "found his feet" in his new land.

A plan unfolds

Again, we are in the realm of surmise, but we can envisage that in his dealings with the Warburtons of Kojonup [23] sometime in 1929, Robert Scott became aware that they had come by a block of land some twelve or so miles to the south. [Details of this later] He would have noted that his nephew had acquired skills not normally associated with a merchant seaman turned motor mechanic from industrial Scotland: the ability to shoot and to ride a horse. He may have suggested that it was time for Mailler to move on and become a farmer in his own right and would presumably have been instrumental in getting Mailler's name on the lease for Kojonup Block 7083. This was land which needed clearing, a job for which Mailler would need the help of another man, one of sturdy stature. That man, of course, was kicking his heels in Denny, Stirlingshire, Scotland.

Thus it was that Robert Scott Yule, unemployed mining surveyor, - with, one supposes, a deal of financial help from the family, prepared to travel half way round the world to take up a new life as a West Australian farmer.

---

[22] "Flowers of the Forest" Royle Chap 12 "In the immediate aftermath of the conflict the economy remained reasonable buoyant, mainly as a result of the wartime boom and the confidence generated by the end of the war, but by the early 1920's the alarm bells were ringing. Between 1921 and 1923 shipbuilding on the Clyde dropped from 510,000 tons to 170,000 tons .... "

[23] Angus Warburton 1891-1960 and Rex Warburton (Senior) 1894 -1962

YULES and SCOTTS

The Yules of Kyle Park about 1924. **Back Row L to R:** Mailler, Johnny, Willie. **Front Row L to R:** John Crawford Yule, Robert Scott Yule, Alex, Bella Yule (née Scott). [Family Collection]

The Scott grandparents: John Train Scott & Isabella. **Above left:** with Bella & Yule bairn plus wee dog (Both unidentified) at Kyle Park and **(Above right)** in a typical formal pseudo-seaside pose with grandson George Young c. 1911. Note the hat! [Family Collection]

OLD UDDINGSTON

From Victorian picture postcards in the Family Collection, two views of a well-set Main Street before the trams. This was the "village" the Yules moved to.

DAD'S UDDINGSTON

The author visited Uddingston in 2017 in search of landmarks in Dad's young life and took the pictures reproduced on this page.

Above left is Cresswell Terrace where he was born and where the Scott grandparents also lived for a time.

Above centre is Church Street looking towards Main Street. The Yules lived on the first floor, a rather noisy location in the days of the trams.

Above right, a door in Kyle Park Avenue bears the numeral "5". The area has been much developed since Dad's boyhood with roads re-named and re-numbered, but it is probable that this is the "5 Kyle Park" villa where the Yules prospered.

Between the rear of the Kyle Park villas and the Caledonian Railway's Main Line was an alleyway called "The Gully", then wide enough for games of cricket. **Pictured left**, much overgrown it remains as a cycle path.

A WEE LADDIE'S UDDINGSTON

An adventure playground for a wee laddie - Uddingston surrounds. **Top:** Bothwell Castle. **Bottom:** the Clyde looking towards the railway bridge.[From the Victorian postcard collection.]

LOCAL RESOURCES

Make use of the facilities. **Above left:** Tunnock's, still extant in Main Street, was the Yules' source of rolls and pies and "a well-fired loaf for Mrs Scott". [Photo author] **Above right:** Dad's Aunt Margaret – Margaret Young [née Scott] -pictured with her son George, was manageress of a café at a Glasgow cinema providing eagerly accepted perks for her family. [Family Collection]

Enjoy the Firth. [See Intro to Vol 1] **Above left:** approaching Lochranza Pier, Isle of Arran, in the heydays of turbine steamers. [Reproduced from *Pleasures of the Firth: Two Hundred Years of the Clyde Steamers* (Stenlake Publishing, 2012), by courtesy of the author, Andrew Clark] and **(Above right)** the same site in 2017 with the ferry for Claonaig at the slip which now does duty for the dismantled wooden pier [Photo author]

WORKING and STUDYING in the 1920's

For more on Mining – see Appendix 3

Above left: A car of the Lanarkshire Tramways Co., whose system Dad would use for cheap if uncomfortable travel round Lanarkshire. [Photo F Inglis. Courtesy of Scottish Tramway & Transport Soc.] **Above right:** a typical drawing office of the time. [Sir William Arrol & Co.]

Above left: The imposing main entrance of the Royal Technical College, now Strathclyde University and **(above right)** Imperial Standards set in stone in George Square, Glasgow. Dad recalled checking his tapes against these standards, still in position today and probably a puzzle to those passers- by who notice them! [Author]

ENTER: A SKETCH BOOK

Tarbert Loch Fyne was a favourite spot for the Yules. **Above** is a scan of Dad's first ever Sketch Book entry and the 2011 panorama **(below)** suggests the whereabouts of his viewpoint as somewhere bottom right [Photo douglas v small. Reproduced through Wiki Creative Commons]

SUMMERS and WINTERS

An active young man. **Upper:** Tarbert Castle, a scan of one of his earliest sketches.
Lower: a sturdy young player with Uddingston RFC 2nd XV 1926-27. (Middle Row 2nd from left)

Dad's Diary – a GENERAL COMMENTARY

A Wee Black Book; Why? When? What? Things unsaid;
The Ardent Correspondent

Author's note

What follows is my attempt at "filling in the gaps" in the diary narrative, clarifying some of the terms or references which may have lost their meaning with the passage of time and offering such opinions or observations which did not occur to me during my transcription from the original.

A Wee Black Book

What I have beside me is a very ordinary piece of stationery. A wee black, octavo sized, hardbacked, fabric-covered, feint-lined notebook which travelled half way round the world one year, back again the following year, took a return trip to a mining camp in West Africa and then remained largely unregarded in personal possessions till long after its author's death.

The entries were written by fountain pen [i.e. a pen with its own refillable ink reservoir] using such blue or blue- black ink as was available, beginning on New Year's Day 1930 in a very legible cursive style of handwriting and ending 5th October 1931 by which time the writing had become much more of a hasty scrawl.

Why?

Dad makes no mention of why he decided to keep a diary. However, one can envisage the scenario wherein his mother, the well-organised Bella Yule, handed him a wee black book and suggested he use it as a diary so as he could record events for letters home. His Engineering training had taught him to record and tabulate, so this would not be a wholly foreign activity to him.

When?

There are entries for every day from 1 I 1930 in Denny to 3 III 31 on SS *Orsova*, when – perhaps understandably, he seems to have lost his enthusiasm for the job. However, he briefly resumed his diarist role on 22 IX 1931 as he was on his travels again having taken up a post with the Sierra Leone Development Company. This continued record, which seems almost to have been an afterthought, appears in this publication as a "Coda". His last entry which has the appearance of being hastily scribbled is dated Monday 5th October when he had just arrived at Marampa mines. Looking at those pages, one gets the impression that several days have been written up in a batch. He had clearly done this before on his Australia venture[24] but might have decided he was going to be too busy in West Africa to keep to the daily discipline and perhaps felt that his writing time was best used to correspond with a certain young lady from Banknock.

What?

"Record and tabulate" he certainly did here. At the back of the book is his meticulously tabulated record of games of Bridge played between 17 III 1930 and 2 III 1930, his cumulative scoring indicating a loss to him and partner. As addenda also there are his "General Notes on the Block" which probably wrote whilst on site and later added to in Katanning when he super-scribed his heading to be "Information Generally". This latter covers a rather wide range of Western Australian information with pages of flora and fauna notes probably gathered from personal experience and a "gazetteer" of climatic information which looks like it came from an encyclopaedia. One can guess that this information would be the substance of the many letters home which he records throughout and totals on 2 II 1931 to have been no less than 116 from 31 III 1930 to 31 I 1931. [See below]

Things unsaid

In any diary, the things which were omitted are often the most interesting. Dad wrote from a perspective from which he would assume everybody would know the circumstances surrounding his travels. Unfortunately, today's readers are not in that position! I have used footnotes throughout to try to clarify terms, references and allusions but questions arise on reading the entries on matters which Dad did not record in particular:

The passage out

Immigration and travel arrangements were a done deal by 1st Jan 1930, so we have no information in the subsequent entries regarding his outward passage. However, he had quite a bit to say regarding his coming home [more on this later] from which we gather that he went out on a "Nominated Passage". This was one of many Australian Government schemes to attract immigrants from UK [e.g. the "Ten Pound Poms" after the Second World War.] in which persons nominated by Australian residents could receive a subsidy towards the fare for ocean trip. It seems reasonable to assume that this procedure was used in the case of Mailler with Robert Scott as nominator and the process repeated five years later for Dad with either doing the honours. The snag in this was that anyone receiving a subsidised passage had to remain in Australia for a set period, at that time apparently two years, or the subsidy had to be repaid. How the train tickets and his hotel were paid for is not plain but, as he records no problems, presumably all was catered for.

---

[24] Entry for 26 XII 1930 reads: *Very warm. Gardening. Bringing diary up to date.*

Luggage

Like those tv programmes where the celebrity presenter zooms all over the place without seeming to have any luggage, the Diary is equally irritating. His outward-bound trip entries make no mention of luggage at all so one presumes, as with ticketing, there were no problems in packing a trunk in Denny and getting it shipped to Freemantle for onward transit. The only mention of baggage comes in the rather hectic entries of his last few days in Australia, in Katanning on 15 II 1931, when his entry reads: *Washing. Partly packing trunk and cases.* The trunk in question would most likely be the black metal trunk which, with adorned with various faded peeling labels, was long part of the Yule family accoutrements, at one time playing a key part in family life as store for the 'O' gauge model railway.

Passport

Dad obviously needed some sort of passport for his outward – assumed one-way – passage but there is no record of what type it was or when he got it. On 1 II 1930, he records: *Tilbury 10.20am. Went through "Y" stile, showed passport, got berth number and went on board. Went to cabin. Bunk Number 263 (top) on C deck.* This document must have had a limited validity because he needed another for the return trip in 1931 and it was on this that he subsequently shuttled to and from West Africa. In these days of tightly controlled international travel and identity fraud, it is illuminating to see that it was renewed with a hand- written annotation by the police in Freetown, Sierra Leone!

Camera

We are fortunate in having a small photographic record of his time in Australia although he makes only two references to his taking them. The family album contains a range of subjects on prints of varies size, some of which may have been commercially produced. One senses that he was keen to fulfil a pledge to send lots of pictures home and thus repair an omission of his brother's voyage and life in Australia. So, the camera – a folding Kodak Brownie - may not originally been his as there are no pictures prior to his setting off. The surmise is that his parents prevailed upon his brother Johnny – who later in life became a keen amateur photographer and may have just acquired a new one– to pass on the camera in the family interest. As mentioned earlier [in Foreword] I include here a selection of those which illustrate an entry. How the snaps were developed is not clear, but he does make one entry [12 II 1930]: *"Sent films"*. This might either indicate a postal service which was the norm at that time or that he sent a roll of undeveloped film home for processing in Scotland.

The Ardent Correspondent

In the hope of simplifying references in the Dairy transcripts, I have followed Dad's example and tabulated below his entry of 2 II 1931 where he listed his correspondence in the previous year. The total represents a noteworthy effort on his part. Not all his recipients have been identified. [See also Appendix 0]

Mother & Father	55	John & Bella Yule
Johnnie	9	Elder Brother
Willie	4	Elder Brother
Alex	8	Younger Brother
Grandma	5	Isabella Scott
Aunt Susan	3	Sister of John (above) m. John Devine
D Devine	3	Son of the above. Later killed in road accident.
Mrs Dickie	3	Uddingston Laundrywoman
Jack Dickie	2	Husband of above
David Black	2	Cousin
Mr Black	1	Presumed father of above
Aunt Jeannie	1	In New Zealand, sister of Bella
Kemps (including Isobel)	2	Gave Dad his writing case. A useful gift!
Woodcock	1	Gave Dad a knife
Flossie Bruce	2	Presumed Uddingston friend
Mr Graham	1	Reference obscure
Mrs Monaghan	1	Reference obscure
Simpson & Rankin	1	Reference obscure
P Keith	1	Reference obscure
Trying for work	11	Sadly, to little effect
TOTAL	116	*Tallies with Diary total!*

COMMENTARY on PART ONE

The Journey Out

In the beginning; On the move - By bus and train to the ocean; On the move - on board Oronsay; *From the ship's rail; Time of his life.*

<u>In the beginning</u>

Having taken an editorial decision to begin the transcription 31 days into the year after Dad's first entry, I must summarise a busy month. The entries mostly concern visits, several to the Glasgow area, to say "Goodbye" to friends and family on the premise that it was unlikely that he would see them again. True to form he lists the presents he received and the scores in the games of Bridge he played. Two of the presents stayed with him for life, a hair brush and shaving set and a writing case. Typically for the age, he received cigarettes: "Mary" at Donaldson's Hotel, Denny giving him 100! His social diary was indeed very full. He records parties, a trip to the Alhambra theatre in Glasgow, a cinema trip with Ina McKechnie [25] and visits to the pub: Donaldson's Hotel in Denny. On Thurs 28th he was there with his younger brother despite the record suggesting Alec was a month short of the statutory age for visiting licenced premises! The only lasting record of his time at Holehouse Farm is a photo taken in the snow of Wednesday 29th January when his entry reads: *Snow. Made Snow Bear sitting on Snow Ball. 8ft high. Johnny photographed it with Glen* [26] *and Myself.* [See Illustrations 2]

<u>On the move - By bus and train to the ocean</u>

That single step which the Chinese tell us is start of the longest journey, for Dad on a dark January morning was from a bus stop in Denny where he, his father and two of his brothers caught the 0810 Alexander's bus to Glasgow. Whether that went by Kilsyth and Kirkintilloch or by Cumbernauld and Shotts, he does not tell us, but the Yules arrived in Glasgow in good time to get from the bus station – perhaps Dundas Street – across the familiar streets of Central Glasgow to an equally familiar Central Station from whence Dad was set out on his adventure. A family group assembled to bid him farewell and, as one might expect, memory of that occasion remained with him. On later family excursions from Central Station, perhaps to catch a train to Fairlie Pier for the Campbelltown steamer, he would point out Platform One as the departure point for the "Royal Scot". [27]

---

[25] Sister of Bet McKechnie whom Alex married. According to Roberta Yule, the families had known each other for some time

[26] Yule dogs were named Glen, Ken and Roy usually in that order of succession. This would be the first "Glen". See the Cloybank photo

[27] For railways and trains please see Appendix 2

As we have seen, he was no stranger to train travel, but this was to far eclipse any previous trip. He may have travelled to Oban by train, as his sketch book contains three freehand drawings of that area, but we know that he had made at least one journey as far as Stranraer with his rugby club. He recalled his team mates' surprise that he did not want to join in a game of cards but preferred to look out the window. So, we can imagine him watching the scenery flash past as he travelled south on the crack "named express" on what he would have known as the Caledonian Railway's Main Line which, of course, ran past the back of the Yule's dormer bungalow in Kyle Park, Uddingston. The fact that there were people waiting at a station (Carstairs) to see him wave as the train passed through would have alerted his travelling companion, whose name and address he notes, that the young man was making a significant trip.

True to form, he notes the snow-covered hills of Scotland and that the train stopped at Symington, Carlisle – surely his first venture into England, Crewe then London Euston and some thought had gone into planning his route to the oceans. Perhaps he was following his brother's footsteps exactly or perhaps a booking clerk somewhere had given helpful suggestions. The locations of the overnight hotel and his route to Tilbury, the use of the St. Pancras line rather than the more direct line from Fenchurch Street were certainly designed to minimise the burden of a luggage laden traveller in central London. Curiously, he was to re-trace his journey eastwards from London several times in later life as he worked on various contracts in Essex for A Monk & Co who had an office at Stanford le Hope. In those days, Tilbury was almost the equivalent of Heathrow in being a major international departure point from the capital. Once there, Dad would be re-living his boyhood in travelling from station platform directly to the quayside just as though he were at Wemyss Bay on the Firth of Clyde. However, that station still performs in interchange function for passengers to Bute, whereas the fortunes of Tilbury Riverside (as it became) declined with the dwindling of ocean travel and the spacious premises now act as a car park as the revived maritime passenger trade brought about by the popularity of Cruising has brought life back to the Tilbury quay.

On the move -on board *Oronsay*

Dad would have been in no way fazed by the prospect of life on board ship. As we have seen, from his earliest years he was familiar with what someone called "liners in miniature" the Clyde pleasure steamer fleet. Thus, he knew his way about a ship, knew, for instance the importance of the Purser's Office. Having sailed on PS *Columba*[28], he was familiar with the concept of a Post Office on a ship. Having sailed on that vessel, however, he may have found the 3rd class Dining Saloon on *Oronsay* did not quite match the splendour of the MacBrayne's paddler!

---

[28] See Appendix 1

Having been brought up in a small house with four brothers and lived under canvas with the Boy Scouts in the wilder parts of the west of Scotland, sharing cabin with 5 others would not have been a daunting prospect. Bound by what we are sure was a promise to his family to keep in touch and tell all his news, he duly recorded [1 II 1930] his cabin- mates' names for posterity. Studying the Passenger List for that voyage reveals that they were:

Sam Dempster, farm labourer, from Moneyrea, Comber, Co Down, bound for Melbourne;

Mr E Fairbrother, Process Manager, Clarence Rd., Brondesbury NW6 [by a coincidence, the author had passed this road many times when living in NW2!],

His son Leslie Fairbrother (also on board was his wife and 3 daughters) all bound for Brisbane [See illustration p2];

Tom Roach (which Dad misconstrued as "Sproach"), bus driver from Pontllanfraith, Monmouthshire (now Caerphilly County Borough, Gwent) bound for Brisbane(also on board was his wife and daughter);

a sea-sick teenager known to Dad only as "Bill" and thus rather difficult to trace on a list.

This sample, with people from all parts of the United Kingdom, gives us an interesting insight into who was emigrating to Australia at that time. Whether they communicated with any efficiency, given the variety of British regional accents which must have been in evidence, was not recorded but Dad may well have talked Rugby Union Football with the Welshman.

He was an enthusiastic passenger, fortunate in that he could echo WS Gilbert's Captain Corcoran who was *"Never, never sick at sea", ["What never?"' "Hardly ever"].* Could it be that childhood experience on the Clyde steamers had given him "sea legs"? A paddle steamer rounding Ardlamont Point or a slim turbine steamer crossing from Ardrossan to Brodick could be quite lively if a near-gale was blowing from the south or south-west [This writer has personal experience of stormy waters between the isles of Arran and Bute.]

Dad, the former Boy Scout joined in all the organised passenger activities. Playing the classic British games of Deck Quoits, Deck Tennis and Shuffleboard perhaps with more enthusiasm than skill though he does record receiving a souvenir spoon as a trophy. [To our everlasting shame, his heirs and successors have mislaid this.] As mentioned earlier, he continued his participation in the craze of the era: Bridge, a game he played in a rather unscientific fashion. With *Oronsay* out of sight of land, his sessions took on a formal aspect. Although he does not name the passengers who made up the four enthusiasts, merely describing "We" as "An Englishman & myself" and "The" as "an Irishman & Englishman", he kept the scores of their games from 17 II 1930 to 2 III 1930 keeping both match and cumulative totals. His meticulously drawn table at the back of the Diary shows that "We" won 11 out of the 22 rubbers recorded in that time although the losses were heavy ones and the final points tally on reaching the Australian shore was "We" 11,693, "They" 12,855. The appearance of this table truly reflects his education and work back in Scotland. Set out with both single and double lining to its nine columns, it draws one to the possibility that, faced with an uncertain future, sub-consciously, he was saying: "*I am really a surveyor. I collect data and tabulate it in a clear fashion*"

From the ship's rail

As we have seen, Dad was an observant passenger by rail and Clyde steamer and so it is not surprising to read that he spent time on deck, not just in the organised activities, but also as an interested spectator of whatever could be viewed from the ship's rail. He must have been a regular visitor to the Purser's Office where details of "what to see" would be posted and noted all this assiduously. So, we have records of both ship and shore. On this trip he did not find time to sketch- maybe his sketchbook was stowed out of reach- but he did make use of his newly acquired camera and the album contains several shots taken both aboard and ashore. [See Illustrations 2] This was a young man whose experience of the world was limited to the coalfields of Lanarkshire and Ayrshire and the hills and lochs of the southern or western coastal Highlands of Scotland. Thus, he made curt notes about *Oronsay's* ports of call where he had a "shore run": Toulon, Naples, Port Said and Colombo, rather than deep insights of socio-economic nature. Although he is rather scathing about the cleanliness of Naples – perhaps not the first nor the last to do so! – in later life he was prepared to admit that the view from out at sea had some scenic value!
 Perhaps the most telling remark comes as *Oronsay* steams through the Strait of Gibraltar [5 II 1930], when he noted: *Left Gibraltar at 12 noon. Part of Morocco like Island of Arran.* On the face of it, this is a very strange comparison – with little geographical justification – but this will have arisen as he looked southward to the other "Pillar of Hercules" - Jebel Musa [2,762ft]. Like the north Arran peaks as viewed from the Ayrshire coast, a sight he would have known from his earliest days "doon the watter" and maybe also when visiting a colliery within sight of the Clyde, he was looking across water to a rugged skyline. The comment may well have been prompted by a sudden realisation that it was unlikely he would ever see those island peaks again

Time of his life

With hindsight, one can see that the outward trip was one of the highlights of his life – an adventure he would often recall. In fact, he was on a state-sponsored, six-week cruise holiday and he was obviously determined to get the best out of it.
Now read this young Scotsman's enthusiastic record of a trip half way round the world on a 1930's liner.

VOLUME ONE

THE DIARY PART ONE

1st Jan 1930 – 3rd March 1930

Dad's diary entries began on 1st of Jan but as they are a rather repetitive list of farewell visits and parting gifts, I have summarised that period in a prior chapter.

<u>Friday 31st Jan 1930</u>

Left home, "Hallhouse" Denny, by Alexander's Motor Service[29] 8.10 am bus. Father, Johnnie and Alex accompanied me. Arr. Glasgow 9.5 am. Had a coffee at Central Station. Uncle John, Aunt Susan, David, Winnie, little John & Mr Kemp came to see me off on 10 am "Royal Scot"[30] train.

Left Glasgow (Central) at 10 am. Waved to Taits at Carstairs. One travelling companion, Jimmy Liddel, Hill St., Wishaw knew Mrs ?Joe Wilson, Wishaw. Scotland snow covered. Train stopped at Symington,[31] Carlisle, Crewe, then London (Euston) at 6.15 pm[32]. Walked to Abbotsford Hotel, Russell Square[33]. Had dinner at 7pm, wrote home then bed. Good accommodation.

<u>Saturday 1st February 1930</u>

Rose 7.15 am. Breakfast at 8am. Walked to St Pancras Station LMSRly[34]. Posted letter home. Left London 9.20 am arr Tilbury[35] 10.20am. Went through "Y" stile, showed passport, got berth number and went on board. Went to cabin. Bunk Number 263 (top) on C deck. Sent wire[36] home and PC of Oronsay to Alex. Oronsay left 12 noon. 4 tugs. Dinner at 1pm. Passed Goodwin Sands[37] in afternoon marked by lightships.[38] Boat Drill 4.30 pm. Travelling companions in cabin[39] (1) Sam Dempster (Irish) 32 years (2) Bill ? English (Devon) 19 years (3) Mr Fairbrother English 48 years (married) (4) his son Leslie 24 years (5) Tom Sproach Welsh 28 years (Married) (6) "Myself". Choppy sea, ship

---

[29] See Appendix 5

[30] See Appendix 5

[31] Edinburgh portion of the train from Princes Street station would be attached.

[32] Journey in 2018 on electrified "Pendolino" trains scheduled 4h 30m!

[33] About a half-mile walk from Euston Station

[34] London Midland & Scottish Railway. See Appendix 2.

[35] See Commentary

[36] Usage at the time means "telegram"

[37] Notorious hazard to shipping in the Strait of Dover 10-mile (16 km) long sandbank 6 miles (10 km) off the Deal coast in Kent, England. Only one lightship remains. See Appendix 5

[38] See Appendix 5

[39] See Commentary on Part 1

heaving and rolling slightly. Tea 6pm. Took walk on 1ˢᵗ class decks. Bed 10pm. Did not sleep much. Oronsay built Glasgow 20,001 tons. Orient Line.[40]

Sunday 2ⁿᵈ February 1930

Rose 7am. Breakfast at 8am. Ship rolling a little. Dropped pilot[41] about Plymouth. Ship did not stop. Skipping ropes in forenoon. Bill went to bed sick. No land in sight after dinner. Later sea a little more rough. Passed Cape Ushant at 6 pm[42]. Saw light at lighthouse. Singing at night. Meal hours: Breakfast 8am, Dinner 1pm, Tea 6pm, supper at 8pm.

Monday 3rd

No land in sight. Bay of Biscay very rough. Ship fairly steady. Bill still in bed. Tom sick and many passengers. Very high seas, lovely sight. Sun warm but strong wind. Thunderstorms in afternoon. During night dishes were broken. Ship heaving a lot. Had a slight headache.

Tuesday 4ᵗʰ

Took two Aspros which put my headache away before breakfast. Passed Cape Tarifa[43] at 7am. Kept near coast of Portugal. My special friend on board June Fairbrother 5½ years of age. Bed 9pm.

Wed 5ᵗʰ

Rose to see Straits of Gibraltar. Calm sea. Porpoises about. Anchored off Gibraltar at 8am. "Bum-boatmen" i.e. men selling oranges etc in rowing boats came round ship. Saw warships. Aeroplanes landing on a flotilla.[44] Did not go ashore. Left Gibraltar at 12 noon. Part of Morocco like Island of Arran.[45] On board 32 English fellows going to join Palestine Police.[46] Passed Cape de Grata at 10pm.[47]

Thurs 6ᵗʰ

Played deck games. Nothing much to be seen.

---

[40] See Appendix 1

[41] Ship would carry a Maritime Pilot during traverse of the busy English Channel.

[42] Franch Ouessant, island of Brittany coast, traditionally marks south western entrance to the Channel.

[43] Punta de Tarifa (Point Tarifa, Point Marroqui) is the southernmost point of the Iberian Peninsula and continental Europe. Point where ships "turned left" for the Med.

[44] Not sure what he meant here. Presumably aircraft carrier.

[45] See Commentary

[46] A colonial police force established during the British Mandate 1920-1948. These would be reinforcements called for after riots in 1929.

[47] Must be Cabo de Gata, Andalusia, SE corner of Spain

Fri 7th

Arr. Toulon 8.15 am. Went ashore after breakfast.[48]Traffic Right-Hand. Tram cars consist of 2 or 3 coaches.[49]Some policemen carried revolvers. Saw a burial. Shape of coffin. Lowered into hole then stone slab laid over top. Lovely cemetery. Artificial flowers made of beads. Bought & ate huge buns[50] in a street where various stalls lined both sides. Dinner on ship. Played Bridge and deck games.

Saturday 8th

Left Toulon 8 am. Saw hilly coast on left. Passed Corsica at 8 pm. Calm sea.

Sunday 9th

 At 7am passed small islands near Naples. Berthed Naples 11 am. Got lovely view of town from sea. Went ashore after dinner. Italians followed us about. Dirty streets. Saw funeral. Men dressed in black with white lace coverings led the procession chanting all the time. Six horses with black plumes pulled hearse. Coffin in a large casket. Men on foot followed then cabs came carrying followers. Top of Mount Vesuvius hidden by smoke and steam. Left Naples at 6pm.

Monday 10th

Passed Stromboli at 1 am but I was in bed.[51] Passed Crete at 8am. Very mountainous. Rough sea, head on wind 70 mph. Concert in evening. Wind 80 mph. Wind through the night 90 mph.[52] Dishes broken.

Tuesday 11th

Deck games etc. Choppy sea but ship still steady.

Wednesday 12th

Bridge in forenoon arr. Port Said 12noon. Anchored behind P&O liner Kaiser I Kahn[53]. Went ashore after dinner. Good streets. Tarmac surface. Verandah buildings. Tramcars drawn (by) mules. Some mounted police carrying swords. Others on foot with batons. Saw funeral. Coffin carried on a sort of table, men walking behind. Lovely European quarters.

---

[48] On foreign soil for the first time!

[49] As distinct from Glasgow's single car vehicles with which he was familiar.

[50] Clearly French Stick or baguette. He often spoke of this & his first encounter with a street market.

[51]Active volcanic island. Presumably he knew this from the ship's daily bulletin

[52] Assuming the ship's course was bearing SE, his use of "head on" suggests the Khamsin wind

[53] P&O was shipping line which eventually absorbed the Orient Line.

Veiled women. Natives wore long shirts or short shirts with sort of bloomers. Others with trousers. Left Port Said midnight. Ship took on oil and pure water.

Thursday 13th
Rose 3.15 am. Ship in canal.[54] Speed about 6 knots.[55] Trees on African side. Sand on the other side. Rose again at 6.15 am. Sand banks on either side. Entered one of the Bitter Lakes[56] at 8.15am. Waited on ships coming through canal toward us. Entered another of the Bitter Lakes at 10.15. Waited till 1pm to get on again[57]. Natives repairing retaining wall on canal banks. Strips of trees on African side. Desert only on Arabian side. Saw camel teams. Dropped pilot at Suez 4.30 pm but did not stop. Red Sea calm. Dutch ship then 3 miles ahead of us, Johan de Witt[58]. We passed it at 6.30 pm.

Friday 14th
Rose at 7am. Warm sun. Played bridge. Got glimpses of African coast. Calm sea. Bed 10pm. Day's mileage 406.

Saturday 15th
Rose 7am. Played bridge in forenoon. Overtook a French ship at 12 noon. Very warm. No land in sight. Played Bridge afternoon. Dance at night.

Sunday 16th
Rose 6.15 am. Passed The Twelve Apostles (or Gebel Tair) Rocks 12 in a long line. At 10.30 am passed Gebel Zubur, Little Hanish, Great Hanish and some reefs. Lounged about in forenoon. Played Bridge in afternoon. My partner[59] and I avenged a long series of defeats. At 4.30 passed Perim, an oil station.[60] Rocky island. Calm sea. Pictures 8.30pm till 10.15pm.[61] Saw Syd Chaplin[62] in "The Missing Link"[63]. Passed Aden at 9.30 pm. Had a pillow fight before bed at 11.45.

---

[54] Suez Canal. 120 miles long
[55] Must be from ship's bulletin
[56] Would be the Great Bitter Lake
[57] The canal is a single lane waterway with only 2 passing places until 2014. Hence a lot of waiting time.
[58] Named after 17th century Dutch politician and statesman.
[59] Bridge partner!
[60] Also called Mayyun in Arabic, a volcanic island in the Strait of Mandeb at the south entrance into the Red Sea, now belonging to Yemen but occupied by Great Britain from 1857 to 1967. Principally a coaling station it did not flourish on the change to oil fuel in ships.
[61] i.e. cinema
[62] 1885 – 1965 Elder half-brother of Charlie Chaplin
[63] Warner Bros 1927

Monday 17th

Rose 7.30 am. Calm sea. Warm sun, cool breeze. No land in sight. Lounged about in forenoon. Afternoon, deck billiards and Bridge. Commenced to keep record of Bridge scores.[64] Passed Cape Guardafui 5.30pm.[65] Whist drive at night. Winning score 160. My score 143. Slept on deck.

Tuesday 18th

Rose 6am. Decks getting washed. No land in sight. Cool breeze. Deck games in forenoon. Bridge afternoon. Evening Parlour Games on deck.

Wednesday 19th

Played deck tennis after breakfast. Pictures at night.

Thursday 20th

Commencement of deck games. Got knocked out 1st round of deck quoits[66] doubles and deck billiards[67] singles. Quiet afternoon. Bridge in evening then concert.

Friday 21st

Very calm sea. No wind. Got knocked out 1st round of deck billiards doubles. Cool breeze in afternoon. Warm sun.

Saturday 22nd

Rose 6.15 am. Arr. Colombo 6.45 am. P&O liner Balranald anchored before us. Went ashore after dinner. Scorching sun. Saw rickshaws, men good runners. Balranald left at 6pm. Oronsay left at midnight. Wonderful lightning in distance.

Sunday 23rd

Calm sea. Pictures at night. Saw "White Wings". Quiet all day.

Monday 24th

Ship quiet. Crossed equator at 11 am, Whist drive after supper.

Tuesday 25th

Got a bye in Deck Tennis doubles. Won the 2nd round. Day's mileage 406.

---

[64] Duly entered at rear of diary with cumulative scores.

[65] Now Somalia. Then Italian Somaliland. Now Ras Asir and the easternmost point of African mainland.

[66] See Appendix 5

[67] Also called Shuffleboard, See Appendix 5.

Wednesday 26th

Won 3rd round of Deck tennis doubles. Pictures at night, saw launch of Orient liner Orontes.

Thursday 27th

Got a bye in Deck Tennis semi-final. Lost the final round. Did a lot of autograph sketching[68]. Pillow fight at night.

Friday 28th

In afternoon, ship gave a children's party. Children's races held Fancy dress dance at night. On board were Lady Fairfax, Hon Mrs Meldon (sister to Duchess of York) and Lady Bedford.[69]

MARCH 1930

Saturday 1st

Prizes given by Chief Officer. I got a spoon for being runner up in Deck Tennis Final.

Sunday 2nd

Largest waves of voyage. Ship heaving greatly. Pictures at night. Many people sick.

Monday 3rd

Arrived at Freemantle. Met Mailler. Stayed in Perth.

---

[68] Not sure what this means. There are no sketches in his book on that outward trip.

[69] Dad may have been conned here! There are a MR Bedford and a MR Fairfax on the passenger list – the clue might be "Fancy Dress party"! However, the Hon Mrs D A Meldon with her husband Lt Col Meldon (of a Pont St address London SW1) were certainly on board bound for Sydney.

COMMENTARY on PART TWO
THE BLOCK OR KOJONUP LOCATION 7083

Where?; What's in a name; The Camp; The work; A hard life; The neighbours; Precursors; Of horses and dogs

Where?

Part Two takes place near Kojonup WA – a name not perhaps as familiar to outsiders as Freemantle or Perth, so to save the reader reaching for an electronic device and "Googling" in a name, a brief description seems to be appropriate.

According to the official website of the Shire of Kojonup accessed in 2017 this is Kojonup:

"Nestling in the rural heartland of the Great Southern region, historic Kojonup is more than just a gateway to the beautiful South. Settled over 150 years ago, this bustling rural town still bears all the trademarks of a traditional country settlement, with its historic buildings and friendly, safe atmosphere."

With a more academic style:

"The early economy of the town was initially dependent on cutting and transporting sandalwood and kangaroo hunting but by the mid-19th century the wool industry began to boom and by 1906 the shire had 10,500 sheep. By 1989 the shire had seen over 1 million sheep being shorn."[70]

So, the great scheme must have been to set up Mailler with Dad to help him (perhaps at the outset only) as sheep farmers on land which had hitherto not been developed.

What's in a name

Determining the whereabouts of the "The Block" became something of a personal odyssey and no excuses are made for relating this personal "story within a story".

After transcribing Dad's diary, I had but the sketchiest idea of whereabouts he had laboured. All I knew was the brothers had about 1,600 acres south of Kojonup WA and that Dad had named the place as "Kanegarup". I contacted Beverley Scott in Palmyra WA to see if she could find out anything about a place of that name. "Kanegarup" does not occur in his daily entries (nor in his photo album) but, in his sketch book(twice) and in his Notes, this is clearly the name by which Dad knew the Block.

---

[70] For Geography fanatics: Coordinates: 33.84°S 117.15°E Population 1,122 (2006 census) Established1845
Elevation 305 m (1,001 ft) Location 256 km (159 mi) S of Perth 152 km (94 mi) N of Albany
Mean max temp 21.2 °C 70 °F   Mean min temp 9.2 °C 49 °F Annual rainfall 531.3 mm 20.9in

Beverley came up with a blank and it appeared the name had vanished. However, she alerted me to the existence of Local History Groups in both Katanning and Kojonup. [see map 3] Irene Doyle in Katanning was the first to get back to me, so in the subsequent exchange of emails helpful to me in other matters, I sent her Dad's description of The Block which appears in Appendix 4. She then put in an exemplary piece of sleuthing in the agricultural land sales notices of 1931 and found a Block which tallied with Dad's description and was in the name of David Mailer [sic] Yule. [Appendix 4] We had found The Block and now knew that the land was legally recognised as "Kojonup Location 7083". In the fullness of time, the Kojonup group made contact, with the information that there were descendants of people Dad mentions still living in Kojonup: the Warburton or Egerton-Warburton family who clearly were the landowners. I was now able to provide more detail when I asked for information about The Block, though I had determined that the name must be Dad's version of "Kengerrup" which DID appear on some maps

To my surprise and delight, I received an email from Joan O'Halloran, a member of the Kojonup Local History Society, whose family were in the process of acquiring land to the south of the township which, by an amazing coincidence, included Location 7083! Scans of Dad's photos of the granite ridge, the dam and the corrugated iron hut which was "The Camp", which he had also sketched, were duly emailed from Sussex to Australia. To my delight, Joan was able to recognise the site of the granite outcrop and was pretty sure her family knew where the Camp had been. The family then undertook a photoshoot of their property which showed the dam as still extant together with the substantial remains of a stone fireplace. Dad described the hut as having a wide, open fireplace so I knew I was looking at the place where in 1930 Uncle Mailler would have cooked their staple diet of kangaroo stew. The granite ridge, which covers several acres and is one of many such scenic features in that part of Western Australia, was well known to the O'Hallorans as a picnic spot and they were able to send me a snap of Rex Warburton (Jnr) and family at the site where Dad had taken his shot all those years ago. [See Illustrations 2] Joan was able to inform me that the Warburton family knew this area as "Kanegarup" and so it will remain in these pages.

Thus were mysteries solved, though, as my cousin Roberta Yule wisely observed, without emails and the World Wide Web, this would have proved an awesome task.

The Camp

From the notes which Dad appended at the back of the Diary, we have a description of the living accommodation:

"Our Camp, 12ft wide;24ft long; and 8ft high, (Lean to roof) built of corrugated iron sheets. 50- gallon water tank. Beds constructed with chaff bags like stretchers resting on

sort of tressles. (sic) Wide open fire-place. Roughly made table. Log raised up for a seat. Boxes to hold food. Letter box (a petrol tin nailed to a tree) 3 miles from the camp."

This was pioneering stuff! He never mentioned who put up this structure. It may have dated from before the Warburtons acquired The Block or might have been the work of the supposed precursors to the Yules. There was building going on in the area at the time, we know that the Warburtons and the Middletons had new houses, so there was a local supply of stone for that substantial (and long lasting) fireplace. At the time of writing this Commentary, neither is it clear who had begun work on clearing The Block or from where the primitive furnishings originated. The sketch and the photos show that the trees around The Camp had been retained – and are still there today. Presumably, the idea was to give some shade as a corrugated iron shed must have been unbearably hot under the Western Australian sun! For the benefit of Kojonup readers, the Historical Society believe the "letter box" must have been at the junction of Jingalup Road and Bokerup Road.

The work

We may assume that the Warburtons had a plan for developing The Block which led to Mailler taking the lease and Dad being there in the first place. This involved clearing the bush – manually – and improving the irrigation. It seems that there was some sort of financial incentive offered by one of the Banks for doing such work as there several references in this section [e.g. 12 VI 1930 ... *Got £52/10/0 from bank re chopping down*]. The family anecdote suggests that the brothers were "given axes and told to get on with it" but the record suggests a much more planned approach with an area of 90 acres marked out as the first stage of clearing. They certainly seem to have stuck to the task manfully. Dad records that they started chopping on 17 III 1930and finished the last tree on 3 VII 1930. Hard labour indeed but we must remember that rugby playing Dad had inherited the strong shoulders of his father and his maternal grandfather together with the stubborn determination shown by his mother and grandmother. More than axes were needed to sink the new dam and the photo [See Illustrations 2] shows considerable horse and manpower supplied by the Warburton family. Dad's basic engineering training would probably be of some value in this task.

The picture of those days would seem to be of long hours of toil. Dad was the sturdier of the two brothers and whilst clearly the "junior partner" in the enterprise, on can see him leading the axe work. Mailler would join him on felling larger trees with the two-man saw but would mostly be working with a horse clearing felled timer and grubbing out tree roots. True to their Scots Presbyterian origins, Sunday was a day of rest!

A hard life

Reading the Diary again after a lapse of many years, the entry from Wednesday 7th May 1930 leapt off the page: *Chopping down. Out of food. Did little work.* That simple phrase: *Out of food* brings home to us the hardships of life in the bush not readily apparent from the usually laconic entries. One can assume that friends and family came to the aid of the hungry Scots, the entry for the next day shows that they were at Kojonup with Robert Scott and Rex Warburton (Snr) and presumably were fed and obtained some stores. (Did a friendly Kojonup storekeeper run a "slate" for the Yules?) Their Uncle must have assessed the plight of his two nephews for on Sunday 18th, Dad writes: *Uncle, Aunt & Cousins visited us. Left cakes, milk, apples, butter, sweets, treacle, meat.* Manna from Heaven indeed!

The neighbours

Other than the Warburtons, other locals are mentioned in the entries and once again I am obliged to Kojonup folk for explaining who these people were and supplying a map to show where their farms were in relation to The Block. The map, which I have appended on Page 42 for ease of access, shows the Middleton establishment some five or six miles from the Camp and on the route of Dad's long walk to and from Kojonup. There are seven entries suggesting he enjoyed some home comforts with the Middleton's and they, in turn, would probably enjoy the company of this smiley, jocular young man with the Scots accent and his tales, no doubt, of Lanarkshire and the Firth of Clyde and his recent ocean trip. Should their descendants be visiting UK, the author and family owe them a lunch!

Precursors

There were people living in the Kojonup area well before the Scotts and Yules were in Western Australia, in fact, well before any Europeans were there. Today we call their descendants the Noongar People and Dad records a few transactions with them in June 1930. Local recollections are of a Noongar settlement, not far from the Camp across the Main Highway and we can assume it was people from there with whom the Yules had contact. He writes using the terminology of the time of "natives" and "blackfellows", but he is perfectly respectful and probably realised they knew more about horses than he did. The transactions appear to have come to nothing [see below] but Dad did remember, years after, that he had met them. His recollections bear out the currently expressed local opinion that the Noongar supplied labour for local farms, were friendly and hard- working people but tended to suddenly disappear, having gone "walkabout".

Of horses and dogs

Dad had come from a smoky world of trams and trains and Alexander's buses. On his excursions into the wilder lands to the north and west of Glasgow, there was always the

Clyde steamer and/or his bike to get him back to that world. The Western Australian bush in 1930 was a different matter – he was twelve or thirteen miles from the nearest store with no vehicular transport. However, the Diary notes: *Brought mare and foal from Mr Newton's,* just two days after arriving on the Block. Thus, every reader of the Diary, when confronted with entries such as: *Walked to Kojonup for stores* [22 IV 1930], asks: Why didn't he ride?

It was not that central Scotland was wholly mechanised – pit ponies were in use and draught horses were common until the fifties – but one cannot envisage an occasion when a mining surveyor would need a horse and so Dad would not have any experience of riding one. Remembered anecdote from his brothers suggests that he had tried to ride but had fallen off and never attempted to mount again. His elder brother, as we know, had been a merchant seaman, an occupation with about the same need for a horse as a mining surveyor, but had clearly adapted to the needs of his new country [28 IV 1930: *Mailler rode to Kojonup*]. What Mailler thought of this accomplishment gap is not recorded nor does it lie in any remembered anecdote but both he and the neighbours must presumably have wondered how the brothers could run sheep on perhaps 1,000 acres with one of them unable to ride.

This must have occurred to Dad, or maybe he was prompted by brother or concerned neighbours, for on 19 VI 1930 we find him writing: *Wrote AJ Bennet about surveying work.* Kojonup memories suggest that neighbour, Fred Cox (brother in law of the Warburtons) was a "surveyor" so maybe the suggestion had come from that direction.

It seems that despite Dad's lack of horse management skills there was an attempt at stock breeding, but this came to naught and the brothers' lack of luck with horses and ill luck generally seems exemplified in Dad's entry for 19 VI 1930: *Found our mare dead in creek.* [The assumption is she had eaten something poisonous which had escaped the clearing.]

Of the foal mentioned above, there is no further mention and indeed the comings and goings of horses are a bit difficult to track. The other "farm stock" recorded is Nell the dog. It seems fair to assume that she was the animal mentioned as Uncle's dog that the brothers were given on 8 V 1930. Although Dad in later life displayed a rapport with dogs – he often spoke of Glen, the collie at Cloybank – Nell never figured in his reminiscences. He did mention having once had a dog that was "no use" and this may have been poor Nell – the dog that no-one wanted. Those readers of a tender-hearted disposition may wish to believe she was found a home with neighbours, but one is forced to conclude that, in the unsentimental environment depicted here, that she came a short, sad, sudden end.

* * * * *

With the reassurance that the following does not contain a record of an accident in the bush befalling a merchant seaman turned motor-mechanic or his assistant, a rugby-playing mining surveyor, it is your turn to read what a young Scotsman far from home put in his diary in the Western Australian bush in 1930.

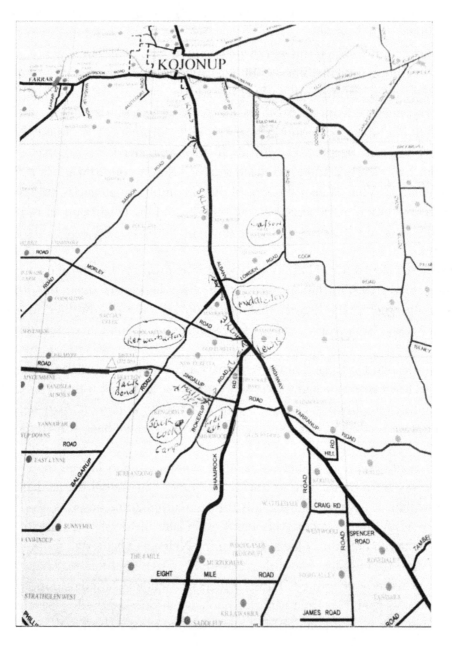

Compiled by the Kojonup Historical Society and reproduced here with thanks, the above shows the location of farms with their owners round about the time of the Diary. The camp of the Noongar People was probably east of the Albany Highway, north of its junction with Jingalup Road.

PART TWO
"The Block" 4ᵗʰ March 1930 – 23ʳᵈ July 1930

MARCH 1930

Tuesday 4ᵗʰ
Seeing around Perth & Freemantle. Saw the P&O liner "Balranald"[71]

Wednesday 5ᵗʰ
Left Perth by Train 7.10 am. [72] Arr. Katanning 8pm. Went to Uncle's house.[73]

Thursday 6ᵗʰ & Friday 7ᵗʰ
At Katanning. Thunder and wonderful lightning.

Saturday 8ᵗʰ
At Katanning. Saw cricket.

Sunday 9ᵗʰ
At Katanning. Looked after the children.[74]

Monday 10ᵗʰ
Uncle ran Mailler and I to the block. Got letters from home.[75]

Tuesday 11ᵗʰ
Met Rex & Angus Warburton[76] at Rex's house. Afternoon setting out fence line for 90 acres clearing. Dull days some rain.

Wednesday 12ᵗʰ
Brought mare and foal from Mr Newton's[77], Kojonup to block 13 miles.

Thursday 13ᵗʰ
At Kojonup. Sale Day. Saw Uncle. Stayed at Warburton's[78] for the night.

Friday 14ᵗʰ
Pegging out fence line for 90 acres.

---

[71] Meaning a ship of P&O Line

[72] A journey no longer possible

[73] And presumably stayed a few nights there.

[74] According to Beverley Scott's "Our Scott Family History", "Uncle" had 5 children: John, Robert, Mary, Hugh, Margaret and the last 2 would have been aged 9 &5 at that time and perhaps not deemed old enough for Church. See Appendix 0

[75] Perhaps waiting in mailbox at end of track

[76] See Commentaries and Sketch Map This would be the new house at Woolareen.

[77] Identified in an email from JO'H thus: *My husband knew where Mr Fred Newton lived. He had a dairy farm just north of town on the Albany highway. I also found out by reading in one of the Kojonup history books that he had a herd of 40 cows and would deliver the milk around town after milking. Another part of the story put in place.*

[78] Presumably Angus Warburton in Kojonup.

Saturday 15th

Finished pegging out fence line. Got letters and "News"[79] from Mother.

Sunday 16th

Spent afternoon at Warburton's[80]

Monday 17th

Locating dam site and chopping down in 90acres.

Tuesday 18th

At Kojonup for stores. Mailler shot first brush[81] I tasted.

Wednesday 19th

Chopping down in 90 acres. Very warm.[82]

Thursday 20th

Mailler helping Angus to sink dam for Fred Cox[83]. I wrote to Johnny through Alex at Hinshelwoods.[84] At night we were at party in Rex Warburton's house[85].

Friday 21st

Helping Angus at Cox's dam.

Saturday 22nd

Chopping down in 90 acres in forenoon. Got letter from home.

Sunday 23rd

At Mrs Middleton's[86] all day.

Monday 24th

Chopping down in 90 acres.

Tuesday 25th

Mailler shot Goanna 3ft 4 ins long[87]. Chopping down in 90 acres. Warm.

Wednesday 26th

Sinking trial hole at dam site.

Thursday 27th

At Kojonup for stores. Got letters from home.

Friday 28th

Sinking trial hole at dam site.

---

[79] Local paper from Scotland.

[80] Rex this time as walkable from the Camp

[81] Assume this to be the Western Brush Wallaby (*Macropus irma*)

[82] Dad's first understatement. Throughout read "very warm" as "hot"!

[83] From Joan O'Halloran: *Fred Cox was also a surveyor and was a brother in law to Angus Warburton*

[84] Reference is obscure

[85] From J.O'H: *This was on Rex's (junior) 2nd birthday which coincided with the celebration of the Warburtons new house.* Reported in local press though Dad's initial wrong.

[86] Neighbours. See sketch map.

[87] Monitor lizard. Dad wrote of "Race Horse" or "Long Tailed" Goanna. Currently unidentified.

Saturday 29th
Forenoon, clearing dam site.
Sunday 30th
Clearing out camp. Washing.
Monday 31st
Chopping down in 90 acres.

APRIL 1930

Tuesday 1st
Chopping in 90 acres. Mailler shot a brush[88]. Had a headache yesterday.
Wednesday 2nd
Chopping down and preventing fires from spreading in 90 acres.
Thursday 3rd.
At Kojonup for stores.
Friday 4th
Chopping down and preventing fires from spreading. 1st heavy rain since Oct 1929[89].
Saturday 5th
Chopping down in 90 acres. Got letter and "Sunday Post" from Mother.
Sunday 6th
Washing. I wrote Mrs Dickie.
Monday 7th
Chopping down in 90 acres. Very warm.
Tuesday 8th
Chopping. Took photo of horses and L to R Bob, Rex, Angus and George[90].
Wednesday 9th
Chopping. Uncle brought letters to Camp. Word of Mrs Kelly's illness[91].
Thursday 10th
At Kojonup. No buyers at sale. Few sheep. Dinner with Uncle. Chopping in afternoon.
Friday 11th
Chopping 90 acres.
Saturday 12th.
Chopping in forenoon. Spent afternoon and evening at Middleton's.
Sunday 13th
Looking for water holes. I shot my first brush. Drinking water finished.
Entries for next 3 days all read: "Chopping down in 90 acres."

---

[88] See earlier note.
[89] Don't know how he knew this
[90] See Illustrations.
[91] Reference obscure

Thursday 17th
Chopping down and burning round 90 acres as boundary.
Friday 18th
Chopping down in 90 acres.
Saturday 19th
Chopping in 90 acres. Letters from Father, Mother and Alex. Mrs Kelly dead.
Sunday 20th
Sharpening tools etc. I mended Alex' flannel trousers.
Monday 21st
Chopping down in 90 acres. Heavy rain showers.
Tuesday 22nd
Walked to Kojonup for stores. Got a lift back to Mail box[92] with Mr Watson.
Wednesday 23rd
Chopping down and burning round 90 acres boundary. Killed Brown Snake[93] 12 inches long
Thursday 24th
Chopping in 90 acres
Friday 25th
Chopping down and burning boundary.
Saturday 26th
Sorting bank at new dam. Got letter from Mother and Alex saying Johnnie, Willie and Alex might be out in 1931.[94]
Sunday 27th
Picking holes for plough at new dam.[95]
Monday 28th
Forenoon at dam. Afternoon Mailler rode to Kojonup to see bank inspector. I burned tree and drew plan of "Oronsay".
Tuesday 29th
Measured new dam. I burned trees. Mailler took Angus' horse back.
Wednesday 30th
Burning down large trees on west side of creek.

MAY 1930

Thursday 1st
Burning on w side of creek. Bank inspector inspected new dam.

---

92 See Sketch Map p42
93 Dad's notes: "About 3ft long. Dangerous. Brown with black markings"
94 See Introduction
95 See Illustrations

Friday 2nd

Burning on W. side of creek.

Saturday 3rd

Burning down. I went for mail. Saw small snake. No letters.

Sunday 4th

Burning down w side of creek. Did some clothes washing.

Monday 5th

Sawed remaining large trees on W side of creek.

Tuesday 6th

Chopping down now on E. side of creek. Short of food.

Wednesday 7th

Chopping down. Out of food. Did little work.

Thursday 8th

Sale day. Saw Uncle. Rex took us in. Uncle ran us back and left us his dog.[96]

Friday 9th

Bailed out old dam.

Saturday 10th

At Middleton's house. Letters said Johnny etc waiting till 1932.[97]

Sunday 11th

Chopped down tree overhanging new dam. Took things easy.

Monday 12th

Worked around camp as Warburtons were clearing out old dam.

Tuesday 13th

Warburtons clearing out old dam. Burning down some trees. At night Mailler rode to Kojonup re payment for new dam.

Wednesday 14th

Burning down in 90 acres. Good steady wind. I shot my second brush.

Thursday 15th

Burning and chopping down in 90 acres. Warburtons finished clearing out old dam.

Friday 16th

Chopping down in 90 acres.

Saturday 17th

Grubbing scrub & suckers in forenoon. Got letter from Mother & Alex.

Sunday 18th

Uncle, Aunt & Cousins [98] visited us. Left cakes, milk, apples, butter, sweets, treacle, meat.

---

[96] Presumably Nell mentioned later
[97] See sketch map. From that it seems he would pass by the "letter box" on his way to Middleton's
[98] See Illustrations

Monday 19th

Chopping down in 90 acres. Went halfway through bush to Middletons but too dark to proceed further.

Tuesday 20th

Chopping down in 90 acres and burning scrub & poison in creeks and round rocks. Very warm day.

Wednesday 21st

Chopping down in 90 acres. Very warm.

Thursday 22nd

Commenced chopping down 2nd half of 90 acres.

Friday 23rd

Chopping down in 90 acres

Saturday 24th

Rose at 5am. Walked to Kojonup.[99] Dinner in town. Got mother's £5 at bank. Called in at Middleton's on way back. Played Bridge. Scores:- We 437 They 504. Arrived back at camp dead tired at 4.30 am.

Sunday 25th

Very tired.[100] Took a walk over proposed 200 acres. Clearing in afternoon.

Monday 26th

Walked to Rex Warburton's and went to Kojonup for stores. Stayed at Rex's overnight. Too dark to go back to camp. Sent £3 with application form for clearing proposed 200 acres.

Tuesday 27th

Raining heavy all day. Wrote Mr & Mrs Woodcock.

Wednesday 28th

Raining all day. Did no work. Drew sketch to send home showing proposed outlay of paddocks.

Thursday 29th

Chopping down in 90 acres. Wrote Grandma. Sun shining all day.

Friday 30th.

Chopping down in 90 acres. Dry warm day. Cold at night time.

Saturday 31st

Chopping down in 90 acres. Letters from Mother, Alex and one from Johnnie in answer to mine through Alex at Hinshelwoods.[101]

---

[99] This was 13 miles!

[100] Hardly surprising!

[101] See March 20th

JUNE 1930

Sunday 1st

Did a little chopping. Mailler shot a brush with a young one in its pouch.

Monday 2nd

Chopping down in 90 acres

Tuesday 3rd

Chopping down in 90 acres

Wednesday 4th

Chopping down in 90 acres

Thursday 5th

Chopping down in 90 acres. Dick Spencer visited us.[102]

Friday 6th

Chopping in 90 acres

Saturday 7th

Chopping in 90 acres. Spent evening at Middleton's.

Sunday 8th

Not working. Wrote Willie.

Monday 9th

Chopping in 90 acres. Mailler shot a brush.

Tuesday 10th

Chopping in 90 acres

Wednesday 11th

Chopping in 90 acres. Angus came to see us about payments.

Thursday 12th

Sale day. Saw Uncle. Angus repudiated his verbal agreement to defer payments for two years. Got £52/10/0 from bank re chopping down.[103]

Friday 13th

Sawing down some large trees to thin out standing timber.

Saturday 14th

Chopping in 90 acres. Got a "Bulletin" and "Sunday Post" from home.[104]

Sunday 15th

In forenoon we went to see "Snowy", a native, about breaking in a horse. In afternoon went to Katanning with Angus Warburton. Stayed with Uncle. Played Bridge.

Monday 16th

Nothing settled with Angus re payments. Came back to block.

---

[102] Reference obscure

[103] See Commentary

[104] Popular Scottish newspapers. "Bulletin" had a long life. "Sunday Post" still extant.

<u>Tuesday 17th</u>

Fixing up horse yard and race[105]. Chopping down in 90 acres.

<u>Wednesday 18th</u>

Chopping down in 90 acres. Black fellows took out all horses including own to be broken in.

<u>Thursday 19th</u>

Chopping in 90 acres. Wrote AJ Bennet about surveying work.[106] Found our mare dead in creek.

<u>Friday 20th</u>

Chopping in 90 acres. Got "Record" & "Post" & letters from Mother, Alex and Isobel Kemp. Letter also from David Black.

<u>Sunday 22nd</u>

Raining all day.

<u>Monday 23rd</u>

Chopping in 90 acres. Showery day.

<u>Tuesday 24th</u>

Chopping in 90 acres. Showery day.

<u>Wednesday 25th</u>

Chopping 90 acres. Black fellows brought back our horse.

<u>Thursday 26th</u>

Raining. Took horse back to natives as it was not quiet enough. [107]

<u>Friday 27th</u>

Raining. Wrote Mother and Alex.

<u>Saturday 28th</u>

Walked to Kojonup and back for stores. "Post" and letter from mother.

<u>Sunday 29th</u>

Raining. Resting in forenoon. Chopping afternoon.

<u>Monday 30th</u>

Chopping in 90 acres.

██████████

<u>Tuesday 1st</u>

Chopping in 90 acres

<u>Wednesday 2nd</u>

Chopping in 90 acres

---

[105] Presumably a paddock.

[106] First sign of disenchantment

[107] See Commentary.

Thursday 3rd

Finished chopping in 90 acres. (Last tree a She- Oak[108] at 3.15 pm).

Friday 4th

Dodging about. Mailler shot a kangaroo.

Saturday 5th

Wrote Johnny. Letter from Mother. Got completely drenched going to Middleton's.

Sunday 6th

Wrote Aunt Susan.

Monday 7th

Brought Mailler's trunk from Angus Warburton's[109].

Tuesday 8th

Angus came to make payment terms.

Wednesday 9th

Washing clothes

Thursday 10th

Walked to Kojonup. Sale day. No sheep. Uncle coming in ten days to take us off block if no agreement made with Angus Warburton.

Friday 11th

Knocked down horse yard. I shot a "28" or Ring Neck parrot[110] and sent tail home.[111] Wrote Mother and Grandma.

Saturday 12th

Wrote Alex. Got an "Express" from Mother.

Sunday 13th

Washing. Wrote Mr Graham.

Monday 14th

Commenced chopping down an extra 10 acres. Some rain. Answered Mr Bennett's (surveyor) letter about no work.

Tuesday 15th

Lounging about. Wet day.

Wednesday 16th

Chopping down.

Thursday 17th

Walked to Kojonup and back for stores. Got letters from Mother, Johnnie, Grandma and David & Winnie Devine.

---

[108] Rather a rude name for a species of beech of which the males bear no fruit.

[109] Though no indication of how that was accomplished.

[110] One of the Bernardius species. Call sounds like "twenty-eight"

[111] Where it was on view for many years

Friday 18th

Stocking firewood and washing clothes. Wrote Mother & Johnnie about giving up the block.

Saturday 19th

Offered our dog "Nell" to Jack Bond who declined the offer.[112] Nothing arranged about payments with Angus.

Sunday 20th

Washing clothes and packing up. Shooting expedition. Mailler shot one out of a large group of kangaroos. I missed with two shots.

Monday 21st

Chopping trees

Tuesday 22nd

Chopping trees

Wednesday 23rd

Walked to Kojonup. Uncle ran us back then took us off block to Katanning.

---

[112] We do not know what became of Nell. Jack Bond was a neighbour. See Map p42

COMMENTARY on PART THREE

KATANNING WESTERN AUSTRALIA JULY 1930 - MARCH 1931

Exits and entrances; Katanning; Back in town; Workless in Western Australia

Exits and entrances

Before the reader finds out what happened next, it seems right that a note is made of those last few weeks in the bush. As stated, this book has not been written to air ancient grievances against inhabitants of Western Australia, alive or dead. The author and family leave it to readers to make up their own minds about the row over the tenancy of Block 7083 which ended the farming project of the far travelled Yule brothers. We would make the point here that Dad could not have been party to any form of contract made in Western Australia in 1929 by Uncle or Mailler as he was far away across the oceans. The reader will probably have come to the opinion that he was very much the junior partner in the enterprise and would have been an embarrassed onlooker in any of those recorded meetings with Angus Warburton.

Across the span of decades, one can construct a scenario of a feasible plan to run sheep on what the North of England calls "intake land" and a very reasonable offer by the landlords to defer rent until the farm had become viable. The trigger for the row seems to have been that £52-10s the Yules received from some still undisclosed Bank for clearing the Block. Perhaps Angus, with possibly some justification, saw that as income which meant that rent for the Block would now be due. Robert Scott ["Uncle"] comes over as a shrewd Scots businessman and one can see it would be he who argued that this was not income from farming but income arising from clearing land for farming. Maybe it is unfair to say so, but it might seem to be in character that he took a very uncompromising view of the situation and, in effect said: "Find somebody else to clear your block". Reading the next part of the Diary, one can conclude that he then showed a strong sense of responsibility in having placed his nephews – one of whom had come halfway around the world specially – in an unfortunate situation and did all that he could to alleviate their circumstances. There is no record or family reminiscence of what his elder sister Bella thought of said circumstances, but one can imagine her reaction.

The reader must be assured that no "clan feud" exists between Yules and Warburtons and, of course, had that misunderstanding long ago not happened, this book would not exist! Other than a continued sense of pride in the physical achievement of clearing ninety acres of bush, the thing Dad took away from that time which stayed with him and which he wished his family to note was the simple rule: "Get it in writing".

Katanning

With the same apologies as were made earlier to the residents of Kojonup, a brief note about Katanning will perhaps help readers in the Northern Hemisphere. Researching various authorities, we learn that Katanning is a town located 277 km [173 miles] south-east of Perth, Western Australia on the Great Southern Highway. [See Map 3] With a population of about 3,600, it is chiefly known as a sheep selling centre.

As with Kojonup, Dad records no dissatisfaction with the place or the people. We must assume that for the first four weeks or so after Uncle brought the Yules back from the Block, that, for a few weeks, they lodged with him in Katanning, a situation which may not have been entirely convenient for either party

This is one part of our story to which we have the record of an eye-witness: Mary Wright (1919-2018), daughter of Robert and Lily Scott, whom Beverly Scott visited in connection with research for this book in January 2016. Although at a very advanced age, Mary could remember the Yules, and Beverley Scott related her recollections to me in an email from which I quote:

"One anecdote Mary related was that Lily Scott sent food down to "the boys". She sent a few cooked chickens and vegetables, and apparently Bob Yule constructed a "ship out of the dried chicken bones" and sent it back to Katanning as a gift for Mary. (By the way, Mary was called "Molly" when she was a child.) Apparently, Bob Scott was not impressed with such time-wasting activities, because the boys were "on the block to work!" Sounds like a very hard taskmaster!!"
"Another anecdote was when Mailler and Bob Yule were staying with the family in Katanning. Lily used to take a shovel of live coals from the kitchen stove into the living room to start the fire there. Bob Yule helped out with this task and used to walk through the house with the shovel of coals warning "Fire, fire" in his Glaswegian accent."

The feeding of the Yules out in the bush tallies with the Diary and these anecdotes have an authentic ring. In the days when a chicken was something of a luxury item in UK, Dad's "party piece" was to assemble chicken bones in the shape of a ship and Dad would often reprise his Katanning "Fire, fire" act [probably learnt in his Uddingston youth] when lighting the fire in the lounge at Fairfield Road, Stockton Heath, Warrington. However, as a proud Uddingstonian, he would have disputed the "Glaswegian accent" tag!

Back in town

After weeks in the bush with little recourse to home comforts, Dad may well have not been too troubled about the move to Katanning. Although he was homeless and out of work he was at least back in a township and a busy industrial (mill and railway hub) and commercial (shops and sale yard) centre, a place he probably found preferable to Denny! The young man from Uddingston was far from the trams and Tunnock's pies he knew but there were trains to be admired, cinema shows and, of course, his lifelong obsession – cricket. The reader will notice no less than 17 references to games of cricket he watched or was involved in, together with the scores in most of the matches. One suspects he was relying on memory rather than press reports for he was not consistent in his spelling. [Forty years on he was painstakingly transcribing match details from the *Warrington Guardian* for the weekly letter to the author.] We are obliged to Arthur Todd for his clarification of Dad's entries and his note on Katanning cricket at that time:

"The Wanderers Cricket Club still operates and plays on the main oval at the Katanning Recreation and Leisure Centre. Australs is now known as Australs North and plays on what is referred to as the "Hockey Fields" at the Rec Centre, but the Railway Cricket Club did not last much longer than the mid 30's. Back then they played on the town oval which, at the time, had a small wooden grandstand with changerooms built in. The ground was basically levelled flat with no grass. "

Dad would have found cricket in Katanning, played on matting wickets on a dry, dusty outfield, very different from Uddingston but it must have provided a focus for him, a framework of familiar surroundings in a far from familiar situation. Is it too much to suggest that watching the game, which had been part of his life since being taken to watch his uncle bowling for Uddingston, had a therapeutic value?
 In later life, his cricket anecdotes were mostly about Uddingston and the Western Union, but he made one telling remark when watching Messrs Lillie and Thomson bowling in the 70's that fast, short pitched bowling was commonplace at Katanning. This seems an interesting memory in view of the furore in the season after Dad went home, when an England touring party adopted a version of this tactic!

Workless in Western Australia
Despite the presence of "civilised" amenities and, one assumes, some provision of home comforts from his Aunt Lily, Dad found himself living like a vagrant and doing such casual labouring tasks as his Uncle could find for the two nephews for whose plight, as we have noted, he surely must have felt some responsibility. The three months of having a tent for his home, which Dad refers to throughout as "camping", as though it were a holiday, were ended when he and Mailler moved to "The Pines" in December. This was a hostel for homeless/ unemployed men which was opened by the Presbyterian Church in response, one assumes, to the plight of many who had found themselves in the same situation as the Yule brothers. Dad was never one to be idle for any length of time and we can envisage him keeping himself busy throughout his days at "The Pines".

We have seen that he was a prolific correspondent and the writing case would still be in constant use. Although he did not "tabulate" letters in and out in the Diary, he had clearly kept a record which he enters on 2 II 1931 showing a total in the year to date of 116, to 20 different recipients! Writing further, he added to the pages of notes about Australian flora and fauna that he made at the back of the Diary with observations he would have taken from newspapers or reference books at "The Pines". As ever, he found time for his sketch book [See Illustrations 2]. The two line-drawings he did, dated December 1930 and January 1931: *"The Pines", Piesse St., Katanning* and *"Shadows of the evening" At "The Pines" Katanning West Australia* represent the very best of his ability.

Like many before him and since, he struggled with the high temperatures of a Western Australian summer though he rather understates this by writing that the day was "Very warm". True to his engineering training, he "tabulates" the temperatures – presumably there was a thermometer at "The Pines" – but at the start of December we get the first sign of negotiations with his family regarding his return home. The thrust of these messages would be that he needed money not only for his passage to UK but also to refund the subsidy he had received for the outward passage as he had not remained in Australia for the qualifying period.

We hear of more "fill-in" bits and pieces of work and then Dad is taken on as a site labourer in the construction on the Hume Pipe Company's plant, of which I have no details. This was something of a return to Engineering but not at the level envisaged when was sitting in the Evening Classes in Glasgow. Of course, he records the details of this uncongenial toil (carefully noting the hours and hourly rate), but each difficult day must have reinforced his inclination to return to Scotland, an inclination which would turn to determination with the abrupt ending of his employment. What he could not have known was that this hard labour under the Western Australian sun was to stand him in very good stead in a few months' time.

But all that lay ahead after Part Three of his Australian saga.

PART THREE
24TH JULY 1930 – 26TH MARCH 1931

The entries for the last week of July are rather terse each beginning "At Katanning", and some with only that. To spare the reader the tedious repetition, I have noted only the additional information and skipped any days when that was the only entry as follows:

Thursday 24th
Weeding garden.
Saturday 26th
Saw Australian Football match[113]
Sunday 27th
At Church[114]
Tuesday 29th
Gardening
Wednesday 30th
Got "Bulletin" from Mother. Wrote Mother and Alex.

AUGUST 1930

As above, the entries for much of the month all begin:"Katanning", so once again, to avoid repetition, I record only a day with an additional entry:

Friday 1st
Letter and "Post" from Mother.
Saturday 2nd
At Australian Football game.
Monday 4th
Wrote home.
Thursday 7th
Letters from Father, Mother and Mrs Dickie[115]
Friday 8th
Got a "Bulletin" from home.
Saturday 9th
Saw an Australian Football game.
Sunday 10th
At Church.

---

[113] Presumably Australian Rules as the term "Soccer" is used later
[114] This would be the "The Scots Church" or Presbyterian Church nowadays the "Uniting Church". The building is now a Heritage Site.
[115] See General Commentary p26

Monday 11th
Wrote David Black.
Wednesday 13th
Wrote Mrs Monaghan.[116]
Friday 15th
Wrote, Mother, Father and Singer Sewing Machine Co in Perth re possible jobs.[117]
Letters from Mother and Mr & Mrs Kemp[118] with photos.
Saturday 16th
"Express" and "Post" from home. "Express" from Mrs Dickie also.
Sunday 17th
Put up tent in one of Elder Smith's paddocks. Killed two sand snakes about 12 inches long.[119]
Monday 18th
Katanning. Gardening. Went to camp.
The entries for the rest of August and to the end of November all begin "Katanning. Camping" or just "Camping" and, as before, for ease of reading, I have omitted that text and any day's entry without additional record.
Tuesday 19th
Made a shelter for Uncle for milking cow. Mailler shot 2 ducks. Warm.
Wednesday 12th
Windy. Burning some stumps and trees. Wrote Mother.
Friday 22nd
Showery. Killed sheep for Uncle.[120] Letter from Mother. PC from J&A.[121]
Saturday 23rd
Wrote Immigration Dept. about a job. Dry & warm.
Sunday 24th
Wrote David & Winnie Devine. At Church.
Monday 25th
Wrote Grandma. Sawing wood for Uncle. Saw a Soccer match.
Tuesday 26th
Wrote Mr& Mrs Kemp, Isobel & Mrs Stewart.
Wednesday 27th
Stormy day. Saw a Soccer match.

---

[116] See General Commentary p26
[117] No idea what these would be
[118] See General Commentary p26
[119] Which Dad lists as "same practically as Grass Snake"
[120] No mention of how
[121] Presumably, Johnnie and Alex.

Thursday 28th
Wrote Mother.
Friday 29th
Commenced work altering Sale Yards. P.C. from Johnnie, Alex and Isobel. "Express" from Mother.
Saturday 30th
Working at Sale Yards. At Soccer Final afternoon.
Sunday 31st
Washing clothes. Wrote J& Alex.

SEPTEMBER 1930

Monday 1st to Wednesday 3rd, entries all read: Camping. Working at Sale Yards.
Thursday 4th
Working at Sale Yards. Wrote Father & Mother.
Friday 5th
Working at Sale Yards. Letter, "Post" & "News" from Mother.
Saturday 6th
Raining. Not working
Sunday 7th
 Wrote Mrs Dickie.
Monday 8th
Stopped work temp[orarily]
Tuesday 9th
Wrote Hume Pipe Company re work.
Wednesday 10th
Wrote Flossy Bruce[122]
Thursday 11th
Got £4-8-6 from the joiner.[123]
Friday 12th
Wrote Mother. Sale Day. Letters from Mother & Alex. Got "Bulletin" & P.C. from Willie.
Saturday 13th
Re-commenced work at Sale Yards.

---

[122] Double underlined but implication uncertain. See General Commentary p26
[123] Presumably as pay from Sale Yard work. 4 pounds, 8 shillings & sixpence.

<u>Sunday 14th</u>
Very warm. Wrote Alex.
From 15th to 24th entries repeat Working at Sale Yards *so will not repeat text.*
<u>Monday 15th</u>
Very stormy.
<u>Thursday 18th</u>
Wrote Mother.
<u>Friday 19th.</u>
Letters from Mother & Hume Pipe Company.
<u>Saturday 20th</u>
East Perth beat Katanning at Australian Football.
<u>Sunday 21st</u>
Answered Hume Pipe Company's letter re possible work
<u>Thursday 25th</u>
Repairing fences in E S's[124] paddocks.
<u>Friday 26th</u>
Letters from Father & Mother re us off the block[125]. Repairing fences E. S's paddocks.
Got a "Sunday Post", "Bulletin" and "Record" from Willie.
<u>Saturday 27th</u>
Repairing fences. Got £5-8-0 for work at Sale Yards.
<u>Monday 29th</u>
Repairing fences on Elder Smith's paddocks.
<u>Tuesday 30th</u>
Finished fence repairs. Wrote Grandma. Sawed wood for Uncle.

OCTOBER 1930

As above, I have omitted repetitive entries: "Katanning", "Camping" and skipped days with any such as sole content.

<u>Wednesday 1st</u>
Sawing wood for Uncle. Letter from Mother in answer to own re left block in Kojonup.[126]
<u>Thursday 2nd</u>
Sawing wood.

---

[124] Elder Smith's
[125] What John & Bella thought of the matter is not known.
[126] Presumably 18th July

Friday 3rd

Wrote Mother. Sent a paper home.

Saturday 4th

Sawing wood. At cricket game.[127]

Sunday 5th

Repaired flannel trousers. At Church.

Monday 6th

Walked to Katanning town dam[128]. Sawing wood for Uncle.

Tuesday 7th

Sawing wood. Walked down Albany line.[129]

Wednesday 8th

Wood sawing. Letter and 2 "Records" from Mother. Letter from Jack Dickie.

Thursday 9th

Sawing wood.

Friday 10th

Wrote Mother and Neal's Retread, Perth for a job. Letter from David Black.

Saturday 11th

Woodnailing 106 all out Railways 126 all out (Mailler 1 not out)

Sunday 12th

At an all day cricket match. Dinner at Uncles. Pictures[130] at night, (Berry Wallace in "A Beggars Life")[131]

Monday 13th

Working in Sale Yards in forenoon.

Wednesday 15th

Got a "Record" and letters from Father & Mother.

Thursday 16th

Wrote Hume Pipe Co for an interview

Friday 17th

Wrote Father & Mother together

---

[127] See Commentary

[128] From an email from Arthur Todd April 2018: *The "Town Dam" he refers to was, in fact, a dam built by Frederick Piesse to supply water to his extensive orchards and vineyards. Frederick is known as the founding father of Katanning. The area is now being developed into a large community space with a large man-made lake. The lake will be used as an evaporation pond for water off the roof of the new sale yards (the largest undercover, animal friendly, livestock saleyards in the Southern Hemisphere*

[129] The railway. See Illustrations 2

[130] An email from Arthur Todd of April 2018 explains: *In the 1930's there were two places films were shown in Katanning. One was the Katanning Town Hall and were known as "Repatriation Pictures". The other was "Kings Hall" which was adjacent to the Town Hall but on the rear street*

[131] His memory at fault! Must be "Beggars of Life", 1928 talkie with Wallace Beery.

Saturday 18th

Spent all day with Mr C McCubbing, an Uddingstonian.[132]

Monday 20th

Painting numerals at Sale Yards. Letter from Hume Pipe Company saying names already noted.

Tuesday 21st

Numbering Sale Yards.

Wednesday 22nd

Repairing netting pens at Sale Yards.

Thursday 23rd

Wrote Father & Mother together. Letters from Father, Mother & Alex.

Friday 24th

Wrote Johnnie & Willie together.

Saturday 25th

Warm. Railways 102 (Spawart 71) Wanderers 62

Sunday 26th

At cricket in forenoon. Commenced letter home to all. Pictures at night.

Monday 27th

Picking peas in one of Elder Smith's fields.

Tuesday 28th

Washing clothes. Darning socks. Picking peas. Cool day.

Wednesday 29th

Washing clothes. Letters from Mother & Grandma. Got a "Record".

Thursday 30th

Finished letter home to all. At Katanning Show.

Friday 31st

Went to Circus at night. Heavy rain.

NOVEMBER 1930

Saturday 1st.

At Cricket in afternoon.

Sunday 2nd

Strong winds

Monday 3rd

Picking peas.

---

[132] Sole reference

Wednesday 5th

Letter & "Record" from Mother. Got letter from Central Agency (Aust.) Perth asking for particulars of myself re possible employment. Replied to Central Agency.

Thursday 6th

Stooking hay in one of E.S paddocks. Uncle told us we got promised work with the Hume Pipe Company.

Friday 7th

Wrote Mother.

Saturday 8th

Weeding Uncle's paddock garden. Mailler shot a Race Horse Goanna[133] 3' – 6" long. Katanning 51 Railways 91 (Spouart 56)

Sunday 9th

I killed a Race Horse Goanna with a stick (3' – 4" long). Commenced letter to all at home.

Monday 10th

Got 8/3 for stooking hay. Took photo of lizard & myself. Also Mailler at tent.[134]

Tuesday 11th

Killed sheep for Uncle.

Wednesday 12th

Posted "Western Mail" home. Repairing fences in and around Sale Yards. Letters from Mother, Johnnie & Central Agency, Perth W.A.

Thursday 13th

Acknowledged letter from Central Agency. Wrote Aunt Susan, Grandma & Jack Dickie.

Friday 14th

Wrote Mrs. Black (Uddingston) about letter from Central Agency[135]. Sale Day. Finished letter home. 12 pages. Wrote Johnnie.

Saturday 15th

Strong winds. Mailler got £10 from A. Warburton re transforming back the block[136]. Wet forenoon

Monday 17th

Washing clothes. Warm day.

Tuesday 18th

Sawing wood for Uncle. Commenced letter home to all. I killed a sheep for Uncle.

---

[133] See Note 17 in Part Two. "A sort of green colour " noted Dad.

[134] See Illustrations 2

[135] No reason given

[136] Joan O'Halloran suggests this should read "transferring" which would make sense. My error!

Wednesday 19th

Elder Smith's Off-Shears Sale.[137] Letters and 3 papers from Mother, the first from Cloybank[138].

Thursday 20th

Did a little wood chopping. Watered garden at night.

Friday 21st

Finished letter home to all. 12 pages. Chopped a little wood. Got buggy ride to town.

Saturday 22nd

Chopping and sawing wood. Very warm. Bathing in dam.

Australs 46 Railways 126.

Sunday 23rd

Killed sheep for Uncle. Bathing in dam.

Monday 24th

Sawing wood and bathing in dam. Letter from a Scotchman[139], C McIntyre of Central Agency.

Tuesday 25th

Sawing wood. Some rain. Commenced letter home to all. Stormy day. Aunt Jeannie[140] sent us £1 each from New Zealand.

Wednesday 26th

Letters from Mother with Mrs Dickie's enclosed.

Thursday 27th

Sawing wood and washing clothes. Wrote C McIntyre.

Friday 28th

Wrote Mr Rankin & Mr McCulloch a 10 page letter. Got a "News". Finished letter home. 4 pages.

Saturday 29th

In forenoon stacking hay. Bathing in dam.

Woodnailing[141] Rovers 213 for 3 wkts Katanning 119 for 8 wkts[142].

Sunday 30th

Sawed a meat chopping block for Uncle. Very warm. Bathing in dam.

---

[137] Sheep who had been recently shorn.

[138] Cloybank Farm, Banknock. See Commentary

[139] Yes he did write that!

[140] Jean Scott b1878 younger sister of Bella Scott who married James Young and moved to New Zealand.

[141] Prob Woodanilling

[142] Sounds like drawn match on a good pitch.

DECEMBER 1930

Most of the entries from 2ⁿᵈ Dec 1930 to 14ᵗʰ Jan 1931, begin: At "The Pines". As with earlier repetitions, I have omitted this and also any day's entry consisting solely of that text.

Monday 1ˢᵗ
Preparing to "flit" and bathing in dam. Very warm. In afternoon Uncle took us to "The Pines", Piese St., Katanning.[143]

Tuesday 2ⁿᵈ
Commenced letter home to all. Stormy day.

Wednesday 3ʳᵈ
Letter with £2 saying my passage money might be sent from home. Letter and socks from D&W Devine.

Thursday 4ᵗʰ
Stormy & wet day. Gathered different leaves and cut samples of woods.[144]

Friday 5ᵗʰ
My 24ᵗʰ birthday. Wrote home to all. Cool day.

Saturday 6ᵗʰ
Wanderers 128. Australs 189.

Sunday 7ᵗʰ
Took down Uncle's tent. Warm. Pictures at night.

Monday 8ᵗʰ
Warm.

Tuesday 9ᵗʰ
Dull and close.

Wednesday 10ᵗʰ
"News" and letter from Mother postponing the sending of my passage money. Wrote to D&W Devine & note to kiddies.

Thursday 11ᵗʰ
Dull & chilly day.

Friday 12ᵗʰ
Stormy & thundery day. Wrote home to all. Sent films.[145]

Saturday 13ᵗʰ
Caught & killed a pet kangaroo[146]. Kept the skin. Wrote home about rate of exchange on passage money paid in Australia.

---

[143] See Commentary
[144] The leaves lasted many years and the wood samples are still with the author.
[145] Presumably camera negatives. See General Commentary
[146] No explanation of "pet"

Monday 15th
Thunder and hailstorm. Largest stone ¾ " in dia.

Tuesday 16th
Thundery heat all day.

Wednesday 17th
Letter from Mother with Xmas card. One from Grandma[147] also. Letter and a handkerchief from Aunt Susan[148]. 2 newspapers. Warm day.

Thursday 18th
Wrote Willie and all at home. Letter & £1 from Grandma. Xmas box from Mrs Dickie.

Saturday 20th
Wrote Mrs Dickie & Grandma. At cricket.

Sunday 21st
Wrote Jack Dickie & Aunt Susan.

Monday 22nd
Warm.

Tuesday 23rd
Thundery-like. Gardening. Wrote Mother & Johnnie.

Wednesday 24th
Letters from Mother, Mrs Dickie & Flossy Bruce.

Thursday 25th
CHRISTMAS. Gardening all day. Warm.

Friday 26th
Very warm. Gardening. Bringing diary up to date.

Saturday 27th
Temperature reached 99⁰. Walked about in the afternoon.

Sunday 28th
At cricket match. Kojonup 73 & 180(?) all out Katanning Railways 71 & 124 all out.

Monday 29th
Wrote Alex

Tuesday 30th
Temp 87⁰

Wednesday 31st
Got two papers and letters from Mother & Johnnie

Unfortunately, the top third of the next page in the notebook has been torn out, whether deliberately or by accident is unknown. The entries for 3rd and 4th January on the reverse of the page are thus similarly affected.

---

[147] See General Commentary p26
[148] His father's sister See General Commentary p26

1931

JANUARY 1931

Thursday 1st

New Year's Day. Looking after Mr Low's house (in Katanning) garden, feeding hens & two cats. Sleeping in house overnight. Wrote Willie also Father & Mother.

Friday 2nd

Looking after Mr Low's property. Taking meals at "The Pines". Wrote Flossie Bruce.

Saturday 3rd

Looking after Mr Low's property. Taking meals at "The Pines". Cricket: Railway Girls all out 21 Sunshine Alley Smilers 95 for 5 wkts. I umpired men's game. Dingoes 124 .....

Rest of this entry is lost as noted above. Some of presumably Sunday 4th remains:

Temp at 12noon 91⁰. Temp at 2.30 pm 95.5⁰. At 8.30 pm 84⁰. Max temp 101.3⁰.

Monday 5th

Temp at 10am 81⁰. Commenced letter home to all. Temp at 3pm 94⁰. Watering garden. Temp at 7.30pm 84⁰. At 8.03 80⁰. Max was 97⁰.

Tuesday 6th

At 3pm 84⁰.

Wednesday 7th

Letters from Mother & Alex. Got 2 newspapers. Answered Alex's letter & continued letter home to all. Made enquiries about Relief work[149]. Told to wait until after the Road Board[150] Meeting.

Thursday 8th

Gardening. In afternoon walked out to the Police Pools about 3 miles S of Katanning[151].

Friday 9th

Completed letter home (10 pages including Alex' note). Washing clothes. Elder Smith's Sale Day.

Saturday 10th

Did drawing of verandah[152].

Railways 150 all out. Wanderers 125 all out. At pictures at night.

---

[149] See Commentaries

[150] Katanning Road Board then the name of the Local Authority.

[151] Named after original Police Station at important Noongar site. Now a Nature reserve. See Katanning Shire website.

[152] See Illustrations

Sunday 11th
Wrote Hume Pipe Company (Saturday 10th date) asking when work would start. At a cricket match in afternoon and saw Uncle. Talked about my going home the best thing to do. Wrote Immigration Dept. about cancelling the diff. in in the Nominated Passage.[153] (Saturday's date 10th)

Monday 12th
Got Orient Line Agent to write trying to cancel difference in nominated passage. Killed a hen for tea.

Tuesday 13th
Cool day 83°

Wednesday 14th
Warm day.

Thursday 15th
Letters from Mother & Father. Commenced joint letter to Father & Mother. Playing cricket with men & girls after tea.

Friday 16th
Letter from Hume Pipe Co. saying we may be able to see Manager when he is at Katanning this weekend. Wrote Mother & Father 8 pages about me possible sending cable re my passage home. Explained things generally about Australia's position and conditions. At night saw Hume Pipe Coy's Manager, Mr Veitch. Promised us a start and said to see the foreman on Sunday 18th.

Saturday 17th
Letter from Officer in charge Immigration saying he cannot cancel the nomination refund if I leave Australia before 3rd March 1932.
Woodnailling [154]213 for 2wkts (Compton 122 not out Fydock 26 not out) Wanderers 119 all out. Uncle at the game. Got an "Evening News" from Home.

Sunday 18th
Got word to start with Hume Pipe Coy.[155] On Monday 19th. Had tea at Uncle's house.

Monday 19th
Commenced work with Hume Pipe Co. Removing & re-erecting fence. Heavy work. Got headache.[156] Early bed. Very warm day. 8¾ hours.

Tuesday 20th
¾ hour removing posts. 3¾hours grubbing trees. Finished forenoon. Tired and faintish. At "The Pines" in afternoon.

Wednesday 21st
Emptying wagon 5¼ hrs. Removing excavated earth 3½ hrs.

---

[153] See Commentary
[154] As before, believe this to be Woodanilling. Perhaps a nickname.
[155] Not sure what this construction was
[156] Very likely dehydration

Thursday 22nd

Cool day. ¾ hrs carrying building material 8 hrs removing excavated earth. Getting hardened to work. Wrote home to all.

Friday 23rd

8½ hrs removing excavated earth. Hands arms & face swollen up at night.[157] The foreman said Mailler & I might have to stop on Friday 30th to give way to Road Board men. Uncle seeing about matter.

Saturday 24th

2 hrs emptying truck. 2½ hrs removing excavated earth. Got note from Uncle saying he could not do anything re getting us kept after Fri 30th. Hands arms & face still swollen. Washing clothes in afternoon.

Sunday 25th

Commenced letter home about having to stop work on 30th inst. to give way to unemployed married men. Very warm day. (Cancelled this letter). *Dad's underlining.*

Monday 26th

 3½ hrs levelling floor in Steam Chamber. 5¼ hrs removing earth.

Tuesday 27th

4½ hrs removing earth. 4¼ hrs excavating for large moulder[158].

Wednesday 28th

1¼ hrs fitting up sheds. 7½ hrs removing excavated earth. Letters from Mother (two), Johnnie & Alex. Sketches of farm[159] & paper cutting also (*unclear)* Records. Got "Evening News" Wrote Johnnie & Alex together.

Thursday 29th

2½ hrs erecting sheds. 6¼ hrs removing excavated earth. Wrote home to all.

Fri 30th

4½ hrs removing excavated earth. 3 hrs excavating for big moulder. 1¼ hrs fitting big moulder. Got paid for Monday 19th to Tuesday 27th:- 61¼ hrs @ 1/10 per hour less 7½d Hospital Tax[160] = £5-11-8½[161]

Saturday 31st

4½ hrs removing excavated earth. In afternoon cleaning out kitchen and washing clothes.

FEBRUARY 1931

Sunday 1st

Washing clothes. Watering garden. Commenced letter home about having to stop work on account of the Katanning Road Board wanting married men to take over in our place.

---

[157] Possibly heat oedema?

[158] Presumably spinning moulds used for pipe construction.

[159] i.e. Cloybank

[160] Insurance scheme?

[161] Author's calculations suggest overpaid by a halfpenny.

Monday 2nd

4 hrs excavating around moulders. 1 hr fitting doors on Steam Chamber. 3¾ hrs levelling earth between tramway sleepers. Very warm day.

Total number of letters written from 31-1-30 to 31-1-31:- Mother & Father 55 Johnnie 9 Willie 4 Alex 8 Grandma 5 Aunt Susan 3 D Devine 3 Mrs Dickie 3 Jack Dickie 2 David Black 2 Mr Black 1 Aunt Jeannie 1 Kemps 2 (including Isobel 1) Woodcock 1 Flossie Bruce 2 Mr Graham 1 Mrs Monaghan 1 Simpson & Rankin 1 P Keith 1 Trying for work 11 Total 116.

Wrote joint letter to Manager Hume Pipe Co re us having to stop work on account of Road Board after being promised work.

Tuesday 3rd

4½ hrs levelling earth between tramway sleepers. 4¼ hrs building ramp for tramway. Finished work. Got paid up to date 52½ hrs - £4-15-4½

The entries from Wednesday 4th Feb to Sunday 15th Feb once again begin with "At The Pines" and, as before, I omit this and entries consisting solely of that text.

Wednesday 4th

Sent cable home asking for passage to be booked. Got letter from Mother with "Express". Pulled plums for Uncle.

Thursday 5th

Letter from Hume Pipe Co manager saying he would look into the matter re us being put off in place of Road men.

Friday 6th.

Finished 12-page letter home to all re having sent cable. Told about being put off work. Washing.

Saturday 7th

Cricket

Monday 9th

Gardening

Tuesday 10th

Washing clothes

Wednesday 11th

Letter from Hume Pipe Co's manager saying work as far as we were concerned was finished.

Thursday 12th

Letter from Mother. Letter from Orient Line[162] saying my passage was booked on "Orsova" (sailing 23/2/31) or on "Orontes" (sailing on 9/3/31). Applied for sales tax clearance[163] and wrote Customs Dept. re passport. Commenced letter home to all.

---

[162] See Appendix
[163] Unsure of meaning here

Friday 13th
Finished letter home. Mailler got word to go Bob Stevenson's farm, Crassburn[164],
Kojonup on Monday 16th to start work. Got pamphlets from Orient Line. "Evening
News" from Home. E.S's[165] sale.

Saturday 14th
Got paid up to date for care-taking £1-7-6[166]

Sunday 15th
Washing. Partly packing trunk and cases.

Monday 16th
Went with Mailler to Bob Stevenson's farm, Mailler's new job. Letter from Orient Line
saying berth booked on "Orsova" for 23rd instant. Packed up.

Tuesday 17th
Left Katanning 12.5 a.m. arr Perth 10.55 am. Put up at Grand Central. Got arrangements
for passage so far on but had to cable home re if nomination is paid, ask immediately
Orient London to cable Orient Perth to that effect[167]. Can't leave if not paid!!
Wrote Mailler.

Wed 18th
At Perth. Spent forenoon in Kings Park. Did drawing of War Memorial[168]. Sent West
Aust. Paper to Mailler.

Thursday 19th
At Perth. Got Income Tax Clearance paper.[169]

Friday 20th
At Perth. Got Immigration clearance. Visited zoo. Handed Passport application &
clearance from Immigration office to Customs Dept.

Saturday 21st
Spent afternoon at Freemantle.

Sunday 22nd
At Perth
*Entries for next four days were originally written in pencil later overwritten in the usual
fountain pen ink.*

Monday 23rd
Sailed from Freemantle at 7.25pm "Orsova".[170] Sent Mailler telegram.

Tuesday 24th
At sea. Ship rolling. Sick before breakfast.

---

[164] Informed by J.O'H that this should be "Crossburn"
[165] Elder Smith's
[166] Was this Mr Low in Jan or from The Pines?
[167] See Commentary
[168] See illustration
[169] See Commentary
[170] He had time to do a last sketch of Australia. See Illustrations

Wednesday 25th
Original lost
Thursday 26th
At sea
Friday 27th
Played Bridge.
Saturday 28th
Won semi- final tennis 6-2 8-6. Scotch tug of war team beat Yugo Slavs.

MARCH 1931

There are only three more daily entries:
Sunday 1st
At sea
Monday 2nd
Sports Day
Tuesday 3rd
Nothing entered

The rest is silence, the page concluding with:
Arrived Tilbury 26/3/31.
A line is drawn below that and this footnote added:
At Cloybank, Banknock, By Bonnybridge, Stirlingshire Scotland from 27-3-31 till 22nd Sept 1931.

Mary Wright (1919 -2018) in her later years [photo: Beverley Scott]

AUSTRALIA BOUND 1930

From a snowbound Scotland ...
Dad at Denny with Glen and the snowman.
[Family Collection]

... to the West Australian bush.
Dad's snap of the bush at Kanegarup.
[Family Collection]

Via the **SS Oronsay** from 1 II 1930 to 3 III 1930. Nearing Freemantle, some passengers dance on deck. The little girl marked is probably June Fairbrother. See 4 II 1930 entry.

[Family Collection]

KOJONUP BLOCK 7083 -1

The Camp "Koneparup" Kojonup, W. Australia

Dad's sketch of The Camp clearly shows the chimney on the right of the hut. Note the axe in the right foreground! [Family Collection]

The same site today shows the remains of the fireplace and the cleared productive land beyond. [Pictures courtesy of the O'Halloran Family]

KOJONUP BLOCK 7083 -2

The granite ridge is a feature of Kanegarup. Dad pictured it top left [Family Collection] and little has changed in the recent view top right courtesy of the O'Halloran Family.

Warburtons on The Block. Above left: in this photo of the horse team on 8 IV 1930, Dad is on the left with the brothers [L to R] Rex (sen), Angus and George. Above right: pictured on the granite ridge by the O'Hallorans in 2017 are Rex (jun), with his daughter Denise and wife Muriel. [Sadly, between the time this shot was taken and going to Press, Muriel died]

KOJONUP BLOCK 7083 -3

In the last weeks at Kanegarup, Dad sketched the Yule's handiwork. [Family Collection]

Dad pictured the hut and the dam and the O'Hallorans captured the same scene with the remains of the fireplace visible top right. [Family Collection]

KATANNING -1

AT Camp. Katanning. W. Australia.

(Above) Living in a tent, Katanning 1930. Fortunately, the family were close at hand
(Below) The Scott Family about 1931 Standing: Hugh, John, Margaret, Robert (jun)
Seated: Mary, Robert (sen), Honoria (Lily) [Family Collection]

KATANNING -2

"The Pines", Piesse St, Katanning.

"Uncle": Robert Scott and his office in Katanning [Pictures supplied by Beverley Scott]

KATANNING -3

Shadows of the evening. At "The Pines" Katanning. West Australia. R.S.Y. 1931

7th October 1930

10th November 1930

THE LEAVING of AUSTRALIA

February 1931

The last snap Dad would ever take of his elder brother. They were at Perth Zoo and Mailler seems to be feeding a rare Black Wallaroo. [Family Collection]

Central if not very Grand in Perth. Dad's last address in WA. [Contemporary photo]

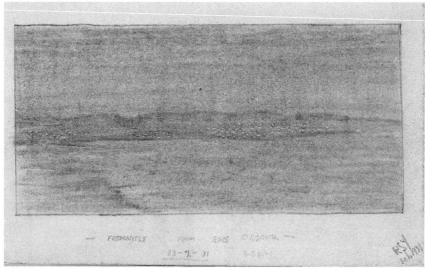

Recording the moment to the hour, Dad's last ever sight of Australia- the lights of Freemantle in the wake of RMS *Orsova*. [Family Collection]

CODA - AN INTRODUCTION & A COMMENTARY

OED *Coda*: *"A passage added after the natural completion of a movement so as to form a more   definite and satisfactory conclusion."*
 The Cassell Concise Dictionary 1997 ed. **"Coda** *...... 3. Any concluding part, event etc."*

But first – a Postscript to Part 3; That Long Trail Home; The Coda – a Commentary; Why Cloybank?; Why West Africa?; Why Dad?; The Sketch Book; Somebody in his life!; At sea again; Landfall and the last of the Diary

But first – a Postscript to Part 3

Reading about Dad's last days in Perth WA, one can sense some feelings of panic as Dad struggled with the necessary financing and documentation for his retreat to Scotland. Also, observing the timings, the reader may be surprised that, in the days before computers and automation that the whole business could take place at such a pace. His cable home, whose contents would not have surprised his family, was on the 4th February which set things in motion in Scotland and by the 16th he knew he was due to sail on the 23rd. He would have said his - perhaps tearful and rather hurried- farewells in Katanning on 17th and then had some clearly hectic days in Perth till all was settled. There must have been a strong foreboding that he wasn't going to make it after all. [17 II 1931: *"Can't leave if not paid"*] and one can envisage him lying awake in the Grand Central Hotel worrying about matters. As so often happened, he immersed himself in his sketch book. Once again, his record is totally free of any sign of self-pity or attempts to blame others for his failed venture. One of Mary Wright's anecdotes, as related to Beverley Scott, suggests a scene at that Katanning farewell where Mary (a.k.a. Molly) had asked this likeable young man why he was leaving. Clearly, he sought to spare the feelings of his cousin (and any family who were listening) by saying that Australia was "Too warrrm!" - an explanation which may have been taken at face value by a young girl, but other family members would have known otherwise. However, our boy was going home to Scotland where his heart had always been.

That Long Trail Home

The reader will have noticed the sharp contrast in the style of entries in that last part compared with those bright daily observations on the voyage out in the previous year. This may not have been such a "happy ship" as was *Oronsay,* full of people looking forward to a new start. It is possible that Dad was not the only one returning home defeated. In the random jottings - undated and unattributed – at the back of the Diary, he noted: "For the period of 9 months ended 30th Sept. 1930, the departures over arrivals totalled 7,101 persons." Dad was not alone in finding disappointment Down Under.

There are only nine entries in the Diary throughout the whole passage back to UK - though the sketch book was in use. Our dejected and cash-strapped diarist does not tell us how he got back to Stirlingshire, so we have to rely on memories of anecdotes. On the author's return from a school trip to the Festival of Britain in 1951 and thereby getting an introduction to the (old) Euston Station, Dad admitted that he had once "dossed down" there. It seems likely that this was the occasion. His sister-in-law [Jean Brown, later Mrs Arneil] much later, recalled that Dad arrived in Glasgow with just enough money in his pockets for his bus fare back to Banknock.

As the old saying has it: It's always darkest before the dawn.

The Coda – a Commentary

On returning to Dad's Diary after decades, I found, to my great surprise, that there were additional daily entries for a fortnight in September and October 1931 which cover the start of his next overseas venture. Whilst these tail away in content and quality of manuscript, as did those on his return from Australia, they provide a good link between Volumes 1 &2 as they record Dad's first encounter with Sierra Leone.

However, as tends to be the case in these records, it is what is left out which intrigues: in this case what he did between returning to Scotland in March 1931 and leaving for Africa the following September. The diary merely records this period as being: *"At Cloybank, Banknock, By Bonnybridge, Stirlingshire Scotland."*

Let us try to fill in the gap.

Why Cloybank?

Dad had returned to Scotland but not to his beloved Uddingston nor the unloved family home he had left the previous year. As we have seen, the Yules who had now become "J&W Yule, Poultry farmers", and were to advertise that they were recognised by the Department of Agriculture for Scotland as a "Class A1 Breeding Station", in a new tenancy at Banknock, just a few miles west of their previous Denny address. [see Map 4] Dad, who would have had little choice but to return to his family wherever they might have been, would have been aware of this typical Stirlingshire mining village and would probably have passed though on the Alexander's bus service. [Routes to and from Stirling and Falkirk via Kilsyth]. The Cloybank farm location is about 250 ft (77m) above sea level, where the land slopes up to the Kilsyth Hills, north west of Banknock, north of the Kilsyth & Bonnybridge Railway and west of the Braeface Road. From the farm, Dad would be able to see much of what was then a continuous belt of collieries and foundries which stretched from Kilsyth to Falkirk. So, whilst he was not exactly in unfamiliar surroundings, there can have been no plan to include Dad as part of the family business, as his immediate past history suggested that Farming was not his forte. One can imagine his feelings, then, having accepted substantial leaving presents and needing financial support from his family, now back on his native soil but once more surplus to requirements.

But developments had taken place whilst he was abroad.

Why West Africa?

This publication is not intended to be an economic textbook on or an industrial history of Scotland but what Dad chanced upon was very much a result of the industrial economy of the time thus, a short note of explanation is needed here.

Scotland's economic success in the 19th century and early 20th century was based upon abundant local supplies of coal and iron ore (especially Splint Coal and Lanarkshire Black Band ore) but by the 1920's these non-renewables were running out. In the short term, the iron and steel industry looked to Spain for supplies of high- grade ore but the long-term solution was going to come from one of Britain's West African colonies: Sierra Leone.

In relating this part of the story, we are fortunate that the estimable Friends of Sierra Leone Railway Museum have preserved a copy of a booklet from 1953 produced by the then still-extant Sierra Leone Development Company ["DELCO"] to celebrate 20 years of production at Marampa. The anonymous corporate author tells us what happened, explaining that haematite ore [Iron III oxide Fe_2O_3] deposits were discovered in the Marampa Chiefdom by Dr. N.R. Junner of the Government Geological Department in 1926. Further exploration in 1927-28, by the African and Eastern Trading Corporation Ltd., confirmed that the deposits on Masaboin Hill were indeed extensive and in 1928, that Corporation obtained a concession from the Tribal Authority of Marampa which permitted the working of iron ore there. Sensing a good investment, an experienced "Merchant Bank", the Northern Mercantile & Investment Corporation, stepped in and further detailed exploration of this rather remote site from 1928 to 1930 proved the deposits to be of such quantity and quality as to present a real commercial opportunity.

The snag was that, as mentioned above, the site was rather remote, lying almost 60 miles [80 km.] from the coast and lacking access to the country's only deep- water port, the anchorage at Freetown, the country's capital. The best way to move bulk goods is by rail, but the expense of building a rail line south across the River Rokel, through the bush and across the mountainous Freetown Peninsula would be prohibitive even if space could have been found on the crowded Freetown foreshore for a railway terminus, bunkers, and loading plant.

However, European ships had been visiting the Sierra Leone River for centuries and other anchorages were known. Hydrographic surveys showed there was sufficient depth of water to allow iron ore carrying ships passage as far as Pepel, a fishing village and trading post some 15 miles north of Freetown. Importantly, building a mineral railway from there to the Marampa site was a feasible proposition. This was the cue for iron & steel manufacturers William Baird & Co., of Coatbridge – erstwhile employers of members of the Yule family – to seize the opportunity to combine with the two previously named bodies and, in 1930, form DELCO to acquire and develop this "greenfield site". That, of course, entailed the construction of port facilities at Pepel, the linking railway [Of which more later and also in Appendix 2], the means of moving and processing quarried ore on to trains at the Marampa terminus, to say nothing of creating a mining town in tropical bushland.

At which point, enter Dad.

Why Dad?

"Cometh hour, cometh man" was never a truer saying for Dad in the summer of 1931. We do not know exactly how he got to hear about the opportunity offered. It may have been through the press -the Yules were avid consumers of both national and local papers - or by word of mouth, as the Yules remained in touch with family and friends in the Lanarkshire mining areas. However, we can imagine Dad going into DELCO's Glasgow office when the managers would see before them this strong, fit, qualified young Mining Surveyor with his experience of working outdoors in the searing temperatures of the West Australian bush and sign him up then and there!

The Sketch Book

By August 1931, Dad was an employee of DELCO and was "under orders for Africa". As such he was reporting to William Baird's offices in 175 Hope Street, Glasgow – a location he may well have been familiar with. Once again, time hung heavily for this ever-active young man for, as we have seen before, the Sketch Book came out. The author was privileged, whilst collecting information for this book in 2017, to be allowed into the premises and to stand in the exact spot from which Dad made his line drawing. Thus, the reader may judge, from the illustrations included in this book, just how skilled Dad was in this activity. [See Illustrations 3]

Somebody in his life!

We can safely assume that, in those Cloybank months, that Dad would be active exploring the new location. He would help around the farm where needed but would spend time walking, perhaps with Glen the Border Collie, a dog of whom he later spoke of with affection. He would have noted that the Banknock coal mines were well-nigh defunct and that the village had a depressed air. [See Vol 2] He would probably have walked up to Braeface or down to Wyndford Lock on the Forth and Clyde Canal [See Map 4]. Importantly, he would walk down to Hollandbush [See Vol2 for explanation of names], maybe to catch the Alexander's bus to Glasgow or on an errand for his mother but for whatever reason, he would have certainly been a regular in Andrew Brown's shop. Of course, the Yules and the Browns would have known each other from Dennyloanhead kirk for some time but suddenly there was a rather exotic addition to the group in the shape of a sun-tanned man just back from Australia whom Anne Brown could scarcely fail to notice! Romance must have blossomed that summer and perhaps Glen had to take second place on those walks. Certainly, something was afoot for Anne came to the station to see Dad depart on the first segment of his trip to Africa and Dad spent much of the voyage composing a very long letter to Anne.

At sea again

So, Dad was off on his travels again but, this time as you will read, in a very different style, he was on a much shorter voyage and on a smaller ship – and that did have an effect on his comfort – but he was now an "old hand" at ocean travel. Sharing a cabin with his boss, he proved to be the better sailor which must have given him a certain cachet amongst his future colleagues, some of whom would have been travelling with him.

Landfall and the last of the Diary

The reader will sense that Dad, when he had got "his sea legs", enjoyed the voyage together with his new-found affluence! (Remember that this was a young man who, six months earlier, had scarce got two coins to rub together in this pocket.) He had gone from emigrant status on an Orient Line trans global liner to the comfort of the Elder Dempster West Africa service[171] – in those days almost a "shuttle" service – travelling with "all expenses paid".

No Bridge sessions this time but he indulged in another passion – cricket. The reader will immediately grasp the problems involved in attempting that game on a pitching deck with limited space and indeed, he records a game being cut short when the ball was lost overboard. In later years, he was to admit being the culprit – a powerful man, he could send a ball a long way over "cow corner" – not exactly what you need in deck cricket!

There were echoes of his younger self too as he spent time in the bow of SS *Apapa* just as he would have done on TS *Duchess of Argyll* speeding from Ardrossan to Arran or on TS *Queen Alexandra* down the Kilbrannan Sound to Campbeltown. There are echoes too, in these final lines as a diarist, of those strong ties to the Firth of Clyde and the West Highlands. Just as he had seen a likeness in the North African peaks to the mountains in Arran, so he saw a resemblance between Freetown Harbour (or the Sierra Leone River) and Loch Lomond[172]. Once again, readers may draw their own conclusions.

Then once again our man is ashore in a strange land, though this time he clearly has a mentor in Mr Buchanan. Or last glimpse of him as described in his own hand, is his making

---

[171] See "Intermezzo" and Appendix 1

[172] Geographers will note that the height of Picket Hill in the Peninsula Mountains above Freetown is 888m (according to Bradt's Guide p3) and Ben Lomond, 973m (OS map). He may have been thinking of the island-studded southern part of the big loch.

his way up country with his new- found colleagues. These were the very early stages of development at Marampa and travel was still by launch up the winding tributary creeks and rivers. Sadly, he left no description of the Marampa site in October 1931 other than to confirm that the railway was not at that time completed. Fortunately, in successive years his camera and sketch book were to rectify the omission. A record of daily life in a West African mining camp was to be left to someone else!

The Rev. David Mailler Yule Dip. Theo. [See Appendix 0] as pictured in the local press thirty years apart. Above left, he featured in an article by the *Falkirk Herald* of 31st March 1909 as part of a series entitled: "MEN YOU KNOW – Prominent Citizens of Falkirk and District". To the right, the *Perthshire Advertiser* was doing its job in June 1939, picturing him at a Parish Sale of Work at Forgandenny. The author had the privilege, in 2019, of speaking to Miss Linda Hendry of the Forgandenny Parish who remembered him as being "*stern and strict*", "*taking his faith very seriously*" though perhaps a little "*too learned*" for a rural parish! [Images via National Newspaper Archive]

CODA

SEPTEMBER 1931

After some decorative underling of the Australian entries, the Diary notes:
At Cloybank[173], Banknock, By Bonnybridge, Stirlingshire, Scotland from 27-3-31 till 22nd Sept 1931.

Tuesday 22nd
Left home at 8.20pm for Mr Brown's[174]. Bus leaving Banknock at 9pm. Anne, Johnnie, Alex, and Devines saw me away from Glasgow Central at 11.5 pm. Long stale train journey to Liverpool[175] arriving 6.5 am.

Wednesday 23rd
Walked to Adelphi Hotel[176] (L.M.S.) washed and shaved. Wrote Mother, and Anne. Breakfast with Mr Buchanan. Wrote Mother again re new address. Did some shopping. I insured luggage for voyage and tour in West Africa. Cashed cheque for expenses at Elder Dempster & Co.'s office. Sent receipt of same to Sierra Leone Development Co. Ltd.[177] Passed time in lounge, orchestra, till 2.20pm. Taxi to ship[178], on board at 2.45 pm. Ship sailed at 3.45 pm. Got baggage insurance papers. Letter from Sierra Leone Development Co Ltd re payment of salary. Answered asking £15 allowance to be paid to Barclay's Colonial Bank, Freetown and balance £25 to Union Bank of Scotland[179], Bridgeton Cross, Glasgow. Wrote David Devine about same and asked him to open an account for me with £1 which he would get from Mother. Got receipt re camp outfit. PPC's of Apapa to Anne, Alex, Devines, Grandma, Mrs Dickie. Wrote letter to C Ryan and D. Hunter. Tea at 4.30pm. Dinner 6.30 pm. Dropped Pilot[180] and letters about 8pm. Bed about 9pm. Took salts, up 4 times at lavvy. Comfortable cabin berth. 2 bunks. Jack exchanged berths so we are both together. Calm sea.

Thurs 24th
Bath 7.10 am breakfast 8am sea calm. Cricket till ball went overboard. Deck quoits. Ship rolling little since 12 noon when we were abreast Land's End. Commenced letter to Anne.

---

[173] See Commentary

[174] See Commentary

[175] Exchange Station then the main terminus for express and local trains to the north. See also Vol 2.

[176] Quite a walk from Tithebarn Street

[177] See Commentary

[178] ss Apapa See App 1

[179] Merged with Bank of Scotland 1955

[180] Liverpool Pilot would go aboard pilot cutter from Amlwch, Anglesey, off Point Lynas.

Lunch about 1pm. Lounging about till tea 4.30 then Dinner at 6.30. Played Draughts with Jack. Bed about 8.15 pm.

Friday 25th

Ship pitching and rolling a good bit, fairly rough sea[181]. Felt alright till my bath at 7 am. After that felt sick. Jack sick. Took breakfast (porridge and herring) lost it immediately after, sick! Went to bed till Lunch. Had a good tuck in. Feeling fine now. Jack still sick. Ship rolling. At 12noon ship nearing Cape Finisterre[182]. 33 miles. PPC's to Mailler, Meg Stark, Jean Wilson, Mr& Mrs Barratt, Mr & Mrs Jamison. Light tea at 4.30. Jack and I feeling [sick?] off and on. Ship getting some large swells. Spray coming over bow in some style, occasionally over stern and centre of ship. Continued Anne's letter. Bed at 8.15 pm.

Saturday 26th

Sea very calm except for slight swell broadside on. Played cricket all forenoon. Very warm. Overtook oil tanker far off on out Port side. Lunch. Resting more or less during afternoon. Commenced letter to Mother. Eclipse of the moon. Continued Anne's letter. Greyhound racing on 1st class deck[183] at night. Day's mileage 346.

Sunday 27th

Sea calm, slight swell. Bath breakfast. Some rain. Lounging about in forenoon. Making up list for 1 month's food. At 12 noon NE of Madeira Islands. Day's mileage 350. Passed ship (cargo) homeward bound on Port Side during afternoon. Got a/c for excess baggage 4/10[184]. Spent an hour after dinner at bow, fine moonrise. Saw rainbow caused by moon rays[185].Continued Anne's letter.

Monday 28th

Sighted Canary Islands at 8.30 am on Starboard. Overtook two ships on Port side. Boat Station Drill. Canvas fitted over decks. Reading and sleeping in afternoon. Commenced letter to David Devine. Boat drill for crew. Islands mountainous[186]. Las Palmas about 5

---

[181] Apapa at 9,333 GRT was a much smaller ship than Oronsay 20,000 GRT so would be livelier in a rough sea. Hence the sea-sickness much worse than on the Australia voyage.

[182] Writing difficult to decipher, have assumed this is what he meant.

[183] Presumably not with real greyhounds!

[184] i.e. 4 shillings and 10 pence

[185] Wikipedia: *A moonbow (also known as a lunar rainbow or white rainbow), is a rainbow produced by light reflected off the surface of the moon (as opposed to direct sunlight) refracting off of moisture-laden clouds in the atmosphere. Moonbows are relatively faint, due to the smaller amount of light reflected from the surface of the moon. They are always in the opposite part of the sky from the moon.*

[186] The author followed in Dad's wake 40 years later and can agree with that.

miles off. At bow at night. Continued Anne's letter. Position at 12 noon 5 miles East of Gran Canaria.

Tuesday 29th
Rose 7.40 am. Cricket in forenoon. Saw shark well behind ship. Fishing boats on horizon. Cricket in afternoon. Usual pastime of sleeping before tea. At bow after dinner. Phosphorus[187] very good. Shoals of fish. Fine moon.

Wednesday 30th
Rose 7.30am. Ship on horizon. Overtook it 2 hours later. Shoals of Flying Fish[188]. Very warm. Completed letter to David Devine. Washed semet[189]. Continued letters to Anne and Mother. Passed Cape Verde, Saw lights of Dakar. Passed MV Apam[190] homeward bound. Bow at night. Saw thundery (wild fire) over Dakar.

OCTOBER 1931

Thursday 1st
Bath 7.30 am. Paid 9/6 to Purser 4/10 re excess baggage. Saw porpoises. Cool wind. Completed Anne's letter 16 pages. Mother's 8 pages. At bow after dinner. Saw 2 sharks swimming at bow. Swimming on one side turning over on the other, diving etc. Cool breeze.

Friday 2nd
(Dad's last few entries must have been written in a rush as much of the writing, in sharp contrast to that his earlier clear style, is very difficult to interpret. Also, there is a tendency towards random jottings.)
Rose 7am. Entering Freetown Bay. Hilly behind town. Bright green foliage. Parts resembling Loch Lomond. Town good sight from sea. Berth at 9am. Disembarked after. Men in canoes diving for coins. One man with tile hat, collar and tie amusing. Another lad quoted bible other chimed in "Hallelujah, Praise the Lord" *(undecipherable)* saying: "Sing Hymn 192, Yes we have no bananas." Went ashore [in] launch. Drive to S.L.D. Co. Ltd's

---

[187] He meant "phosphorescence" these days called "bioluminescence" = light from luminous sea creatures and can be very spectacular.
[188] From Wikipedia: *The* Exocoetidae *are a family of marine fish in the order* Beloniformes class Actinopterygii. *Fish of this family are known as flying fish. Flying fish can make powerful, self-propelled leaps out of water into air, where their long, wing-like fins enable gliding flight for considerable distances above the water's surface. This uncommon ability is a natural defence mechanism to evade predators.*
[189] *Pocket Scots Dictionary Aberdeen University Press:* **semmit** a man's vest or undershirt
[190] Could be SS Appam a ship with a history.

Representative Col. Wardle. Stayed City Hotel. Served soup plate and dinner plated in one pile. Running about. *(undecipherable).* Got Cheque Book from Barclays Colonial Bank. Poor built city but interesting. Got stores.

Sat 3rd

Left Freetown Company's Launch "Lydia" 12 noon with Taylor, Busby (from Perth) Rolfe. Interesting sail to Pepel. Bush, Rice fields, creeks, birds. High "tide mark" on trees. At Pepel I changed to "Delco"[191] went to Sala Marank[192] with Mr Buchanan, Sturgess & Dickie. River narrowing in. Last half hour in darkness. Arr. Sala Marank 6.30 pm "Lydia" 8.30 pm. [193]Goods put in store. Dinner with Mr Moore (store keeper). Slept in Mr Rankin's Bungalow with Jack.

Sun 4th

Walk around with Taylor & Jack. Left camp 11.15 pm[194] car with Mr B. and Jack. 26 miles or so. Dinner with Payne (surveyor). Rough road tall reeds saw natives trying to kill snake 4' long[195].. Road running with railway in construction. Passed native villages. At Marampa at 12.30 (Arrive with Payne) met Sneddon from Bo'ness. Dinner with Mr Buchanan.

Monday 5th

Rose 6.30 am. Breakfast. Walk round hill[196]. Warm. Saw Rice fields. Back 12 had dinner. I shot pigeon.

And there, Dad's diary daily entries cease never to be re-started. If he made any other records, they have not survived. However, the start of his West African experience is not the end of this story.

---

[191] Assumed to be tropical kit

[192] This must be "Sahr Marank" = the name means "Elephant Rock" – a bridging point on Port Loko Creek which was about halfway between Marampa and Pepel and the temporary Company HQ from which the railway was built in both directions according to the SLDCo. booklet of 1953.[See Appendix 2]

[193] Suggests he was not on "Lydia" which followed afterwards.

[194] Perhaps "a.m."?

[195] i.e. four feet long = 1.22m

[196] Assumed to be Masaboin Hill.

INTERMEZZO

1931 -1936

OED*: "Intermezzo: A short movement connecting the main divisions of a large musical work, instrumental or vocal; An interval."*

The Cassell Concise Dictionary 1997 edition. *"Intermezzo: ...... 4. A short dramatic or other entertainment between the acts of a play."*

Author's preface

With Dad's recording finishing in 1931 and Mum's Diary commencing in 1936, there is a gap of several years which needs a narrative. Fortunately, there are "hard" records available in the shape of Dad's snapshots of the Sierra Leone scene [unfortunately, not all dated], his Sketch Book (of course!), a pamphlet of the Sierra Leone Development Co. and professional photos taken for them, the passenger lists of the Elder Dempster Line and – amazingly – a newspaper cutting. From these we can link the two journals and paint quite a happy picture of those busy years in this section for whose title I have chosen once more to borrow a musical term.

INTERMEZZO
1931 to 1936

A Mining Engineer Abroad; A Step Forward; Upwardly mobile; In style, Seeing more of the world, Abroad and at home; FOUR TOURS, Wild Rover No More

A Mining Engineer Abroad

At the time of Dad's arrival, the Marampa mines and the necessary infrastructure were still in a primary stage. So, in the years Dad spent in Sierra Leone Dad had the satisfaction of being part of the development almost from "greenfield site" to the mines reaching their full production capacity. He did four "tours of duty" as a single man, working as a Mining Engineer for which, of course, he was trained. He made no record of his tasks, but he would obviously do a great deal of surveying and setting out, activities in which, from the author's experience, he was highly competent. In addition to the mines complex, he would certainly have been engaged in the construction of the "camp" -the accommodation for the S.L.D.Co. employees -and perhaps also the railway and the loading facilities at Pepel. Looking at his photo album, there are echoes of Kanegarup in his shots of the Bush [See Illustrations] which he describes as the "Permanent Camp Site". This time, however, he had more than just own axe-power to clear the site!

A Step Forward

The West Africa years also played a part in Dad's Career development. At no point in his study course in Glasgow is there any mention of mixing, pouring or curing concrete nor anything of reinforced concrete construction. Mining structures in Scotland, above and below ground, appear in photographs to be constructed mainly from iron and steel – understandable in view of the ready availability of those materials. In contrast, Dad's collection of Marampa photos show a widespread use of concrete, [See Illustrations]in the form of blocks or in reinforced pillars. Probably out of necessity, as staffing the site cannot have been an easy matter, Dad would have been introduced to this facet of engineering. The capacity for "taking pains" served him well here and his skill in supervising concrete work was to be of great value to him and his employers in the years to come.

The Diary was consigned to his kit, but the sketch book and the camera were in use. In contrast to his rather austere life in Australia, Dad now had a group of fellow countrymen for company. One may guess that this was rather rumbustious company too, so studiously recording his observations may have seemed to be out of place.

Upwardly mobile

The lifestyle changed also. For really the only time in his life, there was a touch of luxury. He had a team of "houseboys" at Marampa who would have cooked, cleaned and washed for him. This being a British Overseas Possession, there was, of course, a Club – a little touch of The Raj in West Africa - and a social life revolving round that. As the site developed so too would the facilities and eventually there would be a swimming pool and tennis court. All a very long way from the hut in Kanegarup or the tent or hostel in Katanning!

In style

Travel too reflected his new status. At sea, there was no more being crammed into emigrant cabins as now he travelled Second Class – or better! The Elder Dempster ships on the West Africa run were passenger cargo, twin-screw motor vessels designed to carry colonial administrators and merchant moguls to the then colonies of The Gambia, Sierra Leone, Gold Coast [Ghana] and Nigeria thus well over half of the accommodation was First Class. Freetown being the fourth or fifth port of call for M.V. *Adda* or M.V. *Accra,* Homeward Bound, there were occasions when no Second-Class berths were available for passengers boarding there. Thus Dad – presumably to the annoyance of SLDCo's accountants – on two occasions luxuriated in surroundings clearly designed by the owners to match those of the great Atlantic liners of the time. One can see him reacting as to the manor born and envisage him reclining on those damask cushions in the Smoking Lounge, telling his fellow passengers that the facilities on the Elder Dempster ships were equalled on such Clyde steamers as PS *Columba*!

Seeing more of the world

The West Africa run would call at any of: Las Palmas, Funchal, Bathurst [now Banjul] so he would add to his knowledge of the world, though his only record is a series of what appears to be commercially produced photos of Madeira. His port of departure for the 3000 nautical mile trip of approximately ten days duration, was always Liverpool in which city's Adelphi Hotel he was to become a regular according to remarks he made when passing by in later years. The return trip, save for one celebrated occasion referred to below, was to Plymouth from where he would take the "boat train" to London. No dossing down on a station bench now, for the expenses permitted a more comfortable billet in one of the hotels around Russell Square, and the confident, successful young man "from the colonies" who arrived back in Glasgow Central had a lot more cash to hand than was required for the bus to Banknock!

Abroad and at home

At the risk of turning this into a rather boring "Book of Lists", it seems germane to the theme to summarise the four Tours of Duty Dad undertook in this period. It is the author's understanding that the contract was originally for nine months in Sierra Leone, all tropical kit and travel expenses paid, followed by three months paid home leave though, clearly the overseas period was subject to extension to a year by mutual agreement.

As implied earlier, he spent his leave at Cloybank which he later remembered with some affection. This is understandable as it was a time when he was affluent, was doing his "courting" and would be something of a celebrity to family and family friends as a man doing well in a tropical colony. We can assume that when the season coincided with his time back home that he would make his way to Uddingston to see familiar faces and places and to watch cricket at Bothwell Castle Policies. We know, from the receipt which he retained along with his copy of the Lodge Handbook, that in March 1934, maybe at the instigation of his future father-in-law, he joined the Freemasons. He is recorded as paying the considerable sum of 5 guineas to be initiated into Lodge St Andrew No 176 of the Grand Lodge of Scotland in Denny, who, although his subsequent career prevented him from active participation in Lodge activities, were to respect his memory on his death in 1982.

 We know also, from a photo, that he took Anne to see that family matriarch, his maternal grandmother, Isabella Scott. This is the "Grandma" to whom he wrote from Australia, and for whom, as a wee laddie he had run errands. [He often mentioned going for a "Well fired loaf for Mrs Scott"]. The Scott grandparents, whilst living in Glasgow, had lost their son Hugh at Loos in 1915 [see Addendum1] and their daughter Margaret through illness in 1919, thereafter managed to find their way back to Lanarkshire. The County Council there had a policy based upon improving the housing conditions for those engaged in the Mining Industry – occasionally creating an over-supply – and one assumes it was as an ex-miner that John Train Scott and his wife found themselves in very comfortable Council premises in Woodlands Crescent in Bothwell, not far from Uddingston's cricket ground! John Train Scott died there in 1924 but Isabella survived him for 11 years and would have received regular visits from her family until her death in 1935. Mum would later recall with a smile that, on those visits, whenever Isabella had begun to find the visit a bit tiring, she would enquire: "*What time's yer bus?*"

However, the bus service [the ubiquitous Alexander's or Western SMT] would not be their sole means of transport as the motor car would have come into their lives. As we shall see in Volume Two, Mum obtained a Driving Licence before the Road Traffic Act of 1934 made taking a Driving Test compulsory. Dad was always a bit miffed about the fact that he had to sit the test before he got his licence, so he may not have been driving [legally] during this period. We can picture their having the occasional use of the Brown family car [see Volume Two] with Mum doing the driving and Dad feeling rather uncomfortable about the loss of status shown by his having to be driven by his lassie!

FOUR TOURS

[The ships named are illustrated in the relevant section together with a description in Appendix 1]

First Tour – September 1931 to July 1932

The start of his West African interlude, as we have seen, coincides with the end of his activities as a personal diarist. However, his sketching did continue, and we have four works dating from that tour. Of the photographs in the album there is only which can be confidently ascribed to that tour: a battered shot of Dad on a survey somewhere in the tropical grassland but a SLDCo. photograph shows the railway bridge over the Port Loko Creek still under construction in January. His return to UK by First Class passage on SS *Adda* in the summer of 1932 would, as mentioned above, have been an introduction to a level of luxury of which he could not have dreamed a year previously!

Second Tour – September 1932 to February 1934

When Dad left Liverpool on M.V. *Adda* for his Second Tour, again with colleagues, he may not have known that it was to be by far his longest. The tour, being eighteen months, might not have pleased the folks back in Banknock but we have Press references which explain why his skills were in demand in Marampa. The reader will have noticed that, by 1932, some years had passed since work on the Marampa site had commenced and so may agree that those behind the enterprise might have been anxious for a sign that the site would soon be productive. So, one can readily see that there was pressure on all concerned at Marampa to press for completion of the quite extensive open-cast mine facilities and transport infrastructure and that for Dad - or anyone -to take leave at a key point would not aid progress. However, we have a note on the fly-leaf of a copy of Galsworthy's *The Forsyte Saga* (1932 edition) which shows that Mum was staying with the Barrowcloughs in Agnew Road Fleetwood in December 1932 and if she was away from Banknock the motivation for Dad to be there might not have been so strong.

Progress certainly happened. The 3ft 6in (1067mm) gauge railway, [See Appendix 2] we are told, was complete by February 1933 and the large Marampa complex began exporting haematite ore in September. This outcome turned out to be triumph and disaster simultaneously and was widely reported in the UK press. Family records contain two of many typical articles dated September 22nd 1933, perhaps from the now-defunct *Glasgow Evening Citizen* though it has not been possible to determine with certainty from which paper they were taken.

The copies are rather blurred and battered, so, rather than include difficult to read scans, I have attempted to reproduce the style of the time.

NEW TRADE LINK

IRON ORE FROM SIERRA LEONE

ROMANCE OF WEST AFRICAN DEVELOPMENT SCHEME

To-day the s.s Hindpool will arrive in the Clyde with a cargo of iron ore from Sierra Leone, marking the first stage in an important trade development.

In 1927 iron ore reserves were discovered in Sierra Leone, hitherto believed to be barren of minerals. A railway was built through the bush from the coast to Marampa, where the ore bodies are situated, a loading installation was constructed, for no shipping facilities were available, and now Sierra Leone is regarded as being capable of supplying Britain with a large proportion of its iron ore.

CARGO FOR GLASGOW

**FROM OUR OWN CORRESPONDENT.
LONDON, Thursday**

The end of the first stage of one of the most important developments in a Crown Colony during recent years will be marked to-morrow, when the s.s. Hindpool arrives in the Clyde with a cargo of 8000 tons of iron ore from Sierra Leone. The complete consignment, I understand, has been taken by Messrs William Baird and Co., of Glasgow.

BOUND FOR CLYDE

SHIP STRICKEN WITH MALARIA

OFFICER DEAD: NINE OF CREW ILL

Bound for Glasgow with the first cargo of iron ore from Sierra Leone (the "White Man's Grave"), the steamer Hindpool has put into Fishguard Harbour with nine members of her crew down with chronic malaria and one dead. The Hindpool is expected to reach the Clyde to-morrow with 8000 tons of iron ore to be delivered to Messrs Baird & Co., Glasgow.

The arrival of this cargo marks the first stage in an important Empire trade development. Medical officers of Glasgow Public Health Department are making the customary arrangements to deal with malaria sufferers who are still on board the Hindpool. Quarantine is not necessary, as the disease is not infectious in this country. It must be carried by mosquitos.

FIRST TRIP WITH CERTIFICATE

Glasgow medical officers will take precautions to ensure that there is not a single mosquito on board the Hindpool. It is not expected that the mosquitos will have survived the cold journey north from Africa, but no chances will be taken.

The crew became affected five days ago. The third officer, Charles Brammer (22), of Grimsby, who was making his first voyage after gaining his certificate, died yesterday morning, and the body was landed at Fishguard. Two members of the crew were also landed and conveyed to the County Hospital at Haverford West.

As indicated earlier, the above tidings were widely circulated in the local press throughout Scotland. The Browns in Hollandbush and the Yules at Cloybank would certainly have read the reports with a mixture of satisfaction that Dad was involved and some worry also if they saw the reference to a "White Man's Grave"[197]! However, that did not deter her, for during Dad's Leave, the couple became engaged.

Third Tour – May 1934 to May 1935

Although he had undertaken an extended tour, sailing home on M.V. *Apapa* Dad may well have felt some considerable satisfaction with the part he had played, but there was to be no extended leave. In May 1934 we find him out of Liverpool on M.V *Accra* bound once more for Freetown. This time there was a significant family development as his young brother Alex was with him, not as an engineer but as an accountant, a skill equally needed in the now productive operation at Marampa. We must assume Dad was involved in the on-going construction of the extensive plant needed for raising the ore, treating it and shipping it, together with the necessary expansion of the "camp" and, also the administrative offices where an accountant would be based. We can imagine him settled into a tropical routine, but it is the return from that tour which is noteworthy, as he and Alex made into the local press in Glasgow as a result of their unusual passage home. This extract from a column labelled "*I Cover the Waterfront*" with the by-line of Ross Kennedy - and complete with the inaccuracies common to local newspapers - tells the tale:

'Cargo' of Leopards and Antelopes Landed from Liner presented to Edinburgh Zoo

Two ten-week old leopard cubs and three small antelopes were landed on Saturday from Glasgow steamer Wilston.

She arrived in Rothesay Dock with a 5,200-ton cargo of iron ore from Pepel, North Africa.

I boarded her at Clydebank as soon as she berthed.

I found two Glasgow young men Robert and Alec Yule, surveyor and accountant from the ore station of Marampa, fifty-two miles up country from Pepel, in charge of the livestock.

Dr McKelvie of Edinburgh, medical officer at Marampa, is presenting the animals to the Edinburgh Zoological Gardens.

---

[197] From the title of an 1836 book about a visit to Sierra Leone by F. Harrison Rankin

Before the Yule brothers had sailed with their charges, the doctor had received a cable of thanks from the Zoo authorities which stated that the tiny antelopes – West African duikers – would be new and highly-prized specimens in the new antelope park.

The leopard cubs are about as large as cats, but stronger, and already marked with leopard spots. They had to be fed with diluted milk from babies feeding-bottles. They roamed the bridge by day negotiating steep companion ladders without assistance.

The duikers presented no food problems as they eat anything within reach -paper, string, a spare pair of socks. The eldest of the trio is twelve months old and stands about fourteen inches high.

Robert Yule has been four years at Marampa and has only seen one leopard in that time. Alec saw two in a shorter period.

The brothers were riding through the bush in a trolley, when a full-grown leopard appeared only a yard from the wheel.

"We don't know yet who got the biggest fright!" said Alec.

The Wilston met with head winds and heavy seas as far as the Canaries on the way home, but the least put out by the storm were the animals.

Her cargo is part of a huge weekend ore arrival of more than 17,000 tons in three ships, the others being the Spanish Iciar and Jugo-Slavian Srebeno.

There are copies of the original cutting held as family mementos in households from the West End of Glasgow to Western Australia, representing as it does the nearest the Yule brothers ever came to celebrity status. Alex's story was often repeated. The "trolley" was a two-man rail cart manually propelled by its occupants' hand-pumping a crank, thus its speed was determined by how fast those occupants were pumping the handle up and down. Dad's version of events was that, one evening in the dark, the brothers were ambling along the line in the cart when they saw a pair of glowing eyes closely following them. The pumping rate suddenly increased, and the cart escaped the leopard's unwelcome attention! Given that *panthera pardus* in hunting mode can clock over 30 mph, and that Mum subsequently described the vehicle as a "motor trolley", the reader might be excused thinking that Dad had not allowed facts to get in the way of a good story.

The activities of the omnivorous duikers also remained part of the family folklore. Dad's story was that the First Mate of SS *Wilston* had washed his socks and laid them out to dry only for the grazing duikers to take a fancy to them! According to Dad "the air went blue" with colourful nautical expletives when the Officer discovered the damage!

Dad clearly liked this departure from his customary comfortable trips with Elder Dempster. Not only did the freighter take the Yule brothers directly back to Scotland but, whilst on board as "super cargo", they had the status of ship officers. This meant that they - like the leopards - had access to the Bridge thus surely fulfilling every young boy's dream! No surprise then that Dad remained troubled over the subsequent fate of this vessel - for which story please turn to Appendix 1.

Fourth Tour - August 1935 to August 1936

After the customary three months back home, Dad and Alex were outward bound again on mv Accra with Dad now an experienced "Africa Hand". One can assume that he was keen to do only the nine months as he had plans for 1936 and may well have been due extra leave from the earlier back-to-back tour. That was not what happened, however, as his employers were once more reluctant to lose his services in what now would be a productive but still developing mining site. For instance, the extent of the railways system is shown in Dad's photo collection which he dates as "1935". [See Illustrations 5] The fact that the passport he had acquired at a rush in Perth WA had expired in February 1936 might have affected his plans, though it was a but simple matter for him to renew it at Freetown in the June. It is possible that he was bribed to stay the full year with the offer of a First- Class passage home on mv Accra again but by now his mind would have been on something else.

Wild Rover No More!

That "something else" can be simply described by yet another transcription from a local paper: *the Falkirk Herald* of 16th Sept 1936

> **YULE-BROWN**   -At Dennyloanhead Church, on 9th Sept. 1936, by the Rev. Peter Lovie. M.A., S.T.M., assisted by the Rev. D. Mailler Yule, DipTh., Forgandenny, (uncle of the bridegroom), Robert Scott, fourth son of Mr and Mrs John Yule, Cloybank, Banknock, and Kyle Park, Uddingston,
> To Anne Copland, elder daughter of Mr and Mrs Andrew Brown, Banknock, Stirlingshire.

There is little to add. Mum and Dad would have had a rather busy time! According to custom the Banns were read in Haggs Parish Church on 25th August. *[Collectors of Stirlingshire ecclesiastical curios can note that, although both parties had "Banknock" as a postal address, Dad was residing in the Parish of Haggs but Mum, a stone's throw away "doon the brae" was in the Parish of Banton.]* A familiar name appears again: The Rev. David Mailler Yule DipTh. One might have expected that the "Minister in the Family" would have conducted the ceremony and it seems certain that was what was intended. However, memory prompts and the records show that, Bessie, his wife of 35 years had died a few days before. It is a measure of that man that, in the midst of his undoubted grief, he held to what was surely a promise and that he found his way from Perthshire to Dennyloanhead to play a part on the day.

And, of course, the Yules were still the Yules of Kyle Park, Uddingston and in many ways, always would be. So now it is time to hand over to a recruit to that clan.

Mr. and Mrs. Andrew Brown

request the pleasure of

at the Marriage of their daughter,

Mr. Robert Scott Yule,

at Dennyloanhead Church,

on Wednesday, 9th September, 1936,

at 3 p.m.,

and afterwards in Church Hall.

Hollandbush,
Banknock,   R.S.V.P.
Stirlingshire.

SKETCH BOOK by the CLYDE

Dad's sketch of the bridge & the Broomielaw in August 1931 and the author's view in 2017.

OUT OF THE OFFICE WINDOW in 1931 ...

Dad had time on his hands when in Baird's offices in August 1931 before embarking for West Africa and had his sketch book ready. [Family Collection] See opposite page.

... and MANY YEARS LATER.

The same spot pictured by the author in 2017. Trams gone but the skyline is much the same.

ON LEAVE

As these family snaps show, Dad would be at Cloybank, Banknock when on leave from Marampa with his Collie pals, Glen and Ken [top right] or taking his fiancée to visit his Grandmother, Isabella Scott at Bothwell [top left] [Family Collection]

Whilst on ship, he had his sketchbook with him for quiet moments. [Family Collection]

FREETOWN, SIERRA LEONE

Dad probably sketched this from his ship at anchor in 1932. [Family Collection]

Whilst Helen Ashby of FoSLNRM had a similar view from the ferry in 2018.
[Friends of Sierra Leone National Railway Museum]

A GREENFIELD SITE

The area around Masaboin Hill had to be cleared for accommodation

Virgin bushland.

Clearing a ridge

An early road through the camp

Constructing a bungalow

All the above scanned from a family photograph album. Photographer unknown.

THE VITAL LINK

The railway was key to development of Marampa Mines and bridging Port Loko Creek was the line's major construction feature. This shot has been scanned from a SLDCo publication courtesy of the Friends of Sierra Leone National Railway Museum and shows work in January 1932 with someone looking very like Mr Williams, centre right. [See Appendix 2]

Bridging complete in May 1933, a laden train has a staff coach attached. {Source as above} See also Appendix 2

A SURVEYOR ABROAD

Two surveying pictures. **[Above Left]** A rare shot of Dad at work with a survey party somewhere on the Marampa site in 1931. [Photographer unknown, scan from battered copy in Family Album]. **[Above Right]** From an advert in Whitelaw (op.cit.) p 458, a typical 8" theodolite of the time. The African seen background centre may have been carrying one of these. [Makers' photo]

Two pictures assumed to have been taken on board SS Wilston. Dr McKelvie who presumably found the cubs abandoned is pictured with Dad [after a rainstorm?] on the ship's rail. With their unexpected charges, two suntanned young Scots are about to get their names in the papers. [Photographer unknown. Scanned from battered copies in an album in the Family Collection]

VOLUME TWO

Mum's Diary 1936

Author's Note: What you will find here.

This part of the book is based around the Diary Mum kept on her sojourn as a newly-wed to Sierra Leone in 1936. Following the same pattern as Volume One, I have split the transcript between her outward journey and her life at Marampa. Once more, I have written a detailed "Introduction" explaining the background of the Diarist and the illustrations selected to cover that follow before we look at the Diary.

I start with a contemporary map then some General comments and have written a Commentary on each part of the West Africa saga and the selected illustrations follow. There was more of Marampa in 1937 and I have added an "Afterword" to complete the saga of Sierra Leone.

Also, following my policy of not leaving loose ends to a story, I have added a Postscript to the Volumes.

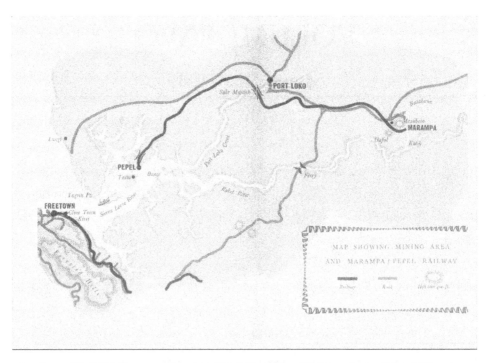

A reproduction of a DELCo map showing the railway from Marampa to Pepel [See Appendix 2] at the time of Volume Two. The bridge at Sahr Marank to where Dad sailed by launch 2 XI 1931 is clearly marked. Lunsar was not then deemed important enough for upper case!

INTRODUCTION TO VOLUME TWO

Rewind; Other Names and Places; Families; … and names; A curious coincidence at Cloybank; Grandparents; … and other animals; A Tale of two villages; … and two coalmines; Doon the watter; A wee lassie and a wider world; At school …; … and after; Accomplishments; Organisations; The Built Environment; Good to Go

Rewind

Unlike Volume One, we have already had much of the "prequel" to a journey into Glasgow Central Station. But before we look at the pages in this second journal, as with Dad, we should look at the background of the diarist and "compare and contrast" the two. But first we should look at a place whose name has already cropped up in these pages: Banknock.

Other Names and Places

A look at the village's name as recorded in 1510 of[198] *Ballinknok* gives the clue to its Gaelic derivation as *baile nan cnoc,* "farmstead on a small hill". However, this leads to a puzzle for the visitor today, seeing a community which stretches from above the Kilsyth Road (A803) down the slope to the Bonny Water's marshy valley floor, will look around and ask: *Where's the small hill?"* For the answer, we must turn to the earliest Ordnance Survey map of the area where we can indeed find a farmstead called Banknock which the map symbolism shows us to be on a small hill but one some distance to the north east of the current village. Further, at about the time of Andrew Brown (jun)'s birth the Gazetteer[199] is recording Banknock as: "*… Banknock, a collier hamlet in Denny parish, Stirlingshire, 2¼ miles SW of Denny town. Three seams of coal here yield large output both for consumption in the neighbourhood and for exportation*". In the same publication there is a record of " *.. a village on the mutual border of Denny and Kilsyth parishes, Stirlingshire, 3 miles SSW of Denny town. It stands contiguous to Haggs village. Pop. of the two villages (1871), 534, (1881) 524, of whom 7 were in Kilsyth"* but that village, which more closely fits the description of modern Banknock, is called "Hollandbush", This is a name we have met previously as it survived into modern times on O.S. maps and was ever used by the Browns as their address and as such it will be used in these pages. There is some justification in this as the mid- 19th century description of Hollandbush (or Hollinbush) is: "*A public house on the side of the T.P. [turnpike]road and the only part of the village of that name which lies in the Parish of Kilsyth.* "[200]

---

[198] See Johnstone p101

[199] Frances Groome's Ordnance Gazetteer of Scotland from GB Historical GIS / University of Portsmouth, History of Banknock, in Falkirk and Stirlingshire | Map and description, A Vision of Britain through Time.
URL: http://www.visionofbritain.org.uk/place/21937

[200] See From: OS1/32/16/98 scotlandsplaces.gov.uk/digital-volumes/ordnance-survey-name-books/stirlingshire-os-name-books-1858-61/stirlingshire-volume-16/98

Having taken a diversion in Volume One into varying Western Australian names, it seems only fair to consider Scottish ones, in particular, how one place could come to be known by another name.

Historians inform us that a mine was frequently given the name of the farm or estate on which it was sunk, so those referred to by Groome (above) would be "Banknock" which would be owned or worked by the "Banknock Coal Company". It was the custom for mine owners to build accommodation for their workers close to their mines and for the subsequent settlement to be named after the pit or its owners. Hence, when the Banknock Coal Company did that by building, to the west of the Hollandbush hamlet, two rows of miners' cottages south of the Kilsyth Road, they would become known as the "Banknock Rows". Later, the Kilsyth & Bonnybridge Joint Railway[See Appendix Two] arrived, saw a suitable site for a station, named it "Banknock" and so, in the course of time, Hollandbush and its surrounds would come to be known by that name.

As noted above, the Browns preferred the distinction of "Hollandbush" from that of "Banknock" which had developed something of a rowdy reputation. The weekly column of local news submitted to the Kilsyth Chronicle by Andrew Brown Senior and Junior for many years perpetuated that distinction!

Families ..

As we have seen, Dad was the fourth of a family of five boys in a family who moved houses quite frequently. In contrast, Mum was the elder of two having a sister, Jean, four years her junior which would tend to make for a rather quieter family environment! Also, in contrast, the Stirlingshire Browns were a much more settled family. Mum's grandfather Andrew Brown (Senior) had forsaken the family farm at Wester Gerchew, near Balfron[201] in Stirlingshire for the Licensed Grocery trade (equivalent of an "off-licence") in industrial Falkirk. Marrying Jane (always known as "Jean") Hamilton in 1882, we understand, from Statutory Records and his obituary in the Falkirk Herald that he bought an "established business"[202] in Hollandbush (together with the house and grounds) about 1893 and there the family remained, built around the family firm of "Andrew Brown & Sons".

---

[201] The father of Andrew Brown (Senior) of Hollandbush was also Andrew Brown (1816 -1900). He was a tenant of Wester Gerchew farm, a substantial holding of 60 acres. The author is obliged to William Douglas of Balfron for his help in locating the site which is to the east of the village north of the B8818 in a loop of the River Endrick. On the death of Andrew Brown, the lands passed into the tenancy of neighbouring farms, the house being occupied by farm workers for many years before it was eventually demolished. See Appendix 0

[202] Valuation Rolls of 1875 and 1885 show two households and a grocers' business at that address. He may have bought the business and property following deaths of occupant and proprietor. Family

.. and names

Both Yules and Browns adhered to the tradition of naming children after their antecedents. On Dad's side ,"Robert" occurs frequently on both sides of the family and, of course, Scott was his mother's maiden name. Similarly, with Mum, "Anne" [or "Annie"] is found in both lines and Mum was intended be the latter, but the name morphed into Anne which she felt was more dignified. Mum's mother was Martha McKinnon Brown, so the perpetuation of her mother's maiden name would have looked rather odd. Instead Andrew and Martha went back a generation to Martha's parents: William and Rose Ann (known as Annie) Copland who married in 1874 in Lesmahagow. The fashion for remembering the roll call of ancestral surnames was splendidly exemplified in the younger Brown sister who was named Jean Hamilton Buchanan Brown!

A curious coincidence at Cloybank

We have met the name "Cloybank" earlier, it being the farm to which the Yules moved from Denny. For a short period before he moved to manage presumably a bigger colliery in Hamilton, the house had been the home to the wife and family of Mum's grandfather, William Brown who was manager of the local collieries (see below). Thus, his daughter Martha would have met an eligible bachelor in the shop down in Hollandbush in a reversal of the situation when the Yules were in Cloybank and Dad would have seen Mum in the shop. The Yule – Brown wedding of 1936, however, would have been easier to arrange than the Brown – Brown wedding of 1911 as by that time William had moved and the wedding was finally fixed for a central Glasgow location.

Grandparents

Grandparents played a major part in both Mum and Dad's upbringing. Bella Yule was never far from her mother, Isabella Scott, in Uddingston but Mum had grandparents who were even closer at hand as Andrew Brown (senior) and Jean (née Hamilton) were part of an extended family living, if not exactly "over the shop", but alongside their business premises in the big house and garden at Hollandbush. This had the effect of bringing Mum, not yet eight years old, up against the harsh realities of life when her grandmother died of stomach cancer in January 1920. She was to speak in later life of the awful atmosphere in that usually cheerful home on that occasion. Thus, Mum would be used to being constantly in the presence of her grandfather, by all accounts a strong personality. She had reason to be grateful to the man, for it was that decision to leave Wester Gerchew Farm (and his twin brother Walter) to come into the licensed trade in Falkirk which was

---

anecdote was: "There was an old man who lived upstairs". The two floors were subsequently converted into one large family house.

the basis of the Brown's prosperity. Also, he came out of retirement to retake his place in the shop when his son was conscripted in the Great War and thus kept the family business afloat in that difficult time. He had a bunch of cronies in and around Hollandbush[203] and their exploits (so the author was told) included a trip to Iceland to buy ponies but he was also a bookish man, being an admirer of Thomas Carlyle whose *Sartor Resartus* was perhaps a surprising item in a considerable collection on the shelves at Hollandbush. Strange perhaps to modern readers but recorded in a talk Mum gave to some women's associations in Cheshire in the 1970's, and not atypical in Presbyterian Scots families, Andrew Brown (Senior) would lead family prayers on a Sunday evening at Hollandbush, a tradition which Andrew (Junior) continued into the lifetime of this author.

It has long been a lucrative trade to sell liquid refreshment – alcoholic and non-alcoholic - in central Scotland. Dad's maternal grandfather, John Train Scott, at one time ran the Clydesdale Inn in Craigneuk (between Motherwell and Wishaw) which enabled him to retire to the pleasant surroundings of Kyle Park and almost certainly provide financial help for his daughter Bella and her five laddies. Thus, both families had reason to grateful for the Licensed Trade.

... and other animals

We have no record or retained memory of the Yules having family pets when in Uddingston and indeed, that would have been something of luxury. On the other hand, there seems always to have been domestic animals around Hollandbush. In older buildings like the house, shop, and "Cellar", one can expect problems with rats and mice. Andrew Brown Senior, brought up on a farm, would have known that the simple solution is The Cat - consequently such animals were part of the Brown's establishment. The trouble with that plan was that the Brown sisters – to the annoyance of their grandfather – treated the cats as pets, despite one of them, Maggie, showing that a house pet can be also be an extremely efficient pest control operative. Perhaps to distract attention from the cats, the girls were given a dog, Dick, a spaniel of unrecorded breed to be their pet. Sadly, this animal does not seem to have led a long life, succumbing [unusually for those days] to a road accident. His spaniel successor, Mac, similarly was doomed to a short life developing a canker in the ear which proved fatal. There were no more family dogs – the Browns presumably decided that they were fated – but they had both lived long enough to accustom Mum to proximity to a dog, so she was quite capable of dealing with Spot[204] and others at Marampa.

---

[203] According to Jean Arneil, they may have been nicknamed "The Three Must- get- beers"!

[204] At the time of the Diary, the Cat in Residence was Jeff, an animal who lived to a great age with such a presence that, as the author recalls, he had his own jealously-guarded chair next the Raeburn stove in the Hollandbush kitchen! [See Illustrations 4]

A Tale of two villages ..

As we have noted, the Yules, together with the other good people of Uddingston, always liked to think of themselves as "villagers". This was despite Uddingston being, in effect, an industrial outer suburb of Glasgow, complete with a handsome Main Street, three railway stations [2 "Caley", 1 "NB"] and - in the fullness of time – access to two tramway systems. The Browns, who were not without knowledge of the Glasgow conurbation, always rather disputed that "village" description of their in-laws considering that it more correctly applied to Hollandbush/Banknock. Readers may judge for themselves, though the author would like to suggest that Mum came from "an industrial village". We must stretch the boundaries here beyond the colliery village along the Kilsyth Road for, before the expansion of coal mining in the second half of the 19th century and making full use of the Forth and Clyde Canal, the Bankier Distillery was established, bringing an industrial complex to the south of Hollandbush[205]. Later, to the west of Hollandbush, in keeping with the major industry of the Falkirk region, came James Dobbie & Co[206] with an iron founders' factory. But no row of shops ever developed, though the Hollandbush Inn – across the road from the Browns -provided a centre of activity, not always of a decorous nature! The Longcroft Co-operative Society set up premises across the Doubs Burn[207] and the Post Office was long established in the old Hollandbush hamlet but that and Andrew Brown & Sons plus the essential fish and chip shop comprised the total dedicated retail premises.[208] So no trams, but a sizeable station [a passing place on the single line] with trains to Glasgow and the Clyde Coast if needed [see Illustrations 4], a mains gas supply [boosted by a gas holder by Banknock House] and then, by the mid-thirties, an automatic telephone system, together with frequent buses to nearby towns with their shops and cinemas gave an urban, industrialised feel to the village. However, in that village, the Browns lived within a small, tight-knit community which is exactly what Mum would be joining in Sierra Leone.

.. and two coalmines.

Banknock stands on the northern rim of an extensive coalfield (geologically the same one as Uddingston) and – as has been indicated previously – the area was well known for coal

---

[205] Geography teachers will note: extensive site; good piped water supply from nearby hills; local coal; adjacent wharf on canal for raw materials and finished product. Falkirk Archives have many illustrations.

[206] One of the partners in the business was Thomas Dobson whose family – part of the Browns' social circle -took over the Dobbie home alongside the foundry. This turreted family house has since upgraded itself to "castle" status and is a multi-starred hotel and restaurant.

[207] Subject of a famous Test Case of 1895 regarding industrial usage priority. See p xii

[208] A great deal of trading was done from pony and cart. [see Illustrations 4] There were also fruit and vegetable traders from Kilsyth or Falkirk.

production. There is more about coalmining and Banknock's Livingstone and Cannerton pits in Appendix Three but, by the time Mum began her Diary, these pits – like many others nearby – were no longer viable, and coalmining was beginning to fade from the Banknock scene, taking the passenger railway service with it. The economy of the area was rescued from total collapse in 1933 by the introduction of a brickworks on the Livingstone site. This was a local initiative in which the Browns were shareholders and, taking its name for the other pit, Cannerton, made use originally of the clay and shale waste in the pit bing and produced a quality brand for almost five decades.

"Doon the watter"

The reader will have noted the Yules' passion for the pleasure steamers on the Clyde and how travel on those "miniature liners" prepared Dad for ocean travel in later life. The Banknock-based Browns were of course much farther from Glasgow's Bridge Wharf or the Clyde piers, but we know from a fragment of script that they certainly indulged in travel "doon the watter". Although Mum also noted trips on the famous steamer *Columba*, the MacBrayne's paddler left Bridge Wharf at too early a time for the Browns to get there from Banknock, so they raced ahead of the ship by train and boarded at a pier further down river. But this was still a long day as Mum's abiding memory of trips to Tarbert or Ardrishaig was having to catch the 0630 train from Banknock Station to Queen Street then crossing Glasgow to catch another train to Greenock or Gourock. Her notes for a possible talk on the topic suggest she preferred a cruise with the North British/LNER steamers from Craigendoran as that did not involve a change of station in Glasgow

As we have seen, the lower Firth can be rough at times and a pleasure steamer, especially a paddle steamer, en route to Rothesay could "rock and roll". This was not to Mum's liking and she must have had qualms about undertaking a ten-day voyage to West Africa. She was much happier on the pleasure craft which – surprisingly to modern eyes – operated on the Forth and Clyde Canal[209], where of course, a boat was unlikely to be tossed about on waves. One can envisage Dad, in briefing his bride on her forthcoming trip, assuring her that the trip from Freetown to Pepel by launch would be just like travelling from Craigmarloch on the canal!

A wee lassie and a wider world

Simple arithmetic shows that Mum was but an infant when the Great War broke out in 1914 and she had no recollection of the events of the conflict save for the announcement of the Armistice in November 1918, when she was stood on a desk in the schoolroom to

---

[209] Aitken's pleasure steamers on the summit level were long a feature of the Canal lasting throughout the 1930's & Mum recalled travelling on them. Maybe, she & Dad went on the popular dance cruises on the capacious triple-decked steamer *Gipsy Queen*.

look out the window and see if her Grandfather had run up a flag on the garden flagpole. However, the War had a direct effect on the Brown household of which she was well aware.

A partner in a Grocery firm and not a sole breadwinner for his family, Andrew Brown (jun.), was not exempt from military service but one of Mum's Talks [See Addendum 2] explained that he was determined to serve as an ambulance driver, which, on being called up in 1917, as 321291 Brown A., Private, Army Service Corps (Mechanised Transport) he eventually became. However, there was a lot of rigorous training on all types of mechanised vehicles, not necessarily to his liking, before he was passed as "efficient" and posted to France late in 1918.

On understanding that the Armistice meant a cessation of hostilities, Mum must have expected her Father to be back home soon but that was not to be the case. There were stores and equipment to be repatriated, and wounded men to be collected from hospitals in France and Belgium and transported to the Channel Ports. Her Father was very much involved in that movement which took him from his Corps base at Wimereux, near Boulogne, down to the damaged towns of the Battle Zone and over war-torn roads back to the coast. We know this from the flood of postcards which he sent, both to his wife "Matt" and to his elder daughter, now in her second year at school and well able to read the largely pencilled messages. Most of the cards were enclosed in an "honour envelope" which he would sign as containing only private messages, thus bypassing the Censor, and passed through an astonishingly efficient postal system to be collected in Mum's specially purchased album which has remained a treasured family heirloom. It was autumn 1919 before the Army decided that 321291 Brown's services were no longer required by King and Country and he could return to Hollandbush, no doubt a sadder but a wiser man.

At school ...

Both Mum and Dad followed a similar educational pathway – Parish School, local academy, specialist college. Mum's school trail took her though Banknock School till age 12 then Kilsyth Academy but we know that, in sharp contrast to Dad's straightforward passage, her schooling was seriously affected by ill health. Family anecdote suggests that she suffered no less than three bouts of pneumonia, an infectious condition which in Mum's childhood days (before the advent of penicillin and other antibiotics together with modern surgical and intensive care techniques) had a mortality rate approaching 30%. These serious episodes would have meant absence from school with its effect on academic progress particularly in a "ladder subject" like Mathematics where, as she related to the author, she missed several key steps. As the School Leaving qualifications of the time were awarded on a group basis, her lack of skill in Mathematics probably resulted in her under achieving in terms of academic qualifications. However, we know from surviving evidence[210] that by March 1930 (when Dad was chopping down West Australian bushland) she had reached a level sufficient for her to be enrolled at Skerry's College in Glasgow on the Civil Service (Executive) course.

... and after

We know from the certificates (see Appendix 3) exactly what Dad studied at Royal Technical College, how well he did and the practical nature of his course. Skerry's Colleges had a similar role in vocational education and, other than academic studies, Mum would have done the "commercial" courses in shorthand and typing. She clearly "satisfied the examiners" and duly moved into the Civil Service. She spoke little of that part of her life, but we gather she worked in Unemployment Bureaux in Stirling, Fleetwood Lancashire and Oldham Lancashire. Given the economic situation of the country in the late 20's and early 30's that may well have been a hectic environment. We know she had a happy time in Fleetwood, lodging with the Barrowclough family who remained lifelong friends. However, something seems to have gone wrong in Oldham causing her father – who must have been mindful of her childhood illnesses - to bring her home to Hollandbush and thereby indirectly ensuring she met Dad!

Accomplishments

Both Mum and Dad acquired the accomplishments – sporting & outdoor in Dad's case, domestic in Mum's - which their families saw as appropriate, but music was an "added extra". One of the "rites of passage" of a young lady was to take piano lessons and Mum reached an acceptable level of competency in the performance of popular ballads. Dad was encouraged to sing. The author has recollections of her accompanying Dad's light tenor in the traditional ballad: *Rothesay Bay,* a number whose waltz rhythm seems to echo the triple beat of the engines of a Clyde paddle steamer and when Mum observed on 31 X 36 that: *"Bob sang very well"* that sad song might well have been in his repertoire.

In one accomplishment however, Mum rather upstaged Dad. For business reasons, the Browns were early into motorised travel [See Addendum 2 for more] and Mum seems to have taken to being behind the wheel at the earliest opportunity which in the days before passing a Driving test became compulsory was one's 19th birthday. One can surmise that, on that or either of the two subsequent anniversaries, her Father – who would have instructed her – or doting Grandfather would have forked out the five shillings (25p) to Stirlingshire County Council for her Driving Licence. Dad, however, had not been so

---

[210]Inscription on flyleaf of: *An Outline of English History* W E Haigh OUP 1917 1929 Impression: *"Anne Copland Brown, Hollandbush Banknock March 12 1930"* And at the foot: *"Civil Service (Executive)"*

fortunate so we had the circumstance – unusual for the time - where the woman in the relationship was a driver whilst the man was not. That situation could scarcely be endured, of course, and at some time Dad duly learned to drive and passed his test but that must have been after June 1935 when it had become compulsory. This lag in accomplishment was ever a matter of some glee amongst the Yules and Browns.

Organisations

As we have seen, Dad belonged to what was then known as the Boy Scouts. Mum also was a member of a uniformed, Christian-based youth organisation: The Girls' Guildry. Formed in Glasgow in 1900 (and thus older than the Scouts), this was the first girls' uniformed organisation in Britain and its spirit lives on today, after mergers, in the Girls' Brigade. As we noted, the Outdoor Activities of the Boy Scouts appealed to Dad and his introduction thereby to living "under canvas" was to be a useful grounding for "roughing it" in Australia and probably also the early months in Sierra Leone. This was definitely not the case for Mum! Though the Guildry did go on annual camps, to the pretty fishing village of St Monans (or St Monance), in Fife, for instance, the girls were accommodated in church halls rather than tents. There is no evidence that Mum ever developed a taste for outdoor living and, one assumes, would have needed some convincing by Dad – perhaps from his photos – that they would be in "serviced" bungalows at Marampa.

The Built Environment

As we have seen, the Yules in their Kyle Park villa, benefitted from the increased demand for coal and the products of coalfired industry during and immediately after the Great War. The Browns also felt the spin off from that rather false national prosperity. The comfortably furnished house at Hollandbush was improved with the addition of a bathroom, an extension to the kitchen, a glazed porch and the conversion of the coal shed into "The Den" -a refuge for the grandparents. Away from the house, a washhouse complete with a coal-fired copper wash tub was built as an extension to the "Cellar" – a former stables lying at right angles to the house which was used as a storeroom. The shop was improved with an office extension built and the yard at the rear enclosed so that the "Cellar" - became directly connected to the sales premises. Pony and trap gave way to motor vehicle [see Addendum Two] and stabling became a garage. The garden retained its fruit and vegetable areas – which became very useful when war returned in 1939 - and the traditional "drying green" for the washing but saw remarkable developments. At the ultimate stage, there was a lawn large enough for tennis or carpet bowls; a rose garden with crazy paved paths, a lily pond with fountain, an ornamental summerhouse "The Clachan", a water feature before they were fashionable and a hothouse. This latter, home to the

Brown's gardener[211], became quite a well- known local feature as – this being Stirlingshire – there flourished within it, a vine grown from a cutting of the great vine at Kippen[212].

This was a rather prosperous family which Dad married into and the fact that his new bride was happy to follow him overseas to a mining camp in the West African bush speaks volumes for their relationship.

Good to Go

We have seen that Dad's training and work as a Mining Surveyor and perhaps his natural, untutored artistic talent made him a person who was used to looking about him and recording, in one form or another, what he saw. So, recording daily events in a Diary at a time of great change in his life was perhaps in keeping with his background. Mum, growing up in a very literate household, would have been enjoined also to look around her. For instance, her Grandfather and Father would have pointed out to her that the "lumps and bumps" just south of the Forth and Clyde Canal were, in fact, the remains of the only previous cross- country work prior to that waterway's construction: the Antonine Wall. However, we must not think of her as living some sort of cloistered existence within the thick walls of Hollandbush. As already noted, she had been close at hand when her Grandmother died. She was living in the centre of a mining community and would be accustomed to hearing, or reading the local paper, about deaths and accidents in the pits. [See Appendix 3] As mentioned above, her home was across the road from a miners' pub with all the Sunday disturbance from its "bona fide traveller" patrons. Unlike Dad, whose journey to Australia began with his first trip out of Scotland, Mum had been out of Scotland with her family [See Addendum 2] and with her work. So, again unlike Dad, she had met plenty of people whose version of English was very different from her own, indeed given that the distillery workers from the Highlands came into the shop, she would have heard people speaking in a tongue she did not understand. So, although she was no aficionado of travel by ship, she was quite ready to join her new husband on the trip of a lifetime to sample a new way of life in a far- off British Colony and she had the skills to produce a written record of the experience.

Having drawn two threads together it is time to look at that record.

---

[211] The Browns were always employers. The 1901 Census shows 2 "live-in" employees: a shop assistant, who probably occupied a small room at the back of the "Cellar", and a "Domestic Servant" who would sleep in the attic room converted from the loft of the big house.

[212] The Kippen Vine, planted in 1891, covering an area of 5,000 square feet and taking up four greenhouses was claimed as the largest in the world. Larger than the much- vaunted Hampton Court vine it was something of a tourist attraction, until the Kippen Vinery had to close in 1964. Delightfully, the local community newsletter in this attractive Stirlingshire village is called the Kippen Grapevine. [See Illustrations Set4]

The BROWNS of HOLLANDBUSH

Tagged as "Paw Maw and the Weans", the Browns posing in formal attire on the steps which led through to the Kitchen Garden at Hollandbush. Note Matt and Andrew stand on the step! [Family Collection]

"Grandpa". A rare picture of Andrew Brown Senior [1854- 1933] who set up the family business. Possibly taken at Hollandbush before the garden was developed. [Family Collection]

The "Clachan", the Hollandbush summerhouse complete with fireplace! [Family Collection]

The very young author at the lily pond at the north end of the rose garden. [Family Collection]

ROUND and ABOUT

This picture from the 1920's [Courtesy EDLC] encapsulated much of Mum's teenage years with the Alexander's charabanc at Craigmarloch on the Forth & Clyde Canal with the pleasure steamer *Gypsy Queen* at the pier. The Kilsyth Hills form a backdrop.

Wyndford Lock, eastern end of the top pound, in 19th century with the pagodas of the Distillery beyond. [Falkirk Archives]

Looking in the reverse direction on the re-opened canal in the 21st century. The lock-keeper's cottage remains. [Author]

AROUND BANKNOCK

Banknock Station in 1923. Note the floral garden. [Falkirk Archives] See Appendix 2

The trains had long ago departed when the author took this picture of the same site.

This picture is believed to be taken in the Banknock Rows with the Longcroft Co-op butcher and his horse and cart posing for the camera. Note the use of the old Scots term: "Fleshing Department". [Falkirk Archives]

"MR. BROON'S GAIRDEN"

A close- up view of the water feature
in the corner of the Wash House and
the Hothouse. [Family Collection]

The grapes of Hollandbush. A cutting
from the Kippen vine thrives in the
hothouse. [Family Collection]

The Cat in Residence in the Diary period
was Jeff, here in the garden with Mum.
[Family Collection]

The Brown's premises lay on the
right between the bridge and the track
of the wagonway. [Author]

WEDDED and AWA'

A very pretty wedding at Dennyloanhead captured by John G Wilson of Bannockburn.

Yules & Browns have a rather hilarious Leaving Picnic Party at Wester Gerchew, Balfron, October 1936. [Family Collection]

Farewell to Hollandbush. Mum & Dad at the sundial in the Rose Garden about to leave for Africa. October 1936. [Family]

FAST REWIND – THE FAMILIES WENT TO WAR

Hugh Scott with unidentified lady at Walsham's Studio Aldershot Nov. 1914 [Family Collection]

Andrew Brown (Jun) with Matt by the newly built Clachan, Hollandbush 1917. [Family Collection]

From a rather battered p/c to his nephew George Young, Hugh Scott with pals from the Section House, at Walsham's, Nov. 1914. 1 JW Scott 2 J Rule 3 R Scott 4 H Scott 5 J? Macrae [Family Collection]

321291 Brown A, Pte. A.S.C [R middle row] with his Section and instructors, at Training Camp, Salisbury Plain. [Family Collection]

SOME GENERAL COMMENTS on the DIARY

Another wee black book; Why keep a diary; ... what went in it; ... and what didn't. The photographic record; Notes in a notebook ...; And a medical note

Author's note

As before, this is where I try to fill in the gaps in the diary narrative, clarifying some of the terms or references which may have lost their meaning with the passage of time and offering such opinions or observations which did not occur to me during my transcription from the original.

Another wee black book

 The leather-bound notebook (usefully labelled "Note Book") would have been easily overlooked amongst Mum's things, it being but 5 ins by 3 ins (130mm x 35 mm) – and may have come enclosed in her Writing Case. Fortunately, it was opened and quickly proved to be the Diary the family knew Mum had kept on her first and only trip to West Africa. As with Dad, the handwriting is firm and legible in Royal Blue Ink and with a few exceptions, Mum used one unlined page to record each day from 7th October 1936 to 31st December 1936. This is a short passage of time perhaps but, as with Dad, a period which had an immense effect on her life.

Why keep a diary ..

Mum, like Dad, never explained why she chose to keep a diary though it was obviously going to make good use of the Note Book in her Writing Case. One can but surmise that her reasons were much the same as Dad's [and may have been prompted by him]: to provide substance for the many letters she wrote and to provide a lasting memento of her trip of a lifetime. In quest of the latter, she may have not very often turned the pages as her household would contain many objects of all sizes purchased in West Africa or Madeira. The reader is once again reminded of Ruth Symes' telling comment quoted on the title page of this book!

.. what went in it..

Mum could cram as much as 80 words onto one of those tiny pages in her daily records and, in contrast to Dad, usually had the time and the energy to make an entry each day. She also had the writing skill to produce a concise account which would perhaps reflect her Civil Service training in précis writing. As one might expect, her style is very different from Dad's. Where Dad tended to use the short descriptive phrase, Mum tends to write in sentences – one can almost hear the voice of her teachers at Kilsyth Academy urging her to do so! This is the writing of a well-read, literate young woman who, the reader might sense, was rather in awe of her surroundings and could perhaps scarce believe that she was finally with her new husband in a far -off land of which he had spoken so much. Mum shared a family attribute: the ability to capture the reader or listener's attention when telling a story. Here she is telling one – or perhaps two for - as I have indicated by so arranging her record - the Diary story falls clearly into two parts: the "honeymoon cruise" then recording the minutiae of setting up home and settling into a domestic regime and a social life in a remote mining community in the West African bush.

.. and what didn't

As before in this publication, there are things unsaid in a diary. The word "Luggage" appears but once in the entries and then, one must surmise, in an insurance context. By now, Dad would be a "savvy traveller" regarding luggage and "no news is good news" in this context.

A surprising omission was that they went to church on Christmas Day 1936. Mum wrote later [See Commentary] that: "*We went to a service in the local church. This church was built of mud walls, shoulder high with a roof of palm branches supported on poles. Very primitive. The preacher was a coloured man and puzzled us by including "Princess Alexandra[213]" in his prayers. We hadn't heard of the Princess's arrival – no radio or papers. In the Church listening to the Christmas message and singing carols brought us nearer home than anything we had done since our arrival.*"

The photographic record

The photographic record of Marampa is much more comprehensive than that of Western Australia. One simple reason would be that Dad in Australia was hard up and paying for films and having them sent away to be developed was something of a luxury. That, as we have seen, was no longer the case! Where photos in the albums – Mum calls them "snaps" - have been dated, they show a range covering all Dad's years there plus some later ones. This suggests that TWO cameras are involved here: Dad's- effectively that of the Yule family- and one which Mum had acquired, perhaps as a 21st Birthday present in 1933 and had used for some years. It seems likely that the former stayed with Alex Yule after Mum & Dad returned to Scotland. Together with some pictures taken professionally for SLDCo., they provide an informative picture of the early years of the Marampa project.

Notes in a notebook ...

There is nothing in Mum's Diary to compare with the lengthy notes in Dad's but there are some intriguing "extras". There are repeated lists of names and numbers which can only

---

[213]Princess Alexandra, The Honourable Lady Ogilvy, (Alexandra Helen Elizabeth Olga Christabel), a member of the British royal family, was born 25 December 1936 so the preacher must have had access to a telegraph or radio.

be an attempt to keep track of who was living in which bungalow. The "A.C. Yule" in this list is, of course, not Mum's newly acquired title but Alexander Crawford Yule, a similarity of initials which seems to have caused occasional embarrassment.

As with Dad, she "tabulated" and in good Civil Service fashion kept a record of correspondence which runs into May 1937 well after the last of her daily entries. From her list of 26 correspondents, she then narrows it to "regulars", still a list of no less than 14. That included both Hollandbush and Cloybank, so one can guess, that with the time on her hands, she had taken over the regular letters to both sets of parents. She remained a regular correspondent with those on that list for much of the rest of her life. She also noted down the dates of sailings from Freetown to Liverpool which indicates there was a fortnightly service which would dictate the times for collection and arrival of mail in that era before regular airmail services.

A surprise entry immediately after her last daily record is a recipe for oatcakes. There were, as in every outpost of Empire, a number of Scots at Marampa and knowing that Mum did some baking of her own may have prevailed on her to produce a "taste o' hame". It is reproduced here but when Mum consolidated her recipes into a new book in 1966, it did not appear, and the author and publisher take no responsibility for its efficacy.

> *"1 lb oatmeal, 1 pint boiling water, ½oz salt butter, melted in water & poured quickly over meal & rolled thin."*

And a medical note

From 13th November, there appears every second day, a most telling note in Mum's record: Atebrin. From that, we may deduce that Mum had been prescribed ATABRINE which at the time was the latest drug for the preventative and curative treatment of Malaria. We have seen earlier [See Intermezzo] that this mosquito-borne disease can prove fatal in some cases, but its effects of fever, fatigue, vomiting, and headaches are clearly debilitating amongst a work-force. Family anecdote and subsequent events suggest that Dad throughout his West African sojourn received the traditional treatment of doses of quinine – of which, more later - but here, Mum seems to have been at the "cutting edge" of medicine. The value of Atabrine, also known as Mepacrine or Quinacrine, which was really a yellow dye synthesised in Germany around 1931, had only lately been recognised by the medical profession[214], so SLDCo. was taking a very responsible attitude to staff welfare. About the [long-lasting] after effects of the tablets, she wrote later: *"These tablets were a deep yellow colour and when I came home, I couldn't understand why folk stared at me, until Mother pointed out that I was more like a Chinese than a Scot!".*

---

[214] The use of Atabrine became widespread during the Second World War when the Japanese conquest of the Dutch East Indies [now Indonesia] removed Allied access to 90% of the world's supply of quinine.

VOLUME TWO

COMMENTARY ON PART ONE

*Not the first "Commentary"; Rewind; Oban; Things to get and things to do ...;
... and people to see; Good Old Aba; A retrospective; Nautical conveniences;
Mal de Mer; Madeira; Landfall.*

Not the first "Commentary"

Mum has rather pre-empted us here. In the 1970's she was very active in the Women's organisations in the Nonconformist churches in the Warrington area and regularly gave talks to them. Prompted by a speaker whose topic was Sierra Leone – but in the 1950's – Mum put together a talk on her experiences twenty years before that. We still have her 12-page type-written script of that talk -which complements her diary in many helpful ways - and those "afterthoughts" are quoted throughout this volume and referred to as "Mum's Talk".

Rewind

Let us return to the thread of the story which we left off with a young couple getting married at Dennyloanhead, Bonnybridge, Stirlingshire, on 9th September 1936 – incidentally, the Certificate has Mum as "Annie", the birth name she disliked. Mum's Talk recorded the event thus: "*Our wedding in church was much as any other couple's*" The reader may disagree here on learning that there were TWO Ministers presiding: Rev. Peter Lovie MA of Dennyloanhead kirk and Dad's uncle: The Rev. David Mailler Yule Dip. Theo. of Forgandenny in Perthshire, clearly honouring a promise though his wife had recently died. Also, the ceremony did attract several column inches in the local press with a 2-column spread photo and their "Wedding Book" lists over 120 presents!
We have six weeks to fill in.

Oban

Some of that time, of course, was the honeymoon. This we know to have been in Oban, in the West Highlands, a wee town well known to Dad whose sketch book has three scenes drawn, presumably, on a visit before he went to Australia. We know they stayed close to the harbourside, perhaps in what is now the Columba Hotel, and thus close to the steamer pier where the summer timetable must have still been in operation for they took advantage of the cruises on offer on the MacBrayne's steamers. These took them to the sheltered waters of the Sound of Mull and Loch Linnhe but also to the far side of the Isle of Mull to Iona and Staffa. Dad may have had a hidden motive in this latter trip in introducing his bride to the rougher seas of the Atlantic and to the practice of disembarking from a steamer onto a small boat as was then a necessity at Funchal or Freetown. Remembered anecdote suggests that this was not a particularly happy trip as Mum succumbed to her old foe, seasickness, on the small craft which took them to the columnar basalt cliffs of Staffa and its famous Fingal's Cave. However, this otherwise carefree holiday clearly made a lasting impression as they later were to name their house in Bridgend, South Wales, after a local Oban landmark: Dunollie Castle!

Things to get and things to do ...

Mum's Talk provides a prequel to her trip: "*We had to leave all our presents at home, but this gave me something to think about when occasionally I was homesick.*" But there were more pressing needs: "*We had a spending spree*" she said in her Talk, "*not on glamorous things, merely plain cotton frocks, shirts, socks, shorts, cotton dresses, large double sun hat, mac,*" and importantly, "*mosquito boots, long white canvas boots which came up over the knees and well up the thighs.*" Not quite enough, as she admitted in the Talk that the visit to Lewis's store [7 X 36] was to buy shoes: "*I bought yet another pair to take with us*". Also, her wardrobe must have proved deficient in shorts – not something she would have worn much in Scotland – as on 3 XI 36 we find her taking delivery of "white shorts". [Mail Order is not an invention of the 21ˢᵗ century!]

Not everything was as agreeable as a shopping spree! Mum continued: "*Next ... horrible things, various injections and vaccinations, medical examinations etc., etc. One of the injections laid me out for a couple of days and I began to wonder if it was worth all the suffering.*"

... and people to see.

Back in Hollandbush, Banknock which was to be their "base camp" in succeeding years, as Andrew Brown (Senior) had died in 1933, there was plenty of space for a household of Andrew, Martha and Jean Brown and the two busy newlyweds. In her 1970's Talk, Mum said: "*... in 1936 there were not such comings and goings as there are today unless you were in the Army or the Diplomatic Corps. There was no TV to bring strange and faraway places into our homes, so my departure was something to talk about in my village.*" Some of that talk would have been filled with doom-laden prophecies, on the "White Man's Grave theme" but about all that – in probably the nicest quote transcribed to this book – Mum commented: "*... when you are young and in love, these things don't worry you*".

One rather out of character event has been recorded on photographs [the daftest illustration herein] and that was a picnic party near Balfron at the farm road end for Wester Gerchew. If one did not know better, one might assume drink had been taken by the Yules and Browns! But the appointed day duly arrived and there is an echo of Dad's first Africa trip in the leaving of Scotland. Once again, it was the Alexander's bus to Glasgow, but Mum does not suggest a farewell group travelling with them perhaps out of consideration for her family, given the lateness of the departure. As in Dad's earlier entry, the Glasgow-based Devines were at Central Station to see them onto the same overnight LMS service from Glasgow Central to Liverpool Exchange, though by now, Dad could command a First-Class sleeping compartment. *("A special treat"*: as Mum judged later.)

Good Old Aba

Ever the enthusiast regarding ships and shipping, Dad would have told Mum of the splendours of the modern Elder Dempster ships and how he knew some of the crew. So, he may have been a bit disappointed to find their passage out booked on the twenty-year-old MV *Aba* on which, as attentive readers will recall, he had not previously sailed. This Clyde -built vessel *[see Appendix 1 for more details]* was not purpose-built for the West Africa trade, having been originally ordered by the Russian Imperial Government in 1916, a contract which was frustrated by well-documented events in the subsequent year. However, she was still serving her owners well in 1936 as Mum – who quickly adopted ship-board ways [see below] -records on 15 X 36 the ship's best progress as 325 nautical miles in the previous 24 hours, which suggests that *Aba* was still capable of nudging her design top speed of 14 knots.

A retrospective

Mum's Talk tells us that her only previous sea-going experience had been on a day trip from Stranraer to Larne and two trips from Fleetwood to the Isle of Man. [These latter would have been when she lodged with the Barrowcloughs who made her one of the family in the days when Fleetwood was the ferry port for the island.] Thus, she remembered on boarding MV *Aba*: *"... to me who had no experience of ships she seemed huge, but I was assured that she was really quite small and after ten days on board, I had to agree."*

From the perspective of the 1970's, Mum was able to take a more detached view of that first ocean trip:

"Life on board ship was really very quiet. The return voyage to the West Coast is not such a happy one. Friends and loved ones have been left behind and another tour has started. As first, it seems very glamorous and romantic but really it is not so. These Elder Dempster ships are no more romantic than the Liverpool to Manchester train, they are just a means of transport to and from work. There were a few travellers going on holiday, but most were just going to work."

However, she notes: *"... the meals were delicious and dressing for dinner exciting."* Yes. Dressing for dinner in Second Class – the British Empire DID have standards.

The voyage as depicted in Mum's Talk is very much a paraphrasing of her Diary entries, but she makes some illuminating additional comments. Of the "swimming pool", which the Diary notes on 13 X 36, she speaks as being: *"... simply a huge canvas bag slung on poles. Not exactly Queen Elizabeth standards"*, though she concedes: *"This proved very popular".* Also, she told her audience: "*Guessing the day's mileage lent some excitement*", so we now know why she regularly recorded that figure though there is no note of a successful estimate! She also enlarged her cryptic entry of 16 X 36: "*I had my hair set*" by pointing out that: "*Getting one's hair done before landing was a must, as in my case, it was 10 months before I could get to a hairdresser again*".

Nautical conveniences

Neither in the Diary or the Talk script does Mum mention on which deck was their cabin, A or B. However, her entry for 9 X 36 suggests the lower of the two, that is one of the 14 outside cabins shown on the Accommodation Plan reproduced on p 169 of Cowden & Duffy's invaluable guide to Elder Dempster ships. Modern readers must note that these cabins were not "en-suite", thus toilets and bathrooms [showers had not become the fashion] had to be shared and were not necessarily on the same deck as the cabin. It is probable, then, that Mum and Dad's bathroom facilities – 2 "Gents", 2 "Ladies" – were on the deck above and had to be shared between nearly thirty Second-Class cabins! Mum did not seem to have considered this to be a problem at the time but later remembered an omission from 8 X 36 where she mentioned unpacking and exploring: "*... oh before that we put our names down for baths, most necessary, otherwise bath time and breakfast can coincide*". Mum, of course, had the advantage of being with a "savvy traveller"!

Mal de Mer.

But the inevitable happened!

On the second day out from Liverpool, [Thursday 8 X 1936] she records herself as feeling "groggy" and she spent the next two days in bed as *Aba* crossed the notorious waters west of the Bay of Biscay. Mum bore all this in a stoic fashion and she was clearly reconciled to the fact that she was not a "good sailor". However, as *Aba* sailed south into calmer waters Mum gained her "sea legs" - Sunday 11 X 36 "*I am feeling OK now & had breakfast in the Dining saloon* " - and thus was fit and well for what was clearly a keenly anticipated highlight of her journey.

Madeira

Dad would have called in at Funchal on his earlier Tours [and possibly also at Bathurst (Banjul) and Vigo] and would have sung the praise of Madeira, illustrating the island's charms with sets of commercial snapshots. Thus, Mum was prepared: "*It is all beautiful. The little park with the swans & boy & girl in the pool are all like the pictures. I felt I knew that part already.* " 12 X 36. Her visit brought out the best of her descriptive writing and her record of that day stretches over five pages of the wee book. There is a freshness about the writing and one may feel that a lot here was owed to her English teacher at Kilsyth Academy, Miss Kirkness – long on Mum's correspondence list – who may have said: "Describe what you saw in your own words"; "Give your story a beginning, a middle, and an end". I leave the reader to decide.

Landfall

There were four more days of this "honeymoon cruise", a bit of rough weather and plenty shipboard activity. Presumably at Dad's suggestion, both took advantage of the ship's hairdressing salon as there is no record of any such facility at Marampa. Mum does not record any instance of standing at the forepeak of the vessel as Dad had recorded in that first voyage. A glance at the illustration of *Aba* [See Illustrations 6] shows a well deck with sizeable cargo facilities forward of the main superstructure and a much shorter forecastle than on *Apapa,* so maybe that access was not available to passengers. [Possibly disappointing to Dad.]

 Then the cruise was over. The ship anchored in Freetown harbour, where Mum had a welcome from the ex-pat community with an exciting new experience awaiting her. There was still some up-country travel by launch and by rail before she was to reach her home for the next few months, but it is now high time to turn to Mum's travel journal.

A lasting memento of the trip out to West Africa: the "tea cloth"
bought at Funchal 12 X 1936 and still a family heirloom.
[Photographed for this book by Esther Lyons.]

VOLUME TWO

Mum's diary is inscribed on the flyleaf:

A C Yule

Started 7.10.36 aboard RMS Aba [and in different ink] *Finished 31-12-37*

(sic) *in Bungalow No 12 Marampa Sierra Leone*

THE DIARY PART ONE
OUTWARD BOUND 6.10.36 TO 17.10.36

Tuesday 6.10.36

We left Banknock at 9.40.[215] The run into Glasgow was as slow as possible. David Devine & Winnie were at the station. The train left up to time 11.5. We had a sleeper[216] which made a big difference. The run down was OK. Bob did not sleep much but I managed about 4 hours.

Wednesday 7.10.36

Wakened up in Liverpool 6.35. [217]We had tea on the train then got dressed & left at 7.15. After strolling around a bit we found a café. Just when we left the station we spoke to a policeman who, true to story was from Bathgate.[218] Breakfast was OK. After breakfast we made our way to Birkenhead where we met Cathie.[219] She was pleased to see us. We had tea. We saw the entrance to the Mersey Tunnel.[220] Lunch we took in Lewis's[221] which was very good. It was early closing so we had to hurry our shopping.[222] Visited Ralph Baker re luggage wrote pc, sent telegrams. We went on board about 3.30 and sailed at 5.5.We had tea then walked around [*next bit unclear*] Hamilton sent a telegram. We unpacked had a sleep then dinner. After dinner we walked round the decks saw the engines. We are now preparing for bed.

---

[215] As before, this would be by Alexander's bus.

[216] See Commentary

[217] Exchange Station – see also Coda – then a large 10 platform terminus. Became redundant in 1970's with local services switched to Merseyrail and long-distance to Lime Street. Site redeveloped but facade retained.

[218] Family myth that if you speak to a policeman in England, he will turn out to be Scots. Perhaps truer for doctors, engineers and Investment Managers.

[219] Cathie Shearer, school friend of Mum's, who had missed her wedding, was a Ship's Nurse on a City Liner, by coincidence, sailing for Bombay same day.

[220] Queensway Tunnel, opened in 1934, and thus still something of a novelty and of especial interest to a mining engineer!

[221] The Department Store. Later a favourite of Mum's.

[222]Until the law was relaxed in the 1990's, UK legislation required shops to close for half a day midweek to compensate their staff for having to work on Saturdays. Local authorities had the power to determine on which day that would be, usually a Wednesday or Thursday.

9 o'clock It has been very cold to day but we will soon have heat. Bob has a cold and is now having hot lemon drink & then bed. Everything has gone well so far.

Thursday 8.10.36

At 12 noon we had done 236 miles, opposite Bristol Channel. We had tea about 7.30 and then a bath. The morning was spent walking around & writing & reading. After lunch we lay down & had afternoon tea in the cabin. We had a walk before dinner when I came down I felt groggy & went to bed minus dinner. We both slept well.

Friday 9.10.36

This morning was a bit rough. The port hole was open & the sea came in. Two windows were broken on the main deck. We had done 235 miles since noon yesterday. The position was 60 miles off Ushant at 12 o' clock. The sea is now much calmer though there is still a good swell. I have spent today in bed. We passed a sailing ship[223] being badly tossed about. She had her top sails down. There is a carnival dance tonight.

Saturday 10.10.36

I spent today in bed but am feeling much better. There has been nothing to write about. Tonight there was Dog Racing, but we didn't go. I managed up in the evening. Mileage 303 opposite Cape Finisterre.

Sunday 11.10.36

I am feeling OK now & had breakfast in the Dining saloon. We have been finishing our mail ready to post. *[Change of fountain pen ink]*. We did 320 miles up to 12 noon today. We got books & spent the afternoon reading. About 6 o'clock I began to dress for dinner. The dinner was OK. We walked round after dinner & then read some mags. We saw one boat to-day. A water spout was seen about 5 o'clock.

Monday 12.10.36

Bob saw Santo Porto[224] this morning at 7.30 on the starboard bow. We passed it about 11 o'clock. The morning was spent reading and watching the Islands. Just abreast Santo Porto we sighted Madeira & abreast NE Madeira we passed the Aboso[225]. She is high out of the water and was dipping her nose into the swell. We gave the usual signals: 3 &1.[226] Lunch was early 12 o'clock. About 2 o'clock we landed[227] at Funchal. Madeira is truly picturesque. The sun was shining beautifully when we landed. We got [incomplete] The diving boys came out in their boats & made a great fuss. They are terribly funny but really [change of

---

[223] Sailing vessels were still in widespread commercial use in the 1930's. Mum may have seen a 4- mast square rigged "windjammer" – perhaps carrying Chilean nitrate or Australian wool – which had "shortened sail".

[224] *From Wikipedia:* Porto Santo Island .. is a Portuguese island 43 kilometres (27 mi) northeast of Madeira Island in the North Atlantic Ocean; it is the northernmost and easternmost island of the archipelago of Madeira,

[225] See appendix 1 for details

[226] Signal code unknown to author

[227] Should be "anchored"

ink] they are good divers. When we got out of the boat[228] down a ladder into a small boat it was 2 o'clock. We got a car as soon as possible and went right up to the Monument du Paz the Funchal War Memorial.[229] The run up was marvellous. We climbed 3200 ft into the heavens. The run up was great. We had a wonderful view of the Bay and the town. The island seems all to be cultivated, bananas melons & pumpkins are growing outside.[230] The houses are interesting. There are several houses which the guide called "English Private Houses". [*Change of ink*] The children all beg & throw flowers for pennies. It seems the lower class are a bit down trodden. The streets are all laid with very small stones which are exceedingly slippery. There is a railway which goes straight up the hillside to the Monument[231]. It is possible to come down in a sledge.[232] The run down was very interesting too, vegetation is everywhere.

We bought two chairs, a table & tray which are very nice. There are funny vehicles driven by two oxen & some by mules. Cars are quite numerous.

We had tea in the open while native women tried to sell us flowers. After tea we did some shopping & then went back to the ship. When we got back the ship looked like a market place. Goods were strewn everywhere. The work is really wonderful. Bob bought me a bracelet & together we bought a tea cloth, a beauty.[233] The man had left the ship and actually came back & gave it to us at our money.[234]

My first visit to Madeira is one I will never forget[235]. It is all beautiful. The little park[236] with the swans & boy & girl in the pool are all like the pictures. I felt I knew that part already.

[*No indication of leaving port*] Until 12 noon we covered 318 miles. Dinner tonight was very nice. We bedded early. It is getting much warmer now.

Tuesday 13.10.36

Rose at 8.15, had breakfast. We took two snaps on board then spent the morning reading. I had a very good book: The Riddle of the Hill by E W Savi. It was about India.[237] We passed several islands to-day Santa Cruz on our Port side & also Tenerife at a good distance. The bathing pool has been erected to-day & an awning over a part of the main deck. We spent the afternoon in bed. After tea we sat near the stern & read. We did 255

---

[228] "Ship" surely!

[229] Madeira was a territory of Portugal, an Allied country in the Great War.

[230] i.e. not under glass!

[231] From Wiki; *There was previously a cog railway from Funchal to Monte in Madeira Island, which operated between 1893 and 1943, and went further up to Terreiro da Luta at 867 m above sea level.*

[232] The "toboggan run" still operates.

[233] It remained for many years for use on special occasions. See illustration p134

[234] Presumably they had haggled and got the price they offered!

[235] True. She would still talk about it in old age.

[236] ?Botanic Gardens.

[237] Riddle of the Hill by Ethel Winifred Savi published 1936. Copies still available. A forgotten but prolific author.

miles to noon to-day. Tea was served in the Lounge. After dinner we had a turn round & then bed.

Wednesday 14.10.36

Today we have come 320 miles at 12 noon. I did not take breakfast this morning. We spent the forenoon reading. I enjoyed lunch & spent the afternoon in bed. There is a moderate[238] sea. While at lunch the water came over the dining saloon portholes. It is terribly blue. We had boat drill today but it wasn't much of a thing. It has been cold this morning but now it is lovely. Dinner was very good.

Thursday 15.10.36

Till 12 noon today we covered 325 miles, (good old Aba).[239] It has been very hazy today caused by sand blowing from the Desert.[240] We saw several flying fish.[241] After tea we tried Deck Golf.[242] Bob was one up (Better luck next time) sez me. We spent most of the day reading. This morning there were sports on deck. We witnessed the Tug of War, a one-sided business for 1st Class[243]. Bob had his hair cut.

Friday 16.10.36

We did 313 miles to noon to-day. Smooth sea – like a pond, a very light swell. Saw one or two flying fish & several shoals of small fish. We saw porpoises jumping right out of the water. Late afternoon one ship overtook us on our starboard side & in the evening her lights were far ahead finally disappearing over the horizon. We overtook a boat during the evening. They signal to each other with lights.[244] There was a Carnival Dinner held tonight. We were all presented with hats. Some costumes were quite good. Had my hair set & after tea we did our packing. Very warm at night. Fans on all the time.

Saturday 17.10.36

Had breakfast & then did our final packing ready to leave. Sea is very calm. Wrote to Cathie & sent it home. We did 318 miles until 12 noon. Bob had a sleep as he had a slight headache. Sighted the hills at Freetown 2.30 & dropped anchor in the harbour at 5.34 pm. Dr Watson & Mr Munro came on board to meet us. We spent the night with Mr Holland, Barclays Bank manager. He made us very welcome.

---

[238] On the recently adopted Douglas Scale: "Moderate" is classed between "slight" and "rough" indicating a wave height of between 1.25 and 2.5 metres.

[239] See Commentary

[240] i.e. The Sahara

[241] As noted by Dad earlier

[242] See App 5 "Games"

[243] Who had numbers on their side! Cowden & Duffy p169: 225 1st class; 140 2nd & 3rd class.

[244] Presumably an Aldis Lamp where Morse Code transmissions can be made using pulses of light produced by opening and closing shutters.

VOLUME TWO

COMMENTARY ON PART TWO

New People; Making a new home …; … and running a household; Entertaining; A Social Scene; Getting about; Beasties; News; In Sickness and in Health

New People

Mum and Dad duly caught the train to Marampa. This was the "Iron Ore Railway" and never a passenger carrying line [See Appendix 2] and the accommodation on the "1.15 from Pepel" as she described in the Talk was nothing more than some camp chairs in a van attached to a train of returning empties. Her arrival can scarcely have been a surprise, as Dad's colleagues – who, of course included his youngest brother who had been his Groomsman – would have been very aware of his plans when he took leave of them in August but a welcome certainly awaited the couple. In her Talk, Mum remembered: "*What a welcome we got at our destination! Everyone returning from Home got a welcome, but we got VIP treatment! We were newly- weds and among the youngest members of the staff.*"[245]

The arrival of a young wife in the male-dominated community of a "mining camp" would certainly have altered the social dynamic. But Mum was not the sole spouse at Marampa as we are soon hearing of "Mrs Williams". In keeping with the formal manners of the time, Mum keeps Mrs Williams' first name hidden from us, but she must have been a great help to the new bride freshly arrived from Scotland. They would have been welcome female company for each other - *I enjoy these cups of tea & talk* [9 XII 36] – as Mum's Talk tells us: "*Bob went to work at 6.30a.m., [was] back for breakfast at 8a.m., lunch at 1p.m. and finished at 4p.m. This was quite a long day in the tropics* [Agreed! Author]*and the days sometimes dragged a bit.*"

Mum always spoke fondly of "Little Mrs Williams" – a description borne out in the photos – and of all the people mentioned and listed, (other than Alex Yule of course), Mr & Mrs Williams were the only listed address. This was Sutton Oak, St. Helens, Lancs., in the heart of coalmining country and by yet another co-incidence, not far from Sutton Manor the site of the only working coalmine ever visited by this author!

We have already met Mr Buchanan who, we must assume, was the General Manager of the Marampa site. He seems to have taken an avuncular interest in the new-comer and would possibly be rather taken aback with the arrival of a young lady who could bake, drive a lorry and play a mean game of snooker!

---

[245] Dad 30, Mum 24

Making a new home ..

The family album gives a good indication of the construction of Mum's new home. We can see that the houses are built on stilts [a common design in both in Freetown and other British settlements in the Tropics] made of reinforced concrete pillars, the concrete being made on site. The construction was of concrete block –[there is a photo annotated "block making]" and we know from Mum's Talk [see below] that the floor was concrete. [See Illustrations 5] Mum's Talk elaborated: "*Our bungalow had a long room [running] the full length of the house. Two rooms opened off it - a Dining Room without doors and a Bedroom with doors. The bathroom led off the bedroom but had an entry from a back porch so that the boys could fill the bath etc. without coming through the house.*" There was an electricity supply to the bungalows but a handwritten note on her script suggests it was turned off at 11.30 p.m., so torches were necessary thereafter though diary entries show a regular bedtime of 9pm. There was no running water in the bungalow and hence no flush toilet. The Talk goes on to explain: "*The toilet had a small door in the outside wall from which the Sanitary Boys removed the bucket so that one had to be careful not to be in the smallest room when they were on their rounds!*"

There was one glaring omission from the point of view of a young woman however as we learn very early on that the rooms were not curtained! We get very good picture of a determined Mum, taking matters into her own hands and rectifying the omission!

... and running a household.

Mum had now become something of a colonial "memsahib" as she oversaw house servants whom in the fashion of the time she calls "boys". There were three whom she would have inherited from Dad's bachelor establishment. In Mum's Talk, she described them, starting with their "Head Boy": "*James S Cole ... was very good and more reliable than a great many. He could read and write which made communication easier. He had attended a Methodist School and had been to America as a member of some ship's crew. Souri, the Second Boy [was] much younger, less reliable and a bit of a lad! He had been put in the stocks in the local village by the Bai Koblo* [local chief] *for misconduct with someone else's wife. Lastly, Saidu [was] just a child and a great breaker of dishes – 'they just slip from my hand missus'.*" Despite those faults, Mum admitted that: "*We couldn't have existed without them.*"

The kitchen, where the boys washed and cooked, as readers may have guessed, was a few yards from the house and as the boys went home in the afternoon, would then be free for Mum to use -though she records that she often took a siesta. As an almost compulsive baker and she regularly records baking – though her first attempt [29 X 36] failed. However, showing the determination which was such a facet of her character, she got the hang of the oven and [12 XII 36] is happy to claim her efforts as "very successful". Sadly, she remains silent on what she made but, judging by well- remembered evidence of her highly acclaimed produce, there would be scones, shortbread, sponge cake and biscuits. The arrangements for cooking were modified as Mum seems to have taken over the preparation of meals or the "chop" as she was soon calling food. Regarding getting the provisions, her Talk tells us: *"Most of our food came from Freetown but somethings such as eggs, chickens, oranges, bread etc could be bought locally very cheaply. There was no fridge, only an ice box – a lead lined box into which ice was put every morning."* Sadly, the Diary and the Talk remain silent on the source of this ice!

Both Mum and Dad in later years, when household help was an unthinkable luxury, were to talk warmly of James S Cole and memory suggests they did try to keep in touch with him and his family.

Entertaining

The bungalow was, of course, Mum and Dad's first married home so Mum had very quickly to learn how to be the hostess. The Diary suggests this to have been a success and one can imagine Mum's baking and home cooking being very welcome to the ex-pats. Mum seems keen to note that the menu when entertaining what seems to be the hierarchy - Messrs Buchanan, Munro & The Doctor -on 5 XI 36, being: *"Scotch broth, fried fish & chips, steak pie, fruit & coffee"*. She must, of course, have been nervous (and Dad too!) and the following day, we can sense her relief as she writes: *"Thank goodness I can make something here"*. The Diary, however, remains silent on a mishap – pure soap opera – which must have occurred at that meal. When the Mine Manager, no less, attempted to add salt to his broth, the top of the salt-cellar fell off decanting its entire contents into Dad's Boss's soup! *"Utter confusion on my part"*, wrote Mum all those years later by which time she could laugh at the incident. *"Luckily we did have another tin of soup."*

A Social Scene

The Marampa "camp" which had, of course, greatly expanded since Dad's arrival in 1931 would typify hundreds of similar ex-pat British communities throughout what was then the Empire. As mentioned earlier, there was a "touch of the Raj" about Marampa and indeed there is a Kiplingesque ring to Mum's entries which speak of Bridge in the evenings and Snooker at the Club. The latter game, of course, is generally reckoned to have been invented in a hill station[246] and the snooker table – almost certainly provided by Messers Burroughes and Watt -would have been open for use by the wives in the afternoon, a facility of which Mum and her new pal "Little Mrs. Williams" seem to have made full use. This would have been as strange an environment to Mum as was the surrounding tropical bushland as Billiards and Snooker Halls were out of bounds to ladies back home and even in the grandest of houses, the Billiards Room was the preserve of the gentlemen.

We read of events at The Club which included dances. An oft told tale was that the Mine Manager, who shared his name with that of a song and dance star of the contemporary movies, invited Mum to dance and often repeated his wise crack: "*Now you can say you have danced with Jack Buchanan.*" [Mum's later comment was that it was difficult to dance on a concrete floor wearing boots!]

Another key leisure facility was the swimming pool [See Illustrations 5] and as the Rainy Season morphed into the Hot Season, - *Today has been very hot.* [18 XI 36] - we read of the ladies taking to its rather murky water just to keep cool.

The arrival of the rather grand sounding Mrs Hunter [26 X 36] made up what seems to be the full complement of Marampa wives [see Illustrations 5] and we read of Mum and Dad breaking what surely would be new ground in attending a cocktail party at *chez* Hunter. There and at The Club, their tipple would have been the fashionable gin and orange or gin and lime for which they retained a taste in later years.

Getting about

Mum's driving ability might have come as something of a surprise to the miners at Marampa, but she seems to have made full use of her expertise as she was quickly allowed the use of a vehicle from what we would now call the "motor pool". That included a lorry, the driving of which in those days would require such skills as "double – de- clutching". We read of her driving into nearby Lunsar to do her shopping just as though she was going from Banknock to Kilsyth.

In 1936, Lunsar, with its new transport link in the railway, was at the start of its development cycle as a mining town – Mum's Talk describes it having: *"... one or two shops and a Post Office. The main store, really only like a big market stall, was owned by a Syrian – Fanny Solomon."* [20 X 36] However, it was still so unsophisticated that crowds gathered to see European women out shopping [20 X 36]. Of course, Mum found driving in Sierra Leone a bit different from delivering the groceries to Cumbernauld or Dennyloanhead as she notes: *I quite enjoyed my run even tho' the road is a bit rough.* [26 XI 36]

---

[246] Its first set of rules was drawn up in 1884 by Sir Neville Chamberlain, a British officer, in Ootacamund – now Ugagamandalam, Tamil Nadu Province, India - on a table built by Burroughes & Watts that had been brought over by boat.

Beasties

Although Mum' Diary does not contain a detailed a list of flora and fauna such as Dad compiled in his idle hours in Katanning, her Talk covered the impact of the animal life. As the Bradt Guide devotes a dozen pages or so to the Natural History of Sierra Leone, to repeat her list of creatures seems superfluous. However, her advice on avoiding stings and bites in the Tropics still rings true: *"Never put your hand any place you can't see into"* and *"never put on your shoes without shaking them"*. But mention must be made of what was the bane of her life: the ant population of Marampa - *"big ones, small ones, black, red, white and the worst of all, flying ones"* she wrote later. Her Talk notes that the wooden furniture legs had to be stood in tins of paraffin to prevent ants climbing and that all food had to be tightly covered. She went on to tell of an occasion, which may be the 21 XII 36 entry, of returning to the bungalow to find there was: *"... a battalion of ants on the march. Our bungalow was in their track, so they came in the back door, right through and out the front. The floors were all concrete so the boys who had our bath water ready soon had the place cleared. There were no baths that night."* Though humans may have ruled in the house and kitchen, the local fauna ruled elsewhere, as Mum related in her Talk: *"We had a shimbeck built in the garden. This was a hut made of palm branches woven together to form a very cool house. Unfortunately, it wasn't much use to us as the insects liked it and more or less took it over".*

News

In these days of instant and almost perpetual communication, it is difficult to envisage a world without radio or television when phones were rare and where news came once a week with the mail and the newspapers and evenings were spent playing games, doing carpentry or embroidery or just reading. In that environment, the times for receiving and sending letters assumes great importance in the household routine and thus Mum made many entries concerning "mail" and in Mum's Talk speaks of looking out for the train which would be carrying letters from Home. The cycle would be based on the arrival and departure dates of ships at Freetown and while this was much a more organised system than experienced by Dad in Kojonup [12 miles walk to the PO or 3 mile walk to the mail box] it still imposed a discipline. The Diary contains lists of arrivals and departures at Freetown which can be assumed to provide a timetable for mails – always remembering they had to allow for a 50- mile narrow gauge railway journey plus a 10- mile launch trip to and from the port.

In this environment it will often fall to the lot of someone to be the bearer of tidings of import. We know there was a Post Office in Lunsar – where Mum went for parcels - and this may have been a telegraph office and that the Mine Office may have been in telegraphic communication with the outside world. In the only case in either Diary where events of world importance make an appearance, there were two such bearers of news. On 3 XII 36 it was Mr Munro – clearly a senior figure with SLDCo. -who visited the bungalow with the news -as Mum put it – that: "*The King wants marry Mrs Simpson, an American.*" The news of the upshot of the crisis which convulsed the entire world at that time was brought to the bungalow by a figure also of importance to the Marampa scene: Mr W.L. Opie. [The surname is Cornish and Cornish folk, like the Scots, were to be found wherever in the world there was mining.] He was the bearer of tidings on 10 XII 36, a day when Mum had other things on her mind [see below] and was to record, almost as an afterthought: "*Mr O. looked in at night & told us that the King had abdicated*".

In Sickness and in Health

At no time did Mum ever write the "M" word in the Diary. When the first cloud appeared on the health horizon in December {10 XII 36], it is a "cold" that Dad had. This is fair enough perhaps as the symptoms of a feverish cold and the onset of Malaria are similar, but readers may make up their own minds as to why Mum never admits that the man she had waited to marry might have a serious condition. And serious enough it was for the site doctor to recommend time in Nursing Home at Kissy - which story awaits the reader.

There is one stand out comment in her entries in December: "*It will be horrid without Bob.* " [14 XII 36]. This is on a par with Dad's "out of food" entry in the Kojonup days – the comment of a young person suddenly alarmed. Although Mum was to stay with the Stilwells, whom she had met, she envisaged herself alone in this foreign land – away from the comforting familiar faces of "Little Mrs Williams", her brother-in-law Alex, Buchanan, Opie and the rest of the Marampa folk.

But now it is time for a "Fast Rewind" to October and Mum's first meeting with her wonderful new world.

VOLUME TWO

THE DIARY PART TWO

MARAMPA 18.10.36 TO 31.12.36

Sunday 18.10.36

We were awakened with a cup of tea at 6.30 and rose soon afterwards. Had breakfast about 7.45. We proceeded to Freetown[247] to meet the others at the City Hotel. From there we went by car to Kissy [248]where we joined the launch. Left 8.05 reached Pepel 10 o'clock. Had rain on the way up. Were nicely received by D Pringle & given lunch before leaving by train at 1.15pm. The run up was really uneventful but quite interesting this time because it was all new. One little kid gave us bananas which were very nice. We were met by Mr Buchanan who gave us tea & dinner.[249] I have met several of the men. Mr & Mrs Williams are very nice & have done their best to make me feel at home. We did some unpacking & went to bed. The crickets make a dreadful noise. There were a great many spark flies[250].

 Monday 19.10.36

I was wakened with the bugle at 6 o'clock, then Cole[251] came with tea. We rose at 7 o'clock& had breakfast at 8. Bob went to work at 9.30. I did the rest of the unpacking & tidied up generally. Mrs Williams came in a wee while. The house is looking not too bad. We got mats today & a box for powder[252] from a man. We had tea in the Williams' house, which was very nice. This morning the boy killed a small snake in the garden. Spot has come back again and seems quite friendly.[253]

Tuesday 20.10.36

Today has been very hot. I went to the Club[254] about 10 o'clock & had tea. Mr & Mrs Stilwell were there. They are very nice. Mr B.[255] gave us the car & we went to Lunsar[256] where I got material for curtains. Mrs Solomon[257] had us upstairs & gave us orangeade & biscuits. The folks all came out to see "Three white misses". I did some sewing & then

---

[247] Means of transport not specified

[248] From Wiki: *Kissy is a neighbourhood on the eastern end of the Sierra Leonean capital of Freetown.* It is still a ferry port and is a noted medical centre.

[249] The Talk records that they were also greeted by a thunderstorm: *"A real humdinger"*

[250] Any of a number of species of fireflies

[251] According to recollection of family tales, James S Cole, Dad's head "houseboy". See commentary.

[252] What sort of powder is not specified.

[253] The dog who presumably had been with the someone else whilst Dad was on leave.

[254] See Commentary

[255] Presumably Buchanan.

[256] See Commentary

[257] See Commentary

went out with Bob. After tea we went to tennis. In the evening we went to the Club for dinner.

Wednesday 21.10.36

Bob went out at 6.30 am this morning. He was back for breakfast at 8.30. I have finished four curtains. I sewed & finished the mail. Bob went to tennis this evening. We dined in the house alone. I like it better that way. We went to bed early 8.45 pm.

Thursday 22.10.36

I rose at 6.45 & did a washing. Bob came in at 8.30 for breakfast. I finished the curtains & Bob helped me put them up. We went a walk into a native village.[258] Everybody came out to see the white missus. I have skinned my heel. We dined alone & played cards. Bed at 9 o'clock.

Friday 23.10.36

I did not rise early today. In fact Bob was back from the mine before I rose. I did my ironing[259] & read a bit. We dined at home today. The heat is fairly strong just now.

Saturday 24.10.36

I rose about 8 o'clock & dressed. Bob came back for breakfast & then in for a few minutes at 10.30. I spent nearly all afternoon talking to Mrs Williams. After tea we went bathing.[260] It was grand. We had a regular storm here tonight. When it died down we went to [the] Club for mail & were lucky in getting 4 letters, a paper & snaps.

Sunday 25.10.36

We did not rise early today. This is the first day of our new chop scheme[261] & it seems ok. At least, Bob is pleased which suits me. We bathed in the afternoon & wrote letters in the evening. We had a walk to the Loko[262] & then played table tennis at the Club.

Monday 26.10.36

Another week started. The cooking is going strong[263] & is very satisfactory. Mrs. H[264] arrived to-night. We heard her singing in the Club. She has a very good voice indeed.

Tuesday 27.10.36

Breakfast as usual. Nothing very much is happening these days. I am getting quite settled now. We had [?tea] in Williams' house on Tuesday & met Mrs Hunter[265]. We went down to the pool but it was very dirty. In we went however to get cool. In the evening we played cards & finished our mail.

---

[258] Presumably Rochendata

[259] According to the Talk, she used a charcoal iron.

[260] In the swimming pool. See Illustrations 5

[261] Chop=meals. See Commentary.

[262] This surely cannot be Port Loko creek which is too far away. Maybe a local name for the Rokel.

[263] See Commentary

[264] Presumably Mrs Hunter.

[265] Guessing this was written up later in the week.

Wednesday 28.10.86

There is not much to write about today. The usual routine was gone through. We have a new watchman who is very much better than the last one.[266] The mail went today.

Thursday 29.10.36

Breakfast as usual. I had tea with Mrs Williams & spent some time with her. I tried to bake but it was no use. Someday I may succeed.[267] In the evening we played cards. Bob has been showing me how to play Crib. It is very interesting and a change.[268]

Friday 30.10.36

Rose as usual about 8 o'clock had breakfast. We[269] washed the bedroom, verandah & dining room floor today. Some performance throwing pails of water on the floor. It is a bit cleaner I must say. The cooking of our meals is helping to take up my time[so] I can't say it is hanging. After dinner we went a wee walk. It was very nice.

Saturday 31.10.36

Did not rise early. I find there is no need to be up too soon. Breakfast bacon & eggs and fried scone. I sent Saidu[270] to Lunsar for more cloth & got the bedroom curtains finished. We bathed in the afternoon. In the evening we went to the Hallowe'en party. It was ever so nice & I enjoyed it very much. Mr B. [271] took me in for dinner & gave me the first dance. We came away at 12. Bob sang very well.[272]

NOVEMBER 1936

Sunday 1.11.36

We rose today at 8.45 am had breakfast. Our curtain material came so we cut the lengths for them & then went to the Club where we played snooker.[273] We rested in the afternoon & had Mr Lorimer & Mr McHaffie[274] in for tea. After Dinner we wrote the mail.

Monday 2.11.36

Rose at 7.30 am & did a washing. We had macaroni & cheese for breakfast. It was VG. Wrote some letters & checked a ps[275] We went bathing in the afternoon. There was a

---

[266] See Commentary for notes on staff

[267] See Commentary.

[268] Time well spent by Dad as Cribbage remained a lifelong pastime.

[269] Presumably Mum and the house staff.

[270] One of the houseboys. See Commentary.

[271] Presumably Buchanan

[272] He always did but there may have been some lubrication on this occasion!

[273] First mention of a game which Mum seemed to enjoy and which she watched on TV

[274] See Commentary for notes on SLDCo personnel

[275] Unsure of the meaning here.

regular thunderstorm this evening. After dinner we played cards. The curtains are finished & up. They look good.

Tuesday 3.11.36

I made a cushion this morning. In the afternoon I read & prepared tea. We had Mr & Mrs Hunter & Mr & Mrs Williams in for tea. We spent a very pleasant time. We played Oh Dear[276] & very good too. They went about 6 o'clock. We dressed, had dinner & played cards. The white shorts came today.

Wednesday 4.11.36

We went down to the bathing pool but it was a bit mucky, however we went in & felt a bit cooler. In the evening we went to Mrs Hunter's for "drinks & small chop"[277]. There were seven of us, all very pleasant. Her house is lovely. We came away about 8 o'clock & had dinner then bed.

Thursday 5.11.36

I was busy today preparing for the dinner tonight. We had Mr Buchanan, Mr Munro & The Doctor. The dinner turned out OK: Scotch broth, fried fish & chips, steak pie, fruit & coffee. There was a storm again tonight. They were late in coming. We played cards afterwards.

Friday 6.11.36

Mrs Williams went down to Freetown today. I spent a few minutes at the Club arranging the food for tomorrow. The afternoon we spent reading. We had Mr Williams in for tea. Then we both dressed for dinner. I made dumplings tonight & they were good. Thank goodness I can make something here. We played cards then bed.

Saturday 7.11.36

Spent quite a busy day preparing for Alex's arrival[278]. Bob & I went along to his bungalow & prepared his bed. The train[279] came in at 7.5. After a bath & change we had dinner. We got lots of letters with the mail this week & several papers. There was some talking on Saturday night!

Sunday 8.11.36

Alex came along about 10.30 & we went a walk up K. Ridge[280], then played snooker. After lunch I wrote some mail. Alex came in for tea. The evening was spent writing mail. Bob has had a headache[281] nearly all day, so we went to bed early.

---

[276] See Appendix 5 Parlour Games

[277] i.e. drinks and snacks

[278] Dad's youngest brother. See Intermezzo and Commentary

[279] See Commentary

[280] Presumably one of the ridges parallel to that with the Club and the bungalows. See Illustrations.

[281] Early signs of a problem

Monday 9.11.36

Bob sent for the Dr. to look at my heel. It is getting on fine now[282]. While he was in, Bob felt a headache. His temp was taken & he was put to bed. He spent a miserable day & was really down at times. Towards night he was slightly better.

Tuesday 10.11.36

Bob is much better this morning for which I am truly grateful. I made steamed fish for him this morning. Alex came in for tea. Bob's temp has been fairly steady all day 98°.[283] We turned early about 8.30 pm. A huge flying beetle[284] came in last night.

Wednesday 11.11.36

Bob spent a quiet night though he did not sleep much. He is keeping in today & if he could have a good sleep would be better. Alex came along in the evening & took his chop with us. We played cards in the evening. Mrs Hunter came in with poppies[285]. Mr McKenzie called to ask for Bob.

Thursday 12.11.36

Bob is still on the bettering way. His temp was normal & he spent all day on the verandah. We had chicken soup[286] which was very much enjoyed by both. Mr Lorimer called this morning. Alex was also in for a wee while. The Dr says that Bob can get up tomorrow.

From here on in her Diary, Mum notes the word "Atebrin" [see Commentary] every second day.

Friday 13.11.36

This morning Bob still had a slight headache but it went away. The dog was killed today. We got the Dr to do the deed. Sawi took him up but he soon came back again. [287] The Dr. came as usual & said that Bob could go out tomorrow. David Pringle called in the evening. He is coming to tea tomorrow.

---

[282] Must have been the wound from 22.10

[283] Fahrenheit. Normal healthy body is 98.6 so he was OK.

[284] May have been one of any species of Rhinoceros Beetle

[285] Remembrance Day

[286] "Jewish penicillin" - a popular remedy

[287] This is presumably the "Spot" mentioned 7/10. Sawi would be one of the "houseboys". May have been one of a pack of feral dogs who hung round the campsite. Dad was always a "soft touch" for any dog!

Saturday 14.11.36

Bob is keeping OK today. We had a game of snooker this morning. Then we went [a] walk in the afternoon but there were too many boys.[288] We had David Pringle & Alex for tea this afternoon. We played cards & in the evening went to the Club to dinner to commemorate the opening of the mess scheme[289]. The dinner was OK. We did not stay late.

Tuesday 17.11.36

One month completed today. This morning I did a washing. We are having tripe for dinner tonight so I prepared it this morning. Mrs W. came in this morning. Mr W gave us a piece of cake[290] which was VG. Alex took his chop with us tonight. He enjoyed [his] share of the tripe.[291]

Wednesday 18.11.36

Bob returned to work this morning. I did my ironing at 7.30am. I wrote some mail. Mr Wm came in [for] a few minutes. Bob had a half day today. We had Mr Opie for tea this afternoon. He is very nice. Alex looked for a few minutes tonight on his way to the Club. We went to bed about 8-45. Today has been very hot.

Thursday 19.11.36

I did not rise till after 8 o'clock this morning. Most of the morning I spent sewing. We got a big load of wood in this afternoon so that should keep us going[292]. Mr Mack & Alex came in for a few minutes then we all went to the Club. We played Bridge at which Bob & I lost very heavily[293]. I wrote some mail.

Friday 20.11.36

Everything was in a fog this morning. One could not see the hill[294] even from our house. Spoke to Mrs Wm a few minutes. Cleaned the tables etc with flit[295]. Today has been lovely, ever so cool. Some have felt it cold. We played snooker & table tennis.[296]

Saturday 21.11.36

I did not rise until Bob returned from work this morning. The Dr called & has given me some antiseptic ointment for my heel. The mail won't be up until tomorrow. The Apapa

---

[288] Could be in Rochendata village. They were probably being followed by youngsters
[289] The communal dining facility?
[290] Presumably some celebration had taken place.
[291] An enjoyment never shared by this writer although tripe is clearly a nutritious dish eaten worldwide.
[292] Assuming this was for a wood burning cooker rather than for a fire!
[293] Might well have been up against very experienced opponents!
[294] Assumed to be Masaboin Hill. May have been dust brought by the Harmattan wind.
[295] This would be the original and popular insecticide with DDT applied via a manual spray pump
[296] Presumably at the Club where she heard the complaints about the cold!

is one day late.[297] We had a small chop party at the Club tonight. Very nice too. Alex took his chop with us tonight.

Sunday 22.11.36

It was terribly wet this morning, in fact it rained nearly all day. We played snooker before lunch. In the afternoon we slept, at least Bob slept. In the evening we read & went early to bed. The mail came tonight. Lots for us.

Monday 23.11.36

Did not rise early this morning. Wrote some mail & shortened the sleeves of my green dress. It is very nice. I baked in the afternoon. After dinner we sat outside in the cool evening air. Alex came along & joined us for a wee while.

Tuesday 24.11.36

This morning Mrs Hunter looked in for a few minutes. The cold chop came today at last. I have written some mail & finished The Story of San Michele [298]which is indeed enjoyable. Bob & I finished our mail & went to bed early.

Wednesday 25.11.36

Did not rise early this morning. I began a little jacket to wear with my floral frock. We played cards a little and as usual I lost. After dinner, Alex came in & we went along to the Club. We had a very enjoyable game of snooker with Alex & Mr Mack.

Thursday 26.11.36

This morning I had a run[299] to Lunsar but the parcel has not come in yet. We went round to the Hospital[300] & then back through the village. I quite enjoyed my run even tho' the road is a bit rough. I spent about ¾ hr at the Club this morning & had tea. I finished my little jacket & it looks OK. I have made a milk jelly which also looks OK. We had another run to Lunsar & I drove[301] the lorry back home. The parcel[302] arrived OK.

Friday 27.11.36

This morning I baked. We had Alex & Mr Clements in for tea. We played Bridge & enjoyed it OK. Alex came back for dinner. After dinner we sat outside & played Bridge. The evening was most enjoyable.

---

[297] SS Apapa – see Appendix 1. Probably held up by November gales in the Atlantic.

[298] Wikipedia:" **The Story of San Michele** is a book of memoirs by Swedish physician Axel Munthe (October 31, 1857 – February 11, 1949) first published in 1929 by British publisher John Murray. Written in English, it was a best-seller in numerous languages and has been republished constantly in the over seven decades since its original release." Content sounds rather bizarre but its popularity probably determined its inclusion in the Club library.

[299] A vehicle run of course. Possibly the lorry mentioned below.

[300] See "Afterword"

[301] As we have noted, Mum had been driving for many years and would be quite capable of handling it!

[302] Content unspecified.

<u>Saturday 28.11.36</u>

I did some reading this morning. In the afternoon I walked down to the bathing pool to see if it was clean. After tea we went bathing. There was not much water in it. In the evening we went to the Club for a Whist Drive but it didn't come off. We had our extra mail this week.

<u>Sunday 29.11.36</u>

We had a nice long lie this morning & breakfasted late 10 o'clock. Alex came in & we went down to the Loko[303]. After walking around a bit, it was suggested that we go up one of the haulages[304]. So we boarded an empty truck & up we went[305]. We walked around several quarries & then came back down[306]. Alex & Mr Mack were in for tea then we went bathing which was very pleasant.

<u>Monday 30.11.36</u>

I washed this morning then tidied the kitchen cupboard & wrote a little. After lunch I read a book & lay down a wee while. We went bathing in the evening & after dinner went to the Club & played Bridge.

DECEMBER 1936

<u>Tuesday 1.12.36</u>

Another month started. I did some writing & prepared lunch. After lunch, I went in to see Mrs W & spent the afternoon with her. After tea we went bathing. I was a bit cold but very refreshing. Bob has fitted up a bell[307] which will be a great help.

<u>Wednesday 2.12.36</u>

I had a nice long lie today. Did some sewing[308] in the forenoon. In the afternoon I baked – very good too. In the evening we went along to the Club & played snooker. Alex was in a few minutes tonight. Cole[309] got me a basket today.

<u>Thursday 3.12.36</u>

This morning I tried to wash the curtains but it is no use. I spent about one hour in the Club this morning. Just before lunch Alex came in to say that he was going down to Pepel indefinitely. We had David Pringle for tea & after dinner we wrote Xmas mail. Mr Munro came in, telling that the King wants marry Mrs Simpson, an American.

---

[303]See earlier remark

[304] A rail track to the mine. See Appendix 3b

[305] See Appendix 3b

[306] See Appendix 3b

[307] Probably a bell which house staff could hear in the separate kitchen.

[308] Embroidery possibly as she has not called it "mending". See Commentary.

[309] Staff. See Commentary.

Friday 4.12.36

I wrote some mail this morning & baked in the afternoon. We had Mrs Williams in for tea as Mr W was away at Freetown. We played cards as usual at night.

Saturday 5.12.36

Bobs birthday:- [*underlined by Mum!*]

I rose early this morning & Souri, Cole & Saidu[310] got to work to clean the bungalow. It is a great business.[311] When Bob came in for breakfast he had word that Alex was coming back again. We had a small party Mrs Wm & Mr McKenzie. Alex came up at 7.30. There was a party at the Club but we waited till 8.45 & it hadn't begun so we came home.

Sunday 6.12.36

This morning we were up early for Sunday. After breakfast we had a walk to the Bata Bana reservoir[312]. We saw several anthills. Alex came in for a wee while. After lunch we slept then Had tea. Mrs W asked us in to see her Xmas present- a beautiful camphor chest[313].

Monday 7.12.36

I had a long lie 8.30. I spent most of the morning reading. Mrs W was not looking too well. Several of the men went home[314] on the 10.00 train today. We have been counting that when they return we will have done five months[315]. We both had out hair cut today. Cole went to Lunsar for stamps today. Souri & Byankee are busy [?making] lanterns for the Mohammedan festival Dec 15[th316].

Tuesday 8.12.36

I had Mr & Mrs Williams in this morning for a cup of tea. We had a right good talk. Alex brought a pineapple in this lunchtime. It was very good indeed. We had a game of snooker after tea & then Alex came in after dinner & we played Bridge. I started my table runner.

Wednesday 9.12.36

I was in Mrs W. house for tea this morning. I enjoy these cups of tea & talk. The mail did not get up until 4 o'clock. We got several letters, the Scots Calendar & a photo of M Barraclough[317]. We went down to the bathing pool. It was fairly cold.

Thursday 10.12.36

I went along to the Club this morning. While I was in, the new Dr came in. Bob has a cold this morning. At tea he came home early & went to bed. Temp 100.2. Dr C. came in but

---

[310] See photo from 1937.

[311] Meaning It's quite a commotion"

[312] A dam on the Batabana stream [see Map] which provided the water supply to the Marampa plant

[313] Maybe that's why Mr W was in Freetown. See Commentary.

[314] Sailings from Freetown to Liverpool were every fortnight.

[315] This confirms the tour pattern of 12 months followed by 12 weeks leave.

[316] Eid al Fitr which can occur as late as mid- December. The Temne are predominately Muslim.

[317] Marjorie Barrowclough d. of Mum's landlady when she worked in Fleetwood.

did not seem worried about Bob. Mr O[318]. looked in at night & told us that the King had abdicated[319].

Friday 11.12.36

Bob is getting along fine today. Temp normal. The Dr. has sent a tonic along. Mrs W. came in this morning & we had a nice cup of tea. In the afternoon, we were asked in next door for tea. Having received the Dr's permission, we went. It was most enjoyable. We met the new boys[320].Alex looked in, in the evening. Just as Bob was going to bed Mr Opie looked in. He is very nice.

Saturday 12.12.36

Bob's cold is much better today. Sent down the mail this morning[321]. I read a bit & sewed a bit. Bob was up in the afternoon for tea. Alex came in this evening & had his chop sent along here. I baked in the afternoon and it was very successful. We played Bridge in the evening.

Sunday 13.12.36

Rose about 8.15 this morning opened PZ[322]'s order & had chop. Prepared chop and went over chits[323]. We slept in the afternoon & Alex came in for tea. The Dr. called in the evening. We went early to bed. Bob's cold is still pretty bad.

Monday 14.12.36

This morning Bob got up but had to come back to bed at once. We sent for the Dr. & after some consultation he advised that Bob should go to Freetown. Maybe there is nothing wrong we can only hope for the best. I shall go down too only I'm not looking forward to it one bit. It will be horrid without Bob.

Tuesday 13.12.36

We left Marampa this morning at 10.10. arriving Pepel 1.50.[324] Mr Cook gave us a cup of tea. We then proceeded by launch to Freetown. A taxi conveyed us to the Hospital. It was dreadful leaving Bob last night[325] only he is much better for which I am very thankful. The Stilwells have been very kind & made me welcome. During the night there was great revelry among the natives Ramidon. (sic)[326].

---

[318] Mr Opie.

[319] News spread by radio presumably as the Abdication document is dated 10th. See Commentary.

[320] Presumably staff joining. There seems to have been quite a bit of staff movement.

[321] Would just about make it for Christmas in UK

[322] The firm of Paterson Zochonis, now PZ Cussons, household & toiletry supplies, had an almost universal presence throughout the British Empire.

[323] i.e. went through household bills etc. See Commentary

[324] Presumably by train but seems a long time.

[325] Presumably she means leaving Dad in the Nursing Home.

[326] Assume she means end of Ramadan and thus Eid el-Fitr.

Wednesday 16.12.36

I had a cup of tea at 8 o'clock, got up, dressed & had breakfast at 9 o'clock. James Cole has gone to Marampa.[327] I went out for a walk this morning & met the Dr. We had a short run round. After lunch I had a rest & went up to the Nursing Home at 3.15. Bob feels much better but is fed up already being in the Home – no wonder. Mr R[328] came here today.

Thursday 17.12.36

This morning I had tea at 8 o'clock & breakfast at 9. I spent most of the forenoon, reading & sewing. Dr. C called in on his way to Marampa. An Indian came in in the afternoon & I bought candle sticks & a bell.[329] I went up to see Bob at 3.30. He is up now & allowed out. Dinner was OK. We had Xmas pudding. Bed 9 o'clock.

Friday 18.12.36

I was awakened this morning to receive some mail. Very nice too. Bob phoned to say he could get out all day. I was up in no time. We had a lovely day together. Alex came down about 4 o'clock. We both went back to the NH[330] with Bob. I think he will be discharged tomorrow. Dinner was quite jolly with Alex & Pat Reilly, Bed 9 o'clock.

Saturday 19.12.36

Rose 8.15 had breakfast. Bob got out for the day only. We had a pleasant day, only it was spoiled by the fact that Bob had to go in at night again. Surely he will be out tomorrow. I am fed-up & so is Bob. Dr W[331] is the limit. If only he knew what we think of him. Alex went back to Marampa.

Sunday 20.12.36

Just after breakfast Bob phoned to say that he was getting out. I went up at once to get him. We spent a very nice day together, visited Lumley Beach which is very nice[332]. We wished we had had bathing costumes. Dinner was very nice. We went to bed early as usual. Stilwell's parrot is funny.

---

[327] Presumably he had accompanied Mum to Freetown.

[328] Not sure who this is. Perhaps "Pat Reilly" mentioned on 18 XII 36

[329] These were "Benares Ware" and remained with the family. See illustration p158

[330] Nursing Home

[331] Must be Dr. Watson.

[332] Still is! A Trip Advisor review in 2016 said: *This beach stretches for some 1.5 miles and it is perfect for a walk. On weekends there are a lot of friendly people playing football and this is a good chance to socialize with the locals. There are also few nice bars and restaurants nearby if you wish to have a cold drink or so.*

Monday 21.12.36

This morning we packed went out & saw a chest, bought shoes. After breakfast we bought the chest. It is a real beauty[333]. I am thrilled. We left at 10 o'clock. The launch was OK but the train journey *[indecipherable]* 4 -8.45. However we've got back. Got plenty mail. Alex had dinner ready. The house was overrun with ants. What a job we had. I won't forget my visit to & return journey from Freetown.

Tuesday 22.12.36

Bob is not going out in the mornings this week. He is feeling OK. Saw Mrs W a few minutes. Mr W has gone to Freetown. Bob saw Mr Opie & he has decided to do his 12 month's tour. We had tea with Mr. O. this afternoon. He is very nice indeed. Alex came in for a wee while. We went to Lunsar & got a parcel, a lovely powder box from Ella[334].

Wednesday 23.12.36

Bob did not go out until 9.30 this morning. Alex is in bed. The carpenter came with a shelf. I cleaned various things including the new chest. I baked in the afternoon & then went to see Alex. After tea we played snooker. In the evening we went along to see Alex again. He is not too bad. Mrs W. in for tea.

Tuesday 24.12.36

I rose at 7.30 this morning & did a washing. After breakfast, Mr Opie called to say Merry Xmas, as he was going away. Souri washed out the bathroom & lavatory & accessories. Mr B[335] called. I went to the Club for a <u>few minutes</u>. *[Mum's underlining!]*. We got an invitation to the Club dinner which turned out very pleasant. Mrs W & I sat with JRB[336]. Left 11pm. I wore my floral frock & coatie[337] which Bob says has improved my dress. Alex better but not at dinner.

Friday 25.12.36

Xmas Day

In the morning, we both began to look for our presents. After some looking, I found mine behind the sideboard, Bob his among the oranges. My tray is beautiful. We had a run to Lunsar. Slept in the afternoon. Did some sewing & played cards. Alex now O.K.

Saturday 26.12.36

In the morning we had a run to Lunsar for parcels. We got two. We slept in the afternoon & in the evening we played snooker & went a walk. Chatted with the Williams. After dinner Alex came in & we played Bridge. There was a concert in the Club but we did not go.

---

[333] Agreed! A wonderful carved camphor chest, it has stayed with the family and is now a proud possession of Steven and Jayne Dandy in Warrington, Cheshire. [See Illustrations 5]

[334] Ella Simpson, a school friend.

[335] Presumably Buchanan

[336] Again presumably Buchanan. See Commentary.

[337] A bolero jacket

Sunday 27.12.36

Rose 8.30 had breakfast saw to the lunch. Played snooker & had a chat with the Williams & Alex. Too hot for a walk in the forenoon. We slept in the afternoon & went a walk after tea.

Monday 28.12.36

I did some cleaning this morning. Polished the chest again. The carpenter came & fitted in the tray & did one or two odd jobs.

After tea we went to the Club & played snooker. Bob won. Alex came in before dinner.

Tuesday 29.12.36

Made the breakfast then finished the lampshade. Saw to the lunch. Had tea with Mrs Williams. I spent the afternoon in bed reading after baking. Played snooker at the Club. Alex looked in for a wee while. After dinner we went to the Club but only stayed an hour.

Wednesday 30.12.36

Did a baking this morning & prepared lunch. Sorted my Black frock & did some reading. In the afternoon, I went to Lunsar for a parcel. It is the cake from home & a beauty too. We had Mr Newton & Mr Cryer for tea. After tea I took along Alex's cake.

We had dinner & played cards, went to bed & did some reading.

Tuesday 31.12.36

Made scones, spent some time at the Club. Read in the afternoon. Alex came in before dinner & had his chop sent along here. We played Bridge & had coffee at 9 o'clock. We meant to go to the Club but we were both too tired so we went to bed instead.

And with that. Mum's daily journal ends.

MEMORIES of MARAMPA

Family mementoes: the candlesticks Mum bought on 17 XII 1936. One of the bells was probably the one she bought from the trader that day, the other being one she already had to ring for the house staff.
[Photographed specially for this book by Esther Lyons]

VOLUME TWO

AFTERWORD 1937

No longer "Remarkable"; A happy routine...; ... cut short.; Ex Africa; An End but not The End

No longer "Remarkable"

At the end of 1936, Mum clearly had the time and the access to writing materials necessary to continue keeping a daily journal, but it may be that she felt settled into a routine which was no longer "remarkable": that criterion cited at the start of this work. [On the other hand – the hot season had started and maybe she did not have the energy.] Thus, the remaining seven months of the Yules' West Africa saga can only be related by piecing together snippets of written information, the script of Mum's Talk, the family photo album, a copy of the Passenger List of their voyage home from Freetown and that old standby: remembered family anecdote.

A happy routine...

We may picture then, Mum quite happy in a leisured if rather humdrum existence, coping with the constrictions of living in a hot climate. Mistress of the household, she was waited on by staff around the home, but still had the opportunity to enjoy baking and preparing meals. With Dad out at the Mine in the day, she would socialise with "Little Mrs. Williams" or maybe drive into Lunsar, play snooker at The Club, or go down to the swimming pool for a cooling dip – mosquitos permitting. In the evenings there were functions at the Club, games of Bridge on the verandah or just doing her embroidery, reading or – for a considerable portion of her time as she lists over a dozen "regulars"– keeping up the correspondence whilst making sure her letters were ready in time for the next boat.

The Talk and the photo album record what Mum calls: "*A bit of excitement*" – a staff picnic by the River Rokel. The SLDCo.'s brochure explains that water from the Rokel would be pumped to the Batabana reservoir when its level fell below optimum and Dad made an annotation on the album to suggest the picnic venue was the pumphouse which explains why there was a track to the river from Marampa. But this wasn't exactly the same as an outing in an Alexander's charabanc, as Mum tells us they travelled, sat on benches, in an open lorry along an unsurfaced road. *"This in itself was bad enough,"* she tells us, *"but the river bridges are only trees stretched from bank to bank"*. [Bradt's Guide Book in an illustration between pp 152-3 suggests that in some parts of the country, things have not changed!]

Mum's Talk records a short holiday in Freetown, presumably staying with the Stillwells. The album shows them having the use of a car and enjoying Lumley beach once more. A flyleaf inscription is dated "Freetown, March 1937" and as the records show Easter Day that year being on March 28th, it may have been the Bank Holiday break. The flyleaf in question is in a collection of poems by Sir Walter Scott [OUP 1925 edition.], though where Mum bought the book is uncertain [It bears a stamp "C.M.S. BOOKSHOP"]. An odd choice perhaps, but maybe in homage to her grandfather, the well -read Andrew Brown Senior of Hollandbush, for the Browns were given to quoting such as the first couplet of the "Lay of the Last Minstrel": *"The way was long, the wind was cold, /The Minstrel was infirm and old;"*. It is a safe bet to assume that Mum would mention that purchase in the letter she wrote to Miss Kirkness, her old English teacher, which she recorded as sending on 1st April and must have written on return to Marampa.

... cut short.

We know from Mum's Diary [22 XII 1936] that Dad, on return from the Nursing Home episode, still planned that they would stay at Marampa for the full contracted twelve months. That plan was to be thwarted.

Mum's Talk suggests that Dad had no less than **FIVE** attacks of malaria whilst she was with him at Marampa. That fifth one, perhaps coinciding with the start of the rainy season in May, was more serious. The doctor would have noticed that the high fever was accompanied by vomiting and jaundice and that his patient's urine was a very dark colour. That last would set the alarm bells ringing and the diagnosis was that Dad now had a complication of malaria which had been first identified in the 1880's and given the name "Blackwater Fever" from its salient symptom. Put simply, the malarial parasites were now destroying Dad's red blood cells at a catastrophic rate and the freed haemoglobin were now passing into the urine and colouring it. Allowed to continue, this situation results in kidney failure and death and indeed the mortality rate from Blackwater Fever amongst Europeans has been recorded as "high".

Fortunately for all concerned in this book, help was close at hand in the presence of a nearby hospital, which we have seen noted by Mum [26.XI.1936].This must have been the Hospital of the Order of St, John of God, where Dad was probably not the first or last patient to be admitted under these circumstances and where the experience and expertise – which probably included changing from quinine as a medication – saved his life.

Mum never recorded this episode or spoke of it, but we can well imagine the reaction a young Scots lass far from home seeing her husband of less than a year in a life-threatening situation.

Ex Africa

The Passenger List of the Elder Dempster flagship, MV *Abosso*, arriving in UK in the first week of July 1937 shows two Second Class passengers: *RS Yule, Engineer, age 30* and *Mrs A.C. Yule, age 25,* no occupation given, address of both: *Hollandbush, By Bonnybridge, Stirling;* Country of Intended Future Permanent Residence: *Scotland.* Those bare facts, of course, must conceal quite a story.

At some point in June, the ministrations of the Order of St. John of God, had pulled a sturdy young Scot back from "death's door". Both Mum and the SLDCo. managers would have said: "Home" and "No more". The shipment of goods and chattels – including that camphor chest – would be arranged – fond farewells would be said to friends and to Cole and the servants. A very weak Dad would then have to cope with the train journey to Pepel and the launch to Freetown. There may have been another stay at the Nursing Home at Kissy, but we know from his sister-in-law's relating of the episode that Dad was on a stretcher and had to be winched aboard M.V. *Abosso* by the ship's derricks. Mum's Talk described that voyage home as a "blur", though remembering they called at Las Palmas and Funchal but at night when there was no carefree "run ashore" for passengers. Of the UK rail stages of the journey, the author remembers being told that Dad had to travel "in the guards van". On the route of Auden's "*Night Mail*", after crossing the border, did he manage to look out of a window and catch a glimpse of his beloved River Clyde at Elvanfoot? Racing through his native industrial Lanarkshire was there a sighting of what Auden described as: "*the furnaces/ Set on the dark plain like gigantic chessmen.*"? Maybe he saved up his strength till the express ran through Uddingston and dragged himself to a window for a fleeting sight of his childhood home at Kyle Park. Mum's Talk describes the end of her odyssey: "*When we arrived back in Glasgow Central Station we were met by my parents. Father had brought us scarves as he thought we might feel the cold even though it was July. The village where I was born is not beautiful by any standards though the country surrounding it is very pleasant but that day I thought it was paradise. No mosquitos or ants, no need for boots or oils to keep insects away, plenty hot and cold water and bread that didn't taste of palm oil*".

An End but not The End

Thus, we reach the end of the records of the overseas lives of Mum and Dad.

Life was never really the same thereafter but memories of Kojonup, Katanning, Madeira and Marampa would never quite fade.

SCOTLAND TO SIERRA LEONE

Mum and ships did not get on! That is probably why she has a rather strained look on board *Lochfyne* [**Above left**] taking a "wee sail" on honeymoon and on *Aba* [**Above Right**] going to West Africa. [Snaps taken presumably by Dad in the Family Collection]

[**Above R.**] Mum and Dad snapped by an unknown photographer on arrival at Pepel 17th Oct. 1936 still in their ship board clothes. [**Above L.**] Mum is more comfortably dressed pictured with the Marampa Wives – Mrs. Hunter and Mrs. Williams – on the staff outing to the banks of the River Rokel the following year. [Scans from an album in the Family Collection]

MAKING THEMSELVES AT HOME

Good neighbours: Mr. & Mrs Williams
[Family Collection]

Relaxing on basket chairs in their new home.
[Family Collection]

The garden shelter or "shimbeck" was a nice idea which didn't
work out because all manner of poisonous creatures made it
their home- as poor Spot found to his cost.
[Family Collection]

HOME COMFORTS

Bought in Freetown on 21 XII 1936 and pictured in the bungalow, the chest made of the strongly scented camphor wood was an insect-proof storage facility which travelled back to UK and, as shown above left in a photo from Steven Dandy, is still a useful item of furniture 80 years later. [Family Collection]

Mum mentions the pool in the Diary. The above left, in a DELCO shot (probably looking east), shows it looking inviting below the bungalows and Dad must have taken the above right showing it in use with Mum and the Williams's on the diving steps. [Family Collection]

THEN and NOW

See also: Appendix 2 and Appendix 3b

Changing times at Pepel. **Above left:** Dad's snap of *River Afton* loading Marampa ore. **Above right:** the FoSLNRM picture of the modern equivalent with ore from Tonkilili loaded into a barge for conveying to a bulk carrier in the deep- water part of Freetown Harbour.

Above left: a DELCO 1935 illustration of ore wagons [plus a stores wagon] in full use as two trains pass on the Pepel – Marampa 3ft 6in. gauge line. **Above right:** a FoSLNRM camera has found a last resting place of one of them.

THIS IS AFRICA -1

Dad's freehand pencil sketch of Port Loko Creek. [Family Collection]

Above left, a view of the African houses in Rochendata which adjoined the Marampa site and **(above right)** an almost timeless photo of palm wine sellers. [Family Collection]

THIS IS AFRICA -2

Dad was clearly fascinated by the shapes shown at the base of a Cotton Tree.

House staff, Saidu, Cole, Sourie (**Above left**) but perils too – a bush fire 7 III 1937 (**Above right**)
All on this page from the Family Collection.

MARAMPA FACILITIES

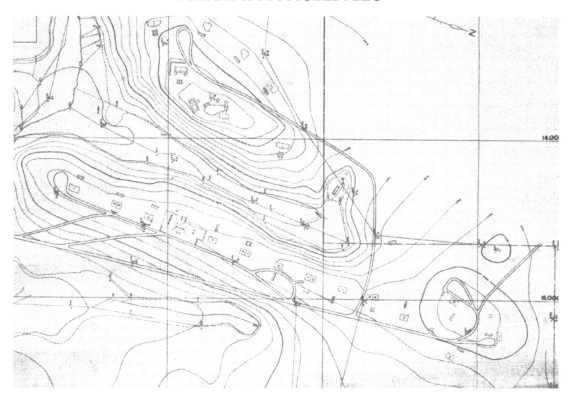

This scan of detail from a faded copy of a 1938 DELCO Plan of Masaboin Hill shows the Club on a N-S ridge with the bungalows widely spaced around. A tennis court is marked adjoining.
[Taken from UGD164/4 Sierra Leone Development Co Ltd, 1927-1974 UGD164/4/3 Rolled plans Archive, University of Glasgow. Ref GB 0248 UGD164/4/3/40/2] Dad's snaps of the building and the tennis court are below [Family Collection]

MASABOIN HILL

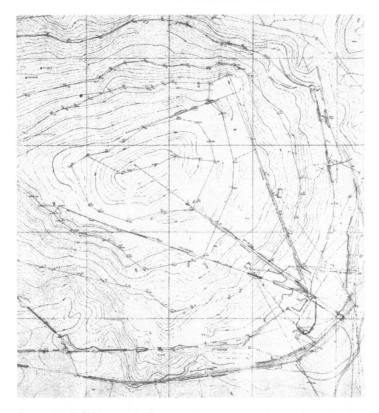

This scan of detail from a faded copy of a 1938 DELCO Plan of Masaboin Hill shows the complexity of 7 haulages converging on the Loading Bank (See also Appendix 3b) [Taken from UGD164/4 Sierra Leone Development Co Ltd, 1927-1974 UGD164/4/3 Rolled plans Archive, University of Glasgow. Ref GB 0248 UGD164/4/3/40/1]

Construction Loading Bank.

Dad's freehand pencil sketch from November 1932 was done before the mines commenced operations. Dad's viewpoint must have been by one of the haulages from where the curve of the Pepel – Marampa Rly. is clearly visible. [Family Collection]

Neither an Addendum nor an Appendix but a

POSTSCRIPT

Concerning the succeeding years **from 1937**

At this point in the publication ...

... the author begs to be relieved of the burden of providing an informed insight into the world of the 1930's through the portal of family Diaries. These closing words arise out of consideration of that eventual readership indicated in the Dedication and are here merely to answer their probable question: "Uncle Donald, what happened next?" In providing as many answers to that as seem suitable, Transport topics (save for one exception below) have been accorded their own Appendices and there is a quick round up of People and Places. So, reader this is where we came in: giving pride of place to the Diarists - - not so much travels but still plenty of travails.

But first that exception

Let us just pause in the narrative to tell of one of the ships, sadly the only one in the Diaries to survive the War, but one to which Cowden and Duffy in their commendable compendium of Elder Dempster ships[338], devote over 12 pages, so a short diversion here seems appropriate.

On the outbreak of war, MV *Aba* was requisitioned as a Hospital Ship and, in the Red Cross markings, had a remarkable record, plucking wounded from conflict zones - sometimes coming under attack- and, when peace came, repatriating thousands of patients. During eight years' service, she circum-navigated Africa – seeing Freetown again -, crossed the Atlantic, even sailed Arctic waters to the land for which she had been originally built. In Mum's words: "Good old Aba"!

Back at home, back at work

A fit and well Dad now found himself in a fast re-arming Britain which meant work for a Civil Engineer, which was how Dad was to describe himself in future. With his proven surveying skills and experience with reinforced concrete he had no difficulty in gaining employment with Sir Lindsay Parkinson & Co Ltd who had government contracts for building armaments factories and military installations throughout UK. Thus, Anne and

---

[338] *The Elder Dempster Fleet History 1852- 1985* See Sources

Bob – now owners of a Hillman saloon Registration Number WG6602 - were soon on the move again, first to Preston area in Lancashire – where they hit the major tragedy of their young lives when Mum's first child died soon after birth. Both families supported, together with the Barrowcloughs from nearby Fleetwood, with whom Mum had lodged in 1932. Then it was Bridgend, South Wales where, they became proud owners of a brand- new Hillman Minx Reg. No. ETG 468. This "10 Horsepower" model was to be the family car for nearly twenty years though out of commission during the Second World War, which broke out shortly after its purchase. [See Addendum 2]

The Blast of War

Dad, in a "Reserved Occupation" and a serial malaria sufferer, was not called into the Armed Services during the conflict- though there was a short period when the Home Guard literally was "Dad's Army". Mum and Dad were spared also any direct effects of enemy action, although there were scares with enemy aircraft overhead and real danger from enemy submarines when crossing from Northern Ireland. Mum, of course appreciated that the life of a civil or mining engineer involves moving to where the work is and that was never truer then in those difficult years when, at the outset, the pre-war construction of military facilities proceeded apace. So, Mum now with the infant author in tow, followed Dad first to the ring of airfields and bases being built around Warrington [then Lancs. now Ches.] and then, with the entry of the USA into the conflict and the need to accommodate their armed personnel, across the Irish Sea to County Antrim. Mission accomplished across the water, it was back to England to work on the eventually massive US airbase at Burtonwood which meant a return to the Warrington area. At this point, with the arrival of the author's sister, Mum and Dad faced the same situation as did John and Bella Yule all those years earlier when they moved from Clyde Cottage to Uddingston: the need to find a school for their youngsters and the "caravan" came to a rest in Stockton Heath, a suburb of Warrington. But that did not mean Mum and Dad were to be together.

Together but separate

Having picked that side of the Pennines to settle in, it was rather ironic that, with the tide of war turning, the need to build new military establishments declined and Dad was now required to reprise his role as a Mining Engineer at his employer's open cast coal sites in Yorkshire. At the Wentworth site, a press photographer covering the visit of King George VI and Queen Elizabeth caught Dad, in his habitual "Donkey Jacket", on the edge of a shot in February 1944 though there is no record of that picture making the papers. [See Appendix 3a] Shortly after that, Dad was called further away to "somewhere in England" where his Marampa experience with reinforced concrete was put to use in the constructing of what the staff were told were massive "fuel tanks". We now know that these were the Phoenix caissons which would eventually form the Mulberry Harbours that played such a major role in the successful Allied invasion of Normandy that summer. However, such was desperate need of the nation for coal in the 1940's, the calls on Dad's time in Yorkshire impinged upon his family life on the other side of the Pennines. In one of those impulsive moves such as took him from Denny to Kojonup or to make an enquiry of the Sierra Leone Development Co. as to whether they might need a surveyor, Dad took himself to the Head Office of a Warrington- based firm of civil engineering contractors, A. Monk & Co. to ask if they had local work. As that firm was then moving into one of its most productive periods with the post-war reconstruction and then the expansion of the UK petrochemical industry, the answer was a definite "yes" and Dad joined the firm where he was to stay until retirement.

A window on Dad's world

So, a decade after that fraught exit from Sierra Leone, Anne and Bob had become used to being Mum and Dad and were sensing that their "Intended Country of Permanent Residences" might not be Scotland after all. As indicated above, it was time to fix their abode and readers will not be surprised that the house Dad's earnings bought was within

sight of a cricket club and a rugby club. [Greenall's CC & Warrington RUFC] Also, it was alongside the Manchester Ship Canal so there were ocean-going cargo passenger liners passing their front door bringing memories of world travel with their cargos of cotton from Egypt or USA, iron ore or timber from Scandinavia or palm oil from West Africa. [Dad would get a wee bit misty eyed if the ship belonged to the Clan Line and displayed on its stern the port of registration as "Glasgow"] Also within sight of the house was one of the canal's swing bridges [pictured above by the author in 1953] which Dad never failed to point out was made of Scottish steel manufactured by Sir William Arrol and Co., back home in Lanarkshire.

No more a- roaming

Save for one trip when they attempted to reprise a brief wartime break in Dublin which was rather marred by their finding the Irish Sea to be as rough as the Bay of Biscay, Mum and Dad never left the UK again. Whenever possible, there were trips "home" to stay at Hollandbush with the Browns and then the Arneils with the Yules just a mile away at No.2 Holding Longcroft where the firm of J&W Yule very successfully shifted their business emphasis from poultry to pigs. Dad's lifelong love affair with the Firth of Clyde meant he took the family – though not always Mum! - on sails to his childhood favourites: Arran, Kyles of Bute, Tarbert, Campbelltown etc out of piers at Fairlie, Wemyss Bay, Gourock or Glasgow Bridge Wharf. As noted in Introduction to Volume 1, he was perhaps disappointed that his children preferred the more modern comforts of the later turbine steamers – *Queen Mary II, Duchess of Hamilton* to those aboard his ageing favourite *Duchess of Argyll.* [For serious studies life in UK in 1940's and 50's, see Sources]

Echoes

In the 1970's, a trip with the author on MV *Balmoral* on the Bristol Channel took Dad to Lundy Island where in those days one went ashore via a small boat and thus was an immediate echo of Funchal or Freetown. But there were other echoes. Mum and Dad's social life centred around their "kirk", St John's Presbyterian Church and the Warrington Caledonian Society and as that town had a goodly proportion of the Scottish diaspora, there were Scots accents forever near.

That camphor chest Mum was so proud, of fulfilled its domestic function and still has a role in her Grandson's household. The Madeira tablecloth they haggled over in Funchal, came out on special occasions, such as when they had a "Marampa" night with "small chop" and gin cocktails.

Their evenings, until the advent of BBC and ITV television were much as at Marampa, reading and writing "home" or playing cribbage. Mum kept up her embroidery and her pictures – like Dad's sketches - are a lasting legacy. Dad discovered one advantage of having a son is that you can play with "boys' toys": Meccano, stationary steam engine, Hornby train. Whilst he was never to sketch regularly again, his creative instinct was to the fore in that last as he designed and built with his fretwork tools the stations, signal box, bridge and engine shed for a sizeable "O" gauge layout and, not to leave out his daughter, a Doll's House still fondly remembered. That capacity for taking pains, such a feature of his personality, was to the fore as he carefully replicated the courses of brickwork in the model buildings. As time passed by, model kits appeared on the market and he was not less painstaking as he built a host of models – of course - locomotives and ships. One model, that of a single screw cargo ship, a successful construction about 2 feet in length powered by a rubber band, had clear echoes of SS *Wilston* upon which he and Alex had been zookeepers back in 1935. The fate of that ship [See Appendix 1] had resonated with him and after several holidays to Cornwall, a county which Mum and he grew to love, he finally gained closure and found the spot where the steamer had come to grief.

Twilight years

Let us then take a last (admittedly sentimental) look at the couple who in their youth considered that what they were doing was sufficiently remarkable to be worthy of recording in a Diary. In those twilight years - early 1970's - Anne and Bob who had in turn become

Mum and Dad, Auntie Anne and Uncle Bob are now Nan and Grandie. They have moved from that big house by the Ship Canal where the smoke from passing steamships' funnels showered Mum's washing with soot. They are in a pleasant 1920's semi-detached house in Parkgate Road, Stockton Heath. Their children- whom they had struggled to feed and clothe in wartime and the ensuing grey years of the 1940's – are now making their own way in the world. Together they visit markets around north west England, as they had once done in West Africa, and tour England and Wales by car. Mum is a leading light in Women's Guild at St. John's and in demand at several associations as a speaker with her well scripted talks on her life. [See Addendum 2]. And on a summer Saturday afternoon, Dad is doing as he had done as a wee laddie in the summers before the First World War, he is on a bench with convivial companions at Walton Lea, watching the Warrington cricket team.

NEAR FRODSHAM.

Twenty years after first opening it at Tarbert, Loch Fyne, Dad took out his sketch book one last time on a warm April day in Cheshire whilst Mum read, and the kids romped around the fields near Frodsham caves. An unremarkable sketch perhaps but that book had seen some remarkable travelling.

Permanent Residence

Close by Warrington cricket club, the Diarists' ashes lie amongst the woods on a sandstone ridge in Cheshire. From that edge one can just see Liverpool – that port they left jointly on an adventure so long ago – and look north up the routes back home to Scotland, that "Intended Country of Permanent Residence" where their hearts forever lay.

ADDENDUM ONE

Hugh Scott

The cricketing Hugh Scott [born 1889 in his father's pub, the *Clydesdale Inn*, Craigneuk] was Bella Yule's wee brother hence Dad's uncle, a fast bowler for Uddingston CC and thus something of a hero to the Yule boys. Legend has it that in one match, between deliveries, he was patrolling the boundary with hands behind his back and head bent forward – clearly in deep thought about the course of the game – when one of his team mates observed: "*Look at Hughie Scott oot there. He looks like a great gull*". As is the way in cricket teams, the nickname "The Gull" duly stuck.

From this distance it is rather difficult to understand that rush to join up in the summer of 1914 and this is not the place to enter into a study of the spirit of that time. For those readers who wish to indulge in that study, I recommend Royle's *The Flowers of the Forest* [see Sources] In summary: industrial Scotland was not perhaps the happiest of lands in those years. A low-wage, undiversified economy was stagnating. Over the years, prices had increased faster than wages leading to industrial and social strife; to the ever-present sectarian tensions was added the problem of immigration from Europe - the Italian influx is well known but, perhaps less well known, was the arrival of many Lithuanians [locally called "Poles"] in and around Bellshill. There may have been a feeling that Imperial Germany was in some way to blame for all this. Remembered Yule Family anecdote spoke of letters from Robert Scott ["Uncle" in Vol 1] speaking of German manufactured consumer goods appearing in the shops in Australia at prices which undercut those of British origin. If there was a dumping of state subsidised goods, then there was a trade war before there was a shooting war and the Scots may have had reason for their suspicion that the Kaiser was up to no good.

That "shooting war" which was occasioned by the invasion of Belgium gave young Scots men a chance to get away from their grey and edgy locality by volunteering for the Army which they did to such effect that, according to Royle, by 1916 half of Scotland's male population aged between eighteen and forty-five was in uniform.

 "The Gull" was one of them and they could claim a moral purpose. Royle [op.cit.] quotes the rather-forgotten Aberdeenshire poet, Charles Murray [1964 -1941] whose lines from "The Sough of War "could be said to epitomise that feeling:

> "*Nae ours the blame, but when it came*
> *We couldna pass the challenge by,*
> *For credit o' our honest name*
> *There could be but the ae reply*"

So, in September 1914, Hugh Scott joined that surge to enlist and, after handing his prized cricket boots to his sister Bella, with instructions to take good care of them, he became

12155 Scott H. with the 5th Battalion (Queen's Own) Cameron Highlanders and, as we have seen in previous illustrations, did his basic training in North Camp, Aldershot.

His section pictured above in training mode [and with an apparently injured Corporal!] still has the air of young men on an adventure holiday. We can see Hugh (back row, left) clearly has the physique of a fast bowler but the rest of the section are also well-built, emphasising the fact that 5th Battalion [or "Locheil's Own"] was selecting the "Flower of Scotland". Basic Training completed, the Battalion moved to Salisbury Plain for Battle Training and then to France in the Spring of 1915. Initially "Line- of -Communications" troops, their baptism of fire was to come that Autumn.

"Battle of Loos" is the official British name for the offensive of September, October and November 1915 fought over a front of 6 miles between the La Bassee Canal and Lens and named after a mining community at the centre of the front, Loos-en-Gohelle. This former coalmining town today is a commune in the Pas-de-Calais department in the Hauts-de-France region of France and not really a magnet for tourists. However, the double- crassier [twin -bings] is a feature of the landscape now as it was in 1915 and the tourist speeding past on the way to Vimy Ridge or the Somme can readily locate the scene of what was then the largest battle ever fought by the British Army.

Hugh Scott by now had the Lance-Corporal's stripes and his Battalion was part of 9th (Scottish Division) forming 26 Brigade with battalions from regiments with illustrious names: Black Watch, Gordons, Seaforths. To get a picture of the first day of the battle, we turn to Gordon Corrigan's *Loos 1915 – The Unwanted Battle* [See Sources].

With the Seaforths, they had to attack the Hohenzollern Redoubt, described by Corrigan as a "*mass of bunkers, dugouts and machine gun nests, many of them concreted in, and surrounded by wire.*" [p59] Ironically for many, they were to fight in a coal mining area just like Lanarkshire, where the bings and pit head gear gave good views of the surrounding country and where the miners' rows [Corons] had been converted to fortified bunkers. (Ibid. p59) "*9 Division was being asked to fight its way through a 600-yard deep defensive complex, and even then, would be still 500 yards from the German second line.*" That would have been a difficult assignment later in this war or in subsequent conflicts following the invention of armoured vehicles and the development of close air support. Attired in kilt and bonnet, armed with rifle and bayonet, the Camerons had a tough job indeed despite a preliminary bombardment which included the British Army's first use of gas. Major Corrigan continues: (on pp 60,61) "*.... the Camerons had an appalling baptism of fire. Firstly, they were held up by gas hanging about in their own front line, and then, when they did advance, they came under very heavy fire from their left, where 26 Brigade had been unable to progress. Taking heavy casualties, the while, the battalion pressed on through the northern part of the Hohenzollern Redoubt through the German firing line and up to Fosse 8* [pithead]*. Fifteen minutes after the Seaforths, the Camerons too were reorganising north of the Corons. They had done all that asked been asked of them but at a terrible price. Of the 800 men who had left the British line, only about 100 were still able to fight and only two of the officers.*"

"The Gull" was not amongst the survivors.

Beverley Scott, in: *Our Scott Family History* (2 Ed 2006 p39) [See Sources] has typed copies of letters about his death:
"One letter (written by "Charlie" to Thomas Grey Esq 16/10/15) states, in part: "*On the 25th of last month we went into the trenches with 1000 men and came out on the Monday afternoon with 160 – so you may judge we had some cutting up. Hugh Scott was killed about 30 yds from our own fire trench by a rifle bullet. We buried him on the morning of the 28th.*"

The subsequent performance of the BEF in eventually winning the War is well chronicled elsewhere – especially in Peter Hart's *1918 A Very British Victory* [See Sources] and we may borrow his summary (Chapter 15 p514): "*Britain and its empire finished the war with the most efficient and deadly army in the world. .... a huge modern, mechanised army that had truly grasped the art of war as far as it existed in 1918.*"

The effects of the Great War on Scotland's society and economy in general are well analysed by Royle (op. cit.), here I would like to emphasise that Loos, which had a casualty rate higher than in the notorious Somme Offensive the following year, cut a swathe through the best of Scotland's youth. One could say that cricket in Scotland never recovered from the two events, certainly never again was the spectator sport it had been pre-war. Dad's principal sport suffered also. Stephen Cooper's excellent "*After the Final Whistle*" [See Sources], the definitive text on the effect of the Great War on Rugby Football worldwide, notes that: "*By November 1918, Scotland topped another dismal wartime table: the flower of its rugby men – thirty- one capped players – had been hacked down, the highest score of all the nations.*"

To end on a personal note, let me take you to a remembered scene sometime in the late 1940's because Bella kept her promise to her young brother. Late in the day, we are in the stone-floored Living Room in the Yule's farm at Longcroft [By Bonnybridge, Stirlingshire, Scotland]. John Crawford Yule, my Grandpa – adorned with the latest batch of kittens - is dozing in his chair by the warmth of the fire sparkling in the old kitchen range; the farm dogs are stretched out and snoring over by the wall. My Grandma, Bella Yule, with her cornflower blue eyes of the Scotts filled with tears, is showing her uncomprehending grandson a pair of old, old cricket boots. And thus, invisibly, a baton was handed on to another generation.

ADDENDUM TWO

Mum and Motoring

Although Mum drove many vehicles over many years, this is the only picture of her at the wheel. Taken on Lumley Beach, Sierra Leone in an unidentified hired car in 1937. (Possible trouble with rear wheels in the sand?)
[Family Collection]

Their first car, a Hillman with a Stirlingshire Registration. This picture probably taken on their first outing.
[Family Collection]

Shiny new car! Bought in Bridgend, South Wales, in 1939 – hence the Glamorgan Registration – "Minnie the Minx" served the family till the mid-1950's after spending most of the War laid up at Hollandbush.
[Family Collection]

Of the preserved scripts of Mum's 1970's Talks, her Motoring one which she called "Early Motoring Recollections in Scotland and Elsewhere" has the most relevance to the subjects in this book. The following extracts are good examples of her story-telling style.

Early motoring recollections.

Cars

The first car I can remember was a Ford Van[339] which father bought in 1916 so that he could learn to drive before he was called up for active service in World War One. He wanted to be an ambulance driver. This he was during 2½ years in France and Belgium.[340] The second car was an Overland 90.[341] It arrived without a body and had to have one coach-built. We were in business[342] so a van it was. This satisfied us for a while and then we had windows put in the sides thus making it much better when we went on an outing - a forerunner of the "Dormobile"[343] as I will tell you.

My father was one of those conscientious people who wouldn't go away for a holiday, "in case things go wrong", so long weekends were our usual vacations until my sister [344] and I were old enough to go on our own.

This Overland 90 was very powerful but it was flat out at 30 mph. Of course, the roads in those days were anything but the smooth tarmac creations of today and motoring was really an adventure, though I think much less dangerous than the congestion on our highways today. A run from here[345] to Chester can tax anyone's patience.

A scary night

Our first stop for the night was on a moorland piece of road not far from Tyndrum. The car had been equipped with a mattress for 3 in the back and I was to sleep on the front seat. We all settled down for the night, a great thrill for us kids. How Father and Mother felt I don't know, suffice it to say we didn't have another "caravan" holiday.

---

[339] This would replace a pony and trap which the Brown's, being Licensed Grocer's, used for deliveries. Presumably a commercial version of a Model T such as Robert Scott drove in Western Australia.

[340] See Vol 2

[341] This would be the Willys Overland 90 from the company best remembered for producing the Jeep. The Browns replaced it with an Overland Whippet, described by Mum as "much speedier" with "proper upholstery". Then came the Wolseley saloon with which they were met in Glasgow in 1937.

[342] See 3 above

[343] The Bedford Dormobile was a 1960s-era campervan/motorcaravan/ motorhome/conversion, based on the Bedford CA van,

[344] Mrs Jean Arneil, 1916 - 2010

[345] Presumably Warrington Cheshire about 20 miles from Chester written before M56 was built.

As the night wore on, the rain began, and you have an idea what that sounded like on the metal roof. Suddenly I became aware of a tap, tap of a stick some way off. This continued for what seemed ages. I lay petrified. My latest story had been *"Treasure Island"* where Jim Hawkins in the inn *"The Admiral Benbow"* heard the tap, tap, tap of the blind beggar's stick [*Blind Pew- ADY*] bringing the sign of the Black Spot to the lodger [*Billy Bones - ADY*.]. My imagination was really on fire. I pictured all sorts of things happening to us. I thought the others were asleep and I would need to face this unknown terror alone!

At last the tapping stopped and a voice called out: *"What time is it?"*

My relief was unbounded when Father replied: *"Who's there?"*

"It's alright, I thought the van was empty. Goodnight."

The tap, tap, tap began again but this time away from us and I knew Father had been alert too & I was not afraid (any more).

Later the next day we passed a tramp with a stick plodding on his way. He (had) only wanted shelter and who could blame him on such a night of rain.

Lost in The Lakes

The next long weekend took us "over the Border into England" – my but we were excited! – you would have thought we were going to a foreign land, it might as well have been Africa! In 1923 there was not the coming and going between Scotland and England that there is today and in our little village, anyone with an English accent was a rarity. On this trip, we stayed in hotels – no more caravanning!

Our first thrill came when we crossed the Sark bridge and we were for the first time out of our own country. As we neared Carlisle, the first week in July, we were horrified to see children going to school. Scottish schools always finish at the end of June, so we were indeed sorry for these boys and girls still hard at work while we were on holiday.

We spent the first night at Glenridding, a lovely place it was.[346]

Now we came as far south as Dalton-in Furness[347] and our aim was to go north again and spend the night at Silloth. We asked directions at a garage and were given some instructions. Now, whether we went wrong, or the garage man hoped for a customer broken down in the hills, I don't know but we got sadly lost. On we went over rough hilly roads, round sharp corners, over a humped bridge. Luckily the tank held plenty of petrol and at 1/3 [one shilling and threepence = approx. 6p] a gallon it was easy to say: "Fill her up". As I said before the 90 was powerful but slow so we anticipated no difficulties with gradients. Once when we met a shepherd and stopped to ask the way, he looked blank, we might have been from Space. I suppose the Scotch [sic] tongue beat him. When Father offered him, a cigarette, he took it but looked at it as if it was doped!

---

[346] On the A592 at the southern end of Ullswater in the Lake District National Park, it still is!

[347] Following what are now the A592 and A590

After leaving him, none the wiser, we turned a corner where some people were in a field – then the car almost stood on its end, the hill was so steep but up it she went, and the folks were left open mouthed and goggle-eyed. Mile after mile we went until we crossed a narrow- gauge railway, there a man was able to direct us to Maryport. He was amazed to hear where we had travelled. This road with gates at intervals was one used for Motor Trials.

Commentary

In keeping with the practice throughout this book, where no piece of writing by Mum or Dad goes without comment, here are some thoughts on that last story – one oft retold to her family.

How was it they got lost?

Mum dates the trip as being in July 1923. It was only in the April of that year that the modern system of numbering and classifying roads in UK was finally adopted, so maps and road signage would not necessarily be available to the motorist. They had chosen a "scenic route" over Kirkstone Pass and along by Windermere [modern A592] down to "The Furness District of Lancashire" [as it then was]. Presumably they had aimed for a similarly attractive route [modern A593 – A591 – A66] back to their northern coastal destination but missed the turn off. It may be that they took the road over Birker Fell from Ulpha which certainly leaves Dunnerdale by a very steep hill and brings the traveller to Eskdale Green where they would meet Mum's "narrow gauge railway", the famous Ravenglass & Eskdale line. One can be pretty sure that the least worried would be Andrew Brown, the ex-RASC driver who had driven all over the war-torn lands of France & Flanders and was unlikely to be upset by a slight diversion in Cumbria!

Mum recorded that the Browns eventually reached their destination at Skinburness near Silloth where they were well-positioned for what was the real object of their trip across the Border – a prize winning visit. Although the surviving script for this talk does not mention it, recalled anecdote suggests that Andrew Brown & Sons, Grocers of Hollandbush, Banknock had won a competition organised by one of their suppliers: Carrs of Carlisle. The prize was a visit to that famous company's factory and the Lakeland trip was all about collecting the prize and more – Mum's script records: "*Oh boy! We had so many samples we had to have bags to carry them away and at the end we each received a box of chocolate.*"

A happy note on which to leave her writings.

DOON THE WATTER

For details of the ships in this set, please see Appendix 1

MacBrayne's paddle steamer *Columba* was, between 1878 and 1935, the most famous Clyde steamer and a favourite with the Yules and the Browns. She departed Glasgow – Broomielaw then later from across the river at Bridge Wharf - at 7.11 each weekday in the season carrying the mails to Ardrishaig for forwarding to the Western Isles. Though fitted with old-fashioned oscillating engines, she was lavishly equipped with Pullman standard saloons the full width of the vessel and even had a Post Office and barbers' shop. [Photo Desmond Banks]

The speedy Caledonian Railway's turbine steamer, *Duchess of Argyll*, launched in the year of his birth was a favourite with Dad. Here she is pictured in a publicity shot, crossing from Brodick to Ardrossan. [Family collection

At 301 ft, Columba's length was not eclipsed until recent times when the car ferry MV *Caledonian Isles* entered service on the same Arran route as opposite. [Pictured at Ardrossan Ferry Terminal by the Author.]

MAILLER in the MERCHANT NAVY

Every wee laddie's dream was to sail on an Anchor Liner. Mailler realised that dream as part of the crew of ELYSIA [above right] sending a very fancy Company Christmas card to the Yules [above left] carrying the standard publicity shot of the liner. Later (inaccurate) annotations were made by Dad. [Family collection]

To be part of the crew of an Anchor Liner on its maiden voyage was beyond all expectations but Mailler was chosen for TUSCANIA [**above left** picture from Book of the Anchor Line 1931]. Unfortunately, by then there was a war on and Mailler was on board when his ship was fatally torpedoed south of Islay by when part of a troop -carrying convoy in February 1918 with over 2,000 US troops aboard. The centenary of the loss of 230 lives -around 200 troops and 30 crew - occurred whilst this book was in preparation and a commemoration on Islay was recorded by the BBC. [**Above right**]

ACROSS the OCEANS

ORONSAY. Dad sailed from Tilbury 1 II 1930 to arrive Freemantle WA 3 III 1930. [From an Orient Line publicity picture postcard in the Family Collection]

ORSOVA. Dad sailed from Freemantle WA 23 II 1931 to arrive Tilbury 27 III 1931 [From an Orient Line publicity picture postcard in the Family Collection]

THE WEST COAST RUN -1

For more details of these ships, please see Appendix 1

APAPA – Dad's first tour outward Sept 1931 and homeward Feb. 1934 [From a contemporary Elder Dempster postcard in the Family Collection]

ADDA – Dad homeward 1ˢᵗ class July 1932 and outward September 1932 [From a contemporary Elder Dempster postcard in the Family Collection]

THE WEST COAST RUN -2

For more details of these ships, please see Appendix 1

ACCRA – Dad outward March 1934 and August 1935. Homeward 1ˢᵗ Class August 1936. [From contemporary Elder Dempster postcard Family Collection]

JULY 1940

THE ACCRA—went down stern first with colours flying.

480 aboard : 461 saved

THE 9,000-ton Elder Dempster liner Accra was torpedoed and sunk in daylight off the north-west coast of Ireland 11 days

Dad's wartime Scrapbook contains this cutting from the Daily Express.

THE LAST of AFRICA

ABA – Mum and Dad outward bound from Liverpool October 1936.
[Scan of contemporary Elder Dempster postcard from Family Collection]

"Good old Aba!" Of the ships on the "West Coast Run" which feature in the Diaries [see Appendix 1] only ABA, launched 1916, survived the Second World War, probably because she was requisitioned as a Hospital Ship – as shown above reproduced from Cowden & Duffy p175. [see Postscript]

When Mum & Dad passed the Elder Dempster flagship ABOSSO in October 1936, they could not have imagined that she would carry them back from a curtailed tour. [see Postscript] Their snap of Abosso, UK bound near Madeira, symbolises that last sad ocean trip. [Family Collection]

APPENDIX 0

People and Places

Neither Genealogy nor Geography just a series of thumbnail sketches.

Some of the people

DAVID MAILLER YULE, the author's great grandfather is a rather shadowy figure as far as this book is concerned. Of concern to us here are two of his sons: John and David but we must mention Susan [1867-1949] whose marriage to John Devine produced the family mentioned in this book.

JOHN CRAWFORD YULE [1870-1960] married Bella Scott eldest daughter of John and Isabella née Smith [see below] in 1899. The five sons were: David Mailler [1900-84] who remained in Western Australia - notably running a café in Geraldton and, in 1949, marrying Thelma Ruddaway who pre-deceased him; John Train Scott[1902-76] – who married Helen Elizabeth "Elaine" Stavert in 1969 - and William [1904-77] who were the J&W Yule poultry and pig farmers and with their purchase of the motor boat *Laughing Water* were "designer uncles" to the author, his sister and cousin; Alexander Crawford [1912-86] returned to Scotland to continue his career as a Commercial Accountant in 1942 and married Elizabeth Stewart "Bet" McKechnie.

REV. DAVID MAILLER YULE [1874 -1952] Classicist and theologian, was ordained into the United Free Church of Scotland in 1900 and was in turn Minister at Roberton, [near Hawick in the Scottish Borders] then Broompark Denny [1906 -1915], Alexandra Parade Glasgow, followed by Forgandenny Perthshire from 1930 to retirement in 1944. He married in 1901, Elizabeth "Bessie" Scott at Mossilee, Galashiels who died at Forgandenny Manse in August 1936, a month before Mum & Dad's marriage. In an article of 31 -03-1909, [see also p86] the Falkirk Herald said of him:

Mr Yule's pulpit ministrations have been found most acceptable by his people. If he is anything, he is in earnest. Withal his discourses are marked by an intellectuality and an originality which are somewhat rare. He sees beneath the surface of things, lays bare the vital underlying causes of movements, and co-ordinates them in well-ordered argument. He often charms by an unexpected image drawn from nature to enforce by analogy some spiritual truth, and then he reveals the literary adept no less than the student and scholar. Noting a man "*devoted to the members of his flock*" and "*popular with his own people*", the unsigned article records a series of lectures he gave as "*eloquent, well-informed, and original in thought and language. They were characterised, however, by more than high intellectuality; they revealed the man in full and loving sympathy with the gospel it is his duty to preach."* Less this seem to portray a dry-as-dust character, the article notes earlier that, whilst in the Borders, he was elected Captain of the local Golf Club.

JOHN TRAIN SCOTT [1847 -1924], a spectacularly broad-shouldered miner- turned - innkeeper, in 1872 married Isabella Kay Smith [1849 -1935]in 1872, she is "Grandma" in Volume 1. They had eight children of whom three: Agnes, John and John Train; died in infancy. Daughters were: Bella [1872 -1957] who married John Yule above; Jean [1878 - 1941]–"Aunt Jeannie" in both Diaries; Margaret [1880 – 1919] – much loved by Dad and mother of his boyhood pal George Young [1906 – 1999]. The sons were: Robert [1882 - 1969], "Uncle" in Volume 1, founder of a dynasty - "The Scott Lot" that includes Beverley, the author's mentor; and Hugh [1889 -1915], subject of Addendum One, buried Pont du Hem Cemetery, La Gorgue, France, Plot 8, Row C, Grave No.6.

ANDREW BROWN, [1816 -1900] the authors' great great grandfather was born in Balfron Parish Stirlingshire, son of John and Agnes (née McEwan). He took over the running over the family farm at Wester Gerchew, Balfron, in 1852 married Jane "Jean" Buchanan [who predeceased him] and died from a stroke at Wester Gerchew. May have been the one who started the family tradition of flavouring ham/bacon with Allspice "Jamaica Pepper".

ANDREW BROWN [1854 – 1933] was the son of the above but moved from the family farm to Falkirk and in 1882 married Jane Hamilton, daughter of William Hamilton & Margaret [née Rutherford], who died of stomach cancer at Hollandbush in 1920. On his death from sepsis, the Falkirk Herald noted: *The late Mr Brown came to Falkirk in 1877 as principal assistant to Mr James Haddow when he established the Falkirk business now known as James Haddow and Company, Limited, and for seventeen years Mr Brown continued in that capacity. Forty years ago, he acquired the old-established licensed grocery business in Hollandbush. which has been successfully carried on since under the firm name of Andrew Brown and Son. ... In years gone by, the late Mr Brown was well known in Falkirk many circles, and for long period took an active interest in Masonic affairs, being a member and office bearer of Lodge, St. John Falkirk No. 16.* He was also known for the garden and hothouse at Hollandbush though by repute he was not fond of some of their products describing salad as "Rabbit food"! [See Illustrations 4]

ANDREW BROWN [1883 -1947], only son of the above, was Mum's father and was born when his parents were in Falkirk. In Glasgow in 1911, he married Martha McKinnon Brown - "Matt" - [1880-1960] one of several children of William and Rose Anne ["Annie"] née Copland. He maintained the garden and the family business till his death when his younger daughter Jean [1906-2010] and her husband William Arneil continued trading until the 1960's. The garden was a delight to his visiting grandchildren, the hothouse being a wonder and the shop a source of goodies -unobtainable in England – such as pies, rolls and Barr's *Iron Brew, Cola* and *Cream Soda.*

Some of the places

Some of the sites and scenes connected with the Diaries have changed beyond recognition, some will see further change, some are still recognizable, and the reader is referred to the Illustration sets. Collieries and steelworks, foundries and brickworks with their attendant smoke and fumes are long vanished. Trams, bus liveries, railway companies and their routes and stations are the subject of books by specialist writers listed here under Sources. Cleared of the soot blackening, Glasgow has re-invented itself and it is still possible to follow Dad's steps across the city though the once busy Broomielaw and Bridge lie silent by a quiet Clyde. It is still possible to catch a train to the Clyde Coast as once did the Yules and Browns and catch a ferry to Arran or maybe take a trip on PS *Waverley* to the Kyles of Bute and Tarbert, Loch Fyne. There is still cricket and rugby in an Uddingston which has the Tunnock's factory at its heart and whose Main Street and sandstone villas now echo its pre-industrial charm.

The name "Hollandbush" is honoured on the street plan of post-industrial Banknock and the site of the Brown's shop and premises, together with Cannerton brickworks, having lain fallow for years is due to be redeveloped. The Yule's last farm, No2 Longcroft has disappeared under modern housing and the farmhouse at Cloybank dating from 1723 fell into disrepair and was demolished. The site of the Yule's poultry farm is now a "country pursuits" centre but in the words of proprietor Jim Penman – whose firm converted Dennyloanhead Church into flats – destined to be a "sporting and educational facility for children and adults with learning disabilities."

Further afield, Block 7083, now part of Burradong Farm, was described in an email to the author in 2018 by Joan O'Halloran as: "V*ery productive land. All cleared now except for shelter belts. Also has some nice dams in the paddocks for water. A big contrast from what it was in 1930"* so the Yule's labours were not entirely in vein. The paddock in Katanning WA, where once two homeless young Scots lived in a tent, is now part of the largest country- based sheep selling complex in Western Australia and the site of "The Pines" is now occupied by the Juniper Bethshan Residential Care Home.

The travails of Sierra Leone have been widely reported over the years, but it may be that the country to which Dad took his new bride is over the worst. Bradt's Guide presents a tantalising picture to potential tourists and the development of the National Railway Museum suggests the advent of a mature nation.

APPENDIX ONE

As a deal of both Volumes concerns ocean travel, it seemed appropriate to provide some background to the 1930's world of ships and the sea as it is so different from the 21st century picture of massive cruise ships and container vessels. Also, many of the ships mentioned in both Diaries came to a sad end – horribly tragic in one case - which Mum and Dad would have noted at the time. As Dad would have wished, I have tabulated some details of ships which are mentioned and or pictured in this book using the works listed in Sources.

Name	Launch	Type	Owner	GRT*	Fate
Home Waters					
Columba	1878	Paddle Steamer 2 cyl oscillating	MacBrayne	543	Scrapped 1936
Duchess of Argyll	1906	3-direct drive steam turbines	CSPCo	583	Sold to Admiralty 1952. Scrapped 1970
Lochfyne	1931	First British diesel electric passenger ship.	MacBrayne	656	Withdrawn 1969. Failed as restaurant ship. Scrapped 1974
Caledonian Isles	1993	Car Ferry Bow Thruster: Caterpillar Diesels.	CalMac	5,221	In service 2017

Mailler					
Elysia	1908	3-cylinder single screw steamship	Anchor Line	6,368	Torpedoed on 5/6/1942 by Japanese aux. cruisers Indian Ocean. Sank 9/6
Tuscania	1914	Twin screw geared turbine.	Anchor Line	14,348	Sunk by torpedo from UB77 s. off Islay 5/28/1918 239 lives lost

Australia					
Orsova	1908	8- cylinder quad expansion steam engine	Orient Line	12,026	Torpedoed but repaired 1917 Scrapped 1936
Oronsay	1924	Twin screw steam Turbine	Orient Line	20,043	Torpedoed & sank off Liberia, 9th Oct 1942. 5 lives lost

Name	Launch	Type	Owner	GRT	Fate
			West Africa		
Aba	1916 Completed 1918	Twin Screw Motor Vessel	Elder Dempster	7,437	Laid down for Imperial Russia. Then *Glenapp.* Hospital ship 1939 -47. Scrapped 1948
Abosso	1935	Twin Screw Motor Vessel	Elder Dempster	11,330	Torpedoed & sank 29th Oct 1942 in N. Atlantic. 172 passengers+ 168 crew lost.
Accra	1926	Twin Screw Motor Vessel	Elder Dempster	9,337	Torpedoed & sank 26th July 1940 in N. Atlantic. 11 passengers + 8 crew lost.
Adda	1921	Twin Screw Motor Vessel	Elder Dempster	7,815	Torpedoed & sank off Freetown 8th Jun 1941. 2 passengers +10 crew lost
Apapa	1927	Twin Screw Motor Vessel	Elder Dempster	9,333	Bombed & sank N. Atlantic 15th Nov 1940. 24 lives lost.
Hindpool	1928	Steamship. Cargo vessel	Ropners (Pool Lines)	4,897	Torpedoed & sank off Cape Verde Is. 8th Mar 1941. Master +27 crew lost
Wilston	1916	Steamship. 3cyl. Triple expansion	W S Miller	3,218	Please read Appendix 1b

For further details please consult sources listed

GRT   *Used above as a measure of size comparison,* Gross Register Tonnage *is a ship's total internal volume expressed in "register tons", each of which is equal to 100 cubic feet ($2.83\ m^3$). GRT is not a measure of the ship's weight or displacement and should not be confused with terms such as* deadweight tonnage *or* displacement. *Not in use for modern Bulk Carriers*

Abbreviations used in the text:

PS *Paddle Steamer;* **SS** *Steam Ship (Reciprocating engines); TS Turbine Steamer;* **MV** *Motor Vessel;* **RMS** *Royal Mail Steamer* **CSPCo** *Caledonian Steam Packet Company*

THE LOSS OF SS WILSTON

23rd January 1939

The scene for this chapter is far removed from Scotland, West Africa or Australia, it being west Cornwall, that granite toe of England stuck out into the Atlantic. The sea girt county is one of the most popular holiday destinations in UK, but its coast is not just a place for surfing, sandcastles and seafood, it has a darker side. The late Clive Carter in his painstakingly researched *Cornish Shipwrecks Vol 2: The North Coast* [p11] sets the scene: "*The northern shore of Cornwall is one of the wildest, bleakest and most dangerous of coastlines, where the Atlantic roars among jagged rocks and breaks in line upon line of white surf on to the long sea strands. Even today the awe-inspiring cliffs and desolate moors tell of their savage past ...*". On the lack of safe havens from the frequent ferocious Atlantic gales, he continues [p12]: "*Shelter from these appalling storms was virtually non-existent; there was no harbour of refuge comparable to Falmouth until a ship reached Bideford Bay or the Bristol Channel. St, Ives, Hayle, Portreath and Newquay were all dangerous to enter during an onshore gale, and Padstow and Bude Haven suicidal.*" In other words, about 100 miles of often storm-wracked shore with no shelter for any save the smallest vessel.

We last met the Wilston carrying a cargo of iron ore and a super-cargo of Yules and zoo-bound omnivorous animals from Freetown to Glasgow in May 1935 when Dad stood on her bridge [in fine weather!] and made the accompanying sketch.

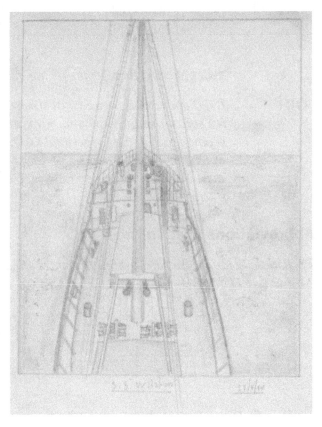

We learn that Wilston was a Clyde-built steamship, launched in 1916, of 3,218 grt., 335 ft long, 48 ft in beam and 22 ft in draught [102.1 x 14.6 x 6.8 m], with a single screw driven by triple-expansion engines which her builders hoped would propel her at 10 knots. After getting her name in the papers in 1935, we assume she went about her lawful occasions as a tramping steamer, carrying iron ore and coal until she hit the headlines in the saddest way in January 1939.

On the evening of Saturday 21ˢᵗ January 1939, SS *Wilston* set sail from Newport, South Wales, carrying a cargo of coal bound for La Goulette, [Ḥalq el-Wād,] the port for Tunis, in North Africa. We shall never know exactly what happened on board but the following day, steaming westwards with the aim of rounding the tip of Cornwall and proceeding into the Atlantic she encountered some of the worst weather those seas could throw at her. Both Dad and his brother Alex remembered the *Wilston* being rather sluggish in heavy seas with her cargo of Marampa iron ore. They both recalled seeing her "shipping it green" - an old nautical expression for taking a lot of seawater on board - and both told of being on the bridge and seeing Wilston duck her forecastle into an oncoming wave and ever so slowly rise out of it.

According press reports, she was last sighted on the afternoon of 22ⁿᵈ January some twenty miles NNW of Longships Lighthouse - about a mile off Land's End -by SS *Corbrook* from the Tyne who exchanged Morse code signals by lamp with her when no distress was apparent. *Corbrook* was a smaller ship on a similar course to *Wilston*'s and had decided to run for port. One can only speculate about what happened to *Wilston* thereafter, a comparatively small ship with a bulk cargo in her holds, facing winds from WNW of Force 10 with higher gusts - more than 60 mph [100kph] - generating waves over 40 feet [12m] high. It may have been that her Master, Captain Stewart of Dundee, decided he too could make no headway against a gale of this ferocity and resolved to head back to port. That would have involved turning the ship about, a highly risky operation in those seas and much could have happened. We know from Press reports, written in the days when her fate was still uncertain, that she had earlier sprung a leak on passage between Glasgow and Newport and had spent Christmas in dry dock in Newport, so this elderly vessel may have suffered that way again. In weather like that night's, she could have lost her propeller or rudder or both, "taken it green" once too often and flooded below deck in her boiler room and/or engine room and thus lost power, or her cargo could have shifted making it impossible to steer her. One or any combination of those would have rendered *Wilston* helpless in the face of the gale which then drove her onto the inhospitable coast where neither ship nor sailor stood any chance.

Carter paints the picture as seen from the cliffs near Gurnard's Head, a prominent headland near the village of Zennor, on the Monday morning:
"*The Wilston's cylinder head lay awash just beside an upended boiler, and from these and from the angle of her shaft tunnel it was clear she had broken her back on the offshore rocks and been driven broadside by heavy seas. Everything abaft the bridge was beaten into a great carpet of flattened plating and girders beneath the swirling water. Close in, several white-painted ribs jutted from the sea, with a great shard of jagged steel the largest intact piece of the hull.*"

That description was borne out by the picture below taken by the celebrated Richards Brothers of Penzance who had, of course, gained some expertise in the photography of wrecks. There being no survivors, it was a few days before it could be confirmed that the heap of scrap below the cliffs was all that remained of *Wilston,* but the owners' ship surveyor was reported in the Press on 30th January as stating: *"... everyone is satisfied that the ship which is found in Wicca Cove is the Wilston. She carried a crew of 32."*

All that remained of *Wilston* Jan 1939 From Carter p62 Photo Richards Bros.

Dad's view of Wicca Cove from offshore 1959

If an example were needed ...

Clyde-built, Glasgow registered, with a Scot as Master and several crew from Scotland, *Wilston* to Dad was a Scottish ship and he felt closer to her than any of the ocean -going vessels mentioned in this book, so he took her loss almost personally. Accordingly, one may fancy there was an ulterior motive in his choice of St. Ives, Cornwall, for family holidays for he knew that it was near there that *Wilston* had met her end and he sought what we now would call "closure". Without the fingertip research facility provided today by the internet, his method was to talk to the locals who pointed him in the direction of Gurnard's Head.

If Dad wanted to point out to his family the dangers of the north Cornish coast, he could hardly have had a better example than was presented on a trip during the family holiday in August 1954. On arrival on the cliff tops near the headland, the family were presented with the sight of a recently wrecked ship, the small German coaster *Traute Sarnow.* This ship, named after the daughter of the Captain and Owner and which was also carrying a coal cargo, had run aground in fog but, in sharp contradistinction to *Wilston*, Gustav Sarnow and his crew had all been rescued by breeches-buoy – a kind of zip-wire system. A few days after the youthful author had taken a snap of the wreck [See opposite], a gale blew up and she ended up in the same sorry state as *Wilston.*

Dad's "closure" came on a later holiday when, on a tourist trip out of St. Ives on a fishing boat, he managed to take a snap of the coast [See above] some twenty years after his favourite freighter had met her tragic end. Would it have been just salt spray misting his eyes as he remembered the day long ago when a delinquent duiker had taken a fancy to the Mate's socks?

In the meantime, the Yules had learnt about another tragedy on the January night in 1939.

For those in peril
In the early hours of 23rd January 1939, the coastguard at St. Just, about ten miles westward along the Penwith coast from St. Ives, reported a steamer struggling in heavy seas about two miles north of Cape Cornwall. We do not know for certain that this was *SS Wilston* for other ships were in difficulty that night and survived but the alarm was sent to the local lifeboat stations. The nearest lifeboat was that at Sennen Cove but launching was impossible because of the high seas and low tide. At St. Ives, in the lee of "The Island" or St. Ives Head, at team of volunteers manhandled the cradle carrying their lifeboat out across the dry sands of the harbour and launched her into the appalling gale. In the previous year, St Ives had lost their lifeboat and the *John and Sarah Eliza Stych* was a replacement sent from Padstow. At roughly thirty feet in length, the motor powered and self-righting boat with a cowl fore and aft, looked very much like those models that today's RNLI have as collecting boxes. What happened to her and her crew is graphically described by Nicholas Leach in *Cornwall's Lifeboat Heritage* [2006 edition p32]:

"Encountering very heavy seas once out of the shelter of St. Ives Head, she was capsized and four of the eight men on board were lost, including the coxswain Thomas Cocking. Although the boat righted herself, the engine could not be restarted and so she drifted helplessly before the storm with no power. Fruitless attempts were made to restart the engine, but when another sea hit her, she again capsized. This time the motor mechanic was lost, leaving only three survivors on board the disabled lifeboat which drifted towards Godrevy out of control. As she approached the rocks another sea hit her and for a third time she was capsized. After righting again, only one man, William Freeman, remained on her. He had only survived by forcing himself under the canopy above the engine controls.

When the lifeboat was thrown ashore by the seas at Godrevy, Freeman crawled out and reached a local farm from where the news of the disaster was sent to St. Ives."

In the remarkable tradition of British Emergency Services whose personnel "run towards danger", so perished Thomas Cocking (Coxswain); Matthew S Barber; William B Barber; John Thomas; Richard Q Stevens; John B Cocking; Edgar Bassett.

Reader – when you are next enjoying a sunny seaside day in a British coastal town – spare some change for the lifeboat.

APPENDIX TWO -THE IRON ROAD

More about Railways mentioned in this book

Merely thumbnail sketches of a subjective content of five railways arranged roughly in order of their appearance in this book. For more detail, the reader is referred to the publications and websites in the "Sources and Further Reading" section.

CAMPBELTOWN & MACRIHANISH LIGHT RAILWAY 1906-1934

A wee train. "Argyll": A rather continental-looking 0-6-2T built by Andrew Barclay & Co in the year of Dad's birth running through the streets of Campbeltown with a single passenger coach. [*Photo reproduced via Wikipedia Commons.*]

"A long name for a small railway" but one of importance to our Diarists. Running across the southern end of the Kintyre peninsula, it was constructed in 1906 to the unusual gauge of 2ft 3in [686 mm] with a length of 4.5 miles [7.24 km], following the route of a colliery tramway. When "Dad was a lad", it was a thriving concern carrying coal from the small Macrihanish coalfield to what was then a Campbeltown bustling with fisheries, distilleries and shipyards. In its lifetime it was Scotland's only passenger-carrying narrow-gauge line and the remotest railway on the island of Great Britain, the nearest mainline connection being in Ireland! The locals were rather proud of their line. In *Eleven Minutes Late*, Matthew Engel reprints an anonymous verse from the local paper:

A railway a' oor ain, nae less,
A railway a' oor ain;
Gin ye've yer doots, jist come an' see't;
This railway o' oor ain.

And "come an' see't" people certainly did, as the passenger carrying activity was a smart addition by the owners who spotted an opportunity when the fast turbine steamers began their service and a day trip from Glasgow became possible. The tourists were thus offered the chance to take a "trip to the Atlantic" on a line which operated rather as tramway with stops rather than stations as the illustration above shows.

Sadly, by the time Mum had begun her Diary, the summer tourist trade had dwindled significantly, and the principal colliery had closed. Facing competition from motorised transport, it abandoned passenger services in May 1932 and the last trains seem to have run in May 1934 though that event seems to have been missed by Dad -outward bound again – as he was still expecting to see the wee train on a family visit in the 1950's.

CALEDONIAN RAILWAY 1847 -1923

Dad's favourite. The named engine of the 1906 "Cardean" class of 4-6-0.
[From *Boys Book of Locomotives* Howden J R (1907) scanned by A Dingley and reproduced here via Wikipedia Commons. UK Public Domain.]

The casual observer could be forgiven for thinking that this Glasgow- based company was Scotland's national railway such were its airs and graces though it was just one amongst others. But it *was* a sizeable and profitable concern: Glenn and Glenn in *Caledonian Cavalcade* (p6) tell us that: *At its zenith in 1910, the Caledonian Railway embraced almost 1,100 miles of track, and had 50 terminal stations. It carried 34 million passengers annually, hauled 23 million tons of minerals and 5 million tons of merchandise. It owned 65,000 vehicles and 927 locomotives.* [Not to mention its subsidiary the Caledonian Steam Packet Company which owned the Clyde steamers] The "Caley" as it was universally known, appears here because, as noted in Volume 1, its Glasgow Central to Carlisle brilliantly engineered main line passed through Dad's birthplace, Uddingston, and the Yule residence of 5 Kyle Park backed on to this key railway artery. What a joy for a young lad to watch the Saltire Blue liveried engines with the chocolate and white coaches racing through the village and it was a spectacle that remained with Dad forever.

Dad fully bought in to the Caley's publicity hype and would repeatedly speak of "the Cardean" referring in fact to the five [reduced to four after 1915] class 903 4-6-0 passenger express locomotives introduced in 1906 and thus his contemporaries. **O.S. Nock's** *Pocket Encyclopedia of British Locomotives,* explaining [p 152] that that the class took its name from the lead engine which was named after the country residence of the Deputy Chairman of the Board, waxes lyrical: *"It is doubtful if any single locomotive built in the first decade of the twentieth century achieved, at the time, a fame greater than that enjoyed by the first of this small class of 5 locomotives",* and again: *"Simply and massively built, they were in every way an epitome of the neat graceful British locomotives of the pre-1914 era."* So perhaps we can excuse Dad's enthusiasm.

Such was the pulling power of the Cardeans, that on hearing the distinctive whistle afar off the Uddingston children would rush to the railway to watch the express rush past. Of that whistle, at the bottom of p26 of "Scottish Railway History in Pictures"[Thomas 1971] [referring to the picture of Cardean at Polmadie he wrote: "*This engine had a very loud two-tone whistle - latterly reduced to one note. Could be heard a long way off from Uddingston."* By "long way off" he meant at Cambuslang and as to the very unusual two-tone sound, the experts at the Caledonian Railway Association suggest that drivers may indeed have found a way to produce a signature note.

Dads' elder brothers – after the way of all such – did not exactly share his starry- eyed enthusiasm for the Cardean and all things Caley. They pointed out the 1909 incident when a crank axle failed at speed with the result that a Cardean class engine became severed from its tender and train – an occasion on which The Caley avoided disaster by a hair's breadth.

The Caley was subsumed into the LMS [see below] in 1923 and the Cardeans were soon overtaken by the more modern Royal Scot 4-6-0's with their larger grate area and higher boiler pressure *[The author's calculations give a Tractive Effort per ton weight for the Cardeans as 288 and for Royal Scots: 390].* All had gone by the time Dad was headed for Australia.

The name "Caledonian Railway" survives today as a preserved line in the north east of Scotland and is hidden in the shipping brand "CalMac" [Caledonian MacBrayne – coupling the names of two major players in Clyde shipping] but as Glenn and Glenn [op.cit.] remark: "*Although the Caledonian's name was submerged in the London Midland & Scottish Railway [See below] its identity can still be recognised – in its stations, bridges, signal boxes, steamer piers, and in its finely engineered lines."* Traveller, if you seek its monument, look around you at Glasgow Central Station.

KILSYTH AND BONNYBRIDGE RAILWAY 1888-1964

A J38 0-6-0, no. 65916, shunting the 7.30 p.m. freight from Cadder Yard at Banknock, 22 May 1961.

Last days of the line. A pick-up goods working at Banknock Station in May 1961. The wagons on the main line may have contained bricks from Cannerton whose well-known chimney appears in the background. Such loose wagons may have spent as little as a sixth of their time actually carrying something! [Scan of photo from the W A C Smith Collection courtesy of Kezlan Images]

Whilst the Caledonian's construction was part of the major rail arteries of the country dating from the 1840's, the single- track line through Banknock [which served as a midway passing point] connecting the eponymous industrial towns was a late comer of the 1880's – almost an afterthought. Despite this being a minor line, the railway which served the collieries played its part in the development of Banknock [including affecting the name – see Volume 2] and until the advent of the motor bus service in the 1920's was the principal means of public transport for the Browns.

This largely forgotten railway was inspired by the ubiquitous Baird's who needed a rail connection for coal and iron ore and finished products running eastward from their increasingly extensive operation around Kilsyth. Unusually, it was a joint enterprise between the rival companies, the Caledonian and its Edinburgh -based rival the North British Railway with both companies running passenger services – the Caledonian from Bonnybridge Central and the North British through to Glasgow Queen Street.

We have noted Dad's almost obsessive interest in the Caledonian Railway and how he and his pals bought into that railway's rather over-hyped "Cardean" class of locomotives. No such mainline glamour attached itself to the wee line through Banknock, but one named loco must have caught the Browns' attention as a long- lasting wooden toy engine was named "*Dominie Sampson*" after one of the North British Railway's "Scott" class *[Note for "gricers": NBR J Class, LNER D29 & D30 BR Power Class 3P]* which must have found its way along this backwater. Ironically enough, the numerous 4-4-0 Scotts [a useful widespread class] were to long outlast the handful of Cardeans and in the author's memory were still working the line in the 1950's long after the much- vaunted Caledonian stars had gone to the scrapyard.

Railways, as exemplified by the Caledonian Railway with its huge coal-carrying capacity, make money from freight not passengers. As with the Campbeltown & Macrihanish, the advent of the motor bus took the passenger trade from the Kilsyth & Bonnybridge, which had become part of the LNER Grouping in 1923, and the passenger service ceased in the year before Mum began her diary. The Bonnybridge connection also went and the line was truncated at Dennyloanhead where the road bridge was removed. Goods services served the Cannerton brickworks for many years, loading by tippling loose bricks directly down a simple lineside staithe and the train moving truck by truck along the line. With British Railways still having "common carrier" status the route was obliged to carry parcels traffic and that too lingered on, keeping Banknock Station open, and the author remembers loco and brake van venturing eastwards to the vestigial remains of Dennyloanhead Station to deliver a parcel. Other memories are of the quality of the lineside wild raspberries and of a never-to-be-forgotten illicit footplate ride to Kilsyth. The line saw its last train in 1964 and, at the time of writing, no part of its route is in use as a railway.

A wee steam story

An interest in steam locomotives was not, in the Diary days, thought to be a suitable concern for a lassie so Mum would always defer to Dad on that subject. Mum often recalled that, on a stay-over visit to "Aunty Mary in Govan", she was awakened one night by the sound of a steam train. She would tell how she looked out of the window of the tenement flat to see a small goods train proceeding through the neighbouring shipyard gates out on to the streets along the lines of the Glasgow Corporation trams. That story would be greeted with remarks from the Yules of the order: "*Ye must hae been dreaming! Trains cannae run on tramlines!*" Generally speaking, the Yules would have been correct but, many years later, as Dad began to accumulate books and pamphlets on rail topics, he found that indeed the Glasgow tramways were built to a gauge which **DID** allow standard gauge trains to traverse their lines. Dad graciously conceded that it had been no dream!

LONDON MIDLAND & SCOTTISH RAILWAY 1923-1948

After the Cardean. A more successful version of the 4-6-0 express passenger class of locomotives was the popular LMS Royal Scot Class. This is 46137 "The Prince of Wales's Volunteers (South Lancashire)"in British Railways days at full tilt near Mangotsfield, Bristol in 1959. [*Photo by Bob & Anne Powell reproduced via Wikipedia Creative Commons*]

Although Dad mentions this railway company but once [1 II 30], the LMS, as it was commonly known, it plays quite a part in both Diaries. Formed 1 January 1923 under the Railways Act of 1921, which required the grouping of over 120 separate railways into four largely geographical monopolies, its importance here is that it incorporated the Caledonian Railway and the London and North Western Railway. [When the LMS became British Railways on nationalisation in 1948, they reverted to separate operating Regions.] Thus, it was the line that took an enthusiastic Dad to London Euston [and on a curious loop round to Tilbury] on the first leg of his outward trip to Australia in 1930 and brought him back to Scotland, penurious and disillusioned a year later. It was the line that took him to Liverpool and the successful tours to Sierra Leone and was his route home via Euston as a sickly passenger when that last trip had proved "one tour too far".

Thus, he knew well what we now call the "West Coast Main Line" with its difficult summits of Shap [915 ft. a.s.l.] and Beattock [1,015 ft. a.s.l.], travelled at a time that O. S. Nock has called "The Zenith of Steam" and on the line which W. H. Auden immortalised in his rhythmical poem *Night Mail.*

An unwieldy entity, with numerous interests other than railway operation, the LMS was – in its time - the world's largest transport organisation, operating 6,870 miles [11,056 km] of track. It was also the largest commercial enterprise in the British Empire and the United Kingdom's second largest employer, after the Post Office. Innovative, in that it electrified both main and suburban lines and introduced all-steel carriages, it is perhaps best remembered for its steam locomotive types: Royal Scots, Jubilees, Black Fives, Duchess Pacifics; several examples of which have been preserved and at the time of writing, are still in steam in UK.   However, the loco type which caught Dad's eye was none of those stars but a lumbering heavy- duty goods loco of a type he had seen before. Working, in the 1940's in the Yorkshire- Nottinghamshire Coalfield, he was reminded of Sierra Leone when he spotted one of the LMS 2-6-0+0-6-2 Beyer Garratts which worked the route from the Toton coal marshalling yards to the London coal trade distribution point at what is now Brent Cross. He and Mum shared a nostalgic moment when he told her about it!

Dad's sense of humour may not be apparent from the preceding pages, but it can be illustrated in a story which involves the LMS Main Line. The LMS followed the practice of attaching roof boards – "Destination Boards" -to the sides of carriages above the windows on its express trains. These boards, laboriously fitted at terminal stations, listed the "station stops" and were a great help to intending passengers before the widespread adoption of efficient station public address systems. According to Andrew Martin in *Belles & Whistles,* [op. cit.] they were about five feet long and five inches high [152 cm x 12cm] and so readable from the platform but never from afar off.
 In the late 1940's, Dad was doing some surveying at a site just north of Warrington within sight of the West Coast Main Line. The petrol restrictions of the time meant the family had often been forced to take the train "home" to Scotland and knew the best train of the day was the regular 10.08 from Warrington Bank Quay. That morning, about 10.15, he looked up from his work and saw in the distance an express train speeding north with little detail visible to the unaided human eye but, looking at his watch, Dad knew could only be one service.
"*Och*", he said. "*There's the Glasgow train!*"
"*How do you know that, Bob?*" said his English workmates.
"*I read the destination boards*" was Dad's entirely untruthful reply to his astonished colleagues who ever afterwards were to tell of Bob Yule's amazing eyesight!

PEPEL TO MARAMPA – THE "IRON ORE RAILWAY" 1933 -1975

Monster. A 2-8-2 + 2-8-2 Beyer Garratt of the type used on the Pepel to Marampa line. The size of the firebox is apparent in this view. [*Photo scanned from a Beyer Peacock Ltd publication in possession of the Friends of the Sierra Leone National Railway Museum*]

We have already met **DELCO**, the consortium formed to develop the iron ore reserves at Marampa [see Coda - an Introduction & a Commentary] and have seen in the Commentaries and Diary entries that this 52-mile [84km] long, single-purpose 3ft-6in [1066mm] gauge railway played a major part - if rather behind the scenes - in Mum & Dad's life in West Africa. [Actually it is something of minnow in terms of later such railways in Africa and Australia which join an "iron ore mountain" to the coast.]

Building and operating such routes was nothing new to the British who had well-documented transferrable expertise in such constructions across their Empire. On the surveying of the route for such lines, Dad's reference work, Whitelaw's *Surveying* [1929 edition P395 Chap XI], summarising a previous publication, advises:

 "... the native route between any two given points in country covered with dense forest is generally the best and most direct that the local features of the country will permit of."

Further on P401, he gives this practical suggestion for a surveying party:

"Fifty or sixty natives may easily be employed in cutting, carrying, shifting camp, making huts, &c., and it is better to have even a greater force of natives if possible, as the whole of the work would be delayed for want of a sufficient number of men."

However, on pages 408 &9 he adds a warning:

 "No engineer should go abroad to take up survey work in unmapped country, jungle or dense forest, without having a pocket compass in case of accident."

This last advice might not be so valuable in an area such as Marampa, for writing about compass work earlier [p105] he noted:

 Deposits of iron or other magnetic ore in the ground attract the needle, so that in such districts compass work is out of the question.

The DELCO booklet of 1953 mentioned earlier tells us that:
"Construction occupied most of three years. The first headquarters were at Sahr Marank (the Elephant Rock) on the Port Loko Creek four miles below Port Loko. It was the best place to bridge the Creek and was about half way between Marampa and Pepel, so that, from Sahr Marank the railway construction could work both towards Marampa and Pepel. Simultaneously with the construction of the railway, work proceeded on the bunkers, pier and loading installation at Pepel and the laying out of the Mines including housing for Africans and Europeans."
[Given Dad's skill set, it seems a good guess that he was involved with those last tasks listed rather than with the railway engineering for which he had no recognised training.]

Purely a single- track freight line with five passing places and laid with heavy-duty rail, which could stand high axle loads, there were no severe gradients or tight curves and DELCO sought for the most economic means of propelling trains carrying of up to 1,000 tons of processed ore.
Their solution was one which had been widely adopted world-wide: to use the articulated steam locomotives built by Beyer Peacock Ltd. of Manchester, England. This design had been patented in 1907 by an English engineer employed in Australia, Herbert William Garratt [1864-1919] and the locos became known as Beyer Garratts or Garratts – the name by which our Diarists recalled them. The design used on the DELCO line comprised a boiler, cab and firebox slung between two power units each with the power of a 2-8-2 engine, with a 4,600- gallon capacity water tank at one end and a tender holding 9 tons of coal at the other. Weighing 151 tons and with a total wheel base length of 70 feet, these were indeed monsters and eventually the line used four of them and seems to have been unique in using Garratts as the sole motive power as this was never a public, passenger-carrying railway. Running equally well in either direction, they were built for power not speed, usually averaging a standard for their class of about 20 mph and thus traversing the line in about 2.5 hours – though "Up" trains to Marampa would have to yield to the loaded "Down" traffic as must have been the case when Mum recorded 4.75 hours on 21 XII 36.

Taking four or five loads to Pepel each day, these locos served the line well until the 1950's when they were superseded by diesels which formed the motive power until the DELCO operations collapsed in the 1970's and the mines ceased production in the 1980's. The railway along with the mines complex suffered severe depredations in the civil wars of the 1990's but DELCO -as shown by documents in the Glasgow University archive – had been aware of even larger deposits of ore the east round Tonkilili as early as 1932. These have been developed and at the time of writing, the route of Mum and Dad's Pepel to Marampa Railway is in use as part of a modern freight carrying line and seems destined to be so for some time to come.

APPENDIX THREE

Mines & Mining Home and Away

Part 1 Home

Dad was not a coalface worker (though his grandfathers may have been) but the above shows a typical scene with an Anderson Boyes chain coal cutter of a type introduced in 1906. In Dad's time about 50% of Scottish coal was cut by machine.
[Courtesy of the National Mining Museum Scotland Trust]

Beginners – Start Here!

This is a book built around the Diaries of a young Scot who trained and worked as a Mining Engineer in Scotland and Sierra Leone and his wife, from a Mining Community, who was the granddaughter of a Colliery Manager. Thus, there is a lot about Mines & Mining in the foregoing and this section starts with some basics for the benefit of those readers unfamiliar with that Industry – greatly changed from the time of our Diarists. Students of the Industry may skip this bit and find some rarer information further on.

King Coal

From today's perspective where the power for heating, lighting, cooking or running machinery can come at the touch of a switch it is difficult to appreciate the importance of coal at the time when our Diarists were born. At that time, the many varieties of coal provided: heat for homes via open fires; a safe means of cooking via "kitchen ranges" or stoves such as the Raeburn at Hollandbush; lighting for urban streets, factories, shops, offices and homes via its derivative – coal gas; fuel for the iron and steel industry either directly via "splint coal" or through conversion to coke; and, of course, the heat which turned the water to steam which pushed the piston or turned the turbine which powered the stationary or locomotive engine. Thus, the production and distribution of what seemed to be an endless resource was a mainstay of the industrial society of the late 19th and early 20th centuries and thereby, directly or indirectly, the Yules, Scotts and Browns made their living. However, this versatile product of our planet's geological evolution was extracted from the strata at great cost in treasure and human life -in 1913 440 miners were killed in one accident alone: the Senghenydd Disaster in South Wales. Whilst the need to transport it had spawned the transport infrastructure of canals and railways, the products of its combustion polluted the atmosphere in towns and cities and begrimed every building. Unburnt flecks of carbon flew out of every smokestack, chimney and funnel and were the housewife's despair and not just a plot device in the classic film: *Brief Encounter.*

Now we can talk about its extraction.

An Extractive Industry

To begin at the beginning, my copy of the *Shorter Oxford English Dictionary* [1983 OUP] has this definition:

Mine. *An excavation made in the earth for the purpose of digging out metallic ores, or coal, salt, precious stones etc. Also, the place yielding these.*

Dad worked with the first two of the above- named targets for digging so we should look at the types of excavation with which he was involved as a "Mining Engineer". That is defined by *The Wordsworth Dictionary of Science & Technology* (Wordsworth Editions 1995) as: *That branch of engineering chiefly concerned with the sinking and equipment of mineshafts and workings and all operations incidental to the winning and preparation of minerals;* a broad description covering Dad's surveying tasks above and below ground and his Father's concerning "Coal Washers" on the surface.

The following is the author's collation from various sources and is intended as illustrative rather than definitive.

Coal. Coal is a combustible black or brownish-black firm but brittle sedimentary rock occurring in strata called coal seams. These seams can vary in height from a few inches to several feet, often dip steeply and form part of strata subject to many Geological faults [as in Stirlingshire]. Thus, driving tunnels to extract coal from the seams is a complex engineering operation. Derived from vegetable debris which has been altered by pressure, temperature and chemical process, coal is mostly carbon with variable amounts of other elements; chiefly hydrogen, sulphur, oxygen, and nitrogen. Thus, there are many varieties with widely differing calorific and chemical properties. Also, the constituent elements have combined in various ways to produce explosive or poisonous gases which provide a hazard during mining.

Fireclay. Clay consisting of minerals predominantly [silicon & aluminium oxides] which soften only at high temperatures are used widely as refractories in metallurgical and other furnaces. Fireclays occur abundantly in the Carboniferous System as "seat earths" underneath the coal seams so, in Lanarkshire and Stirlingshire, a pit would often produce both and Bonnybridge emerged as a centre for fireclay products such as domestic fireplaces.

Refractories. Materials used in lining furnaces etc. They must resist high temperatures, changes of temperature, the action of molten metals and slags and hot gases carrying solid particles.

Colliery. [*Obsolescent term found on maps*] An industrial site containing a coal mine or mines together with the plant for processing the won coal for transport or coal products such as coke, gas or tar.

Viewpark Colliery at Uddingston was opened in the 1890's and was a modern colliery in its time. The above picture from North Lanarkshire Libraries shows the two shafts as required by statute but also aiding ventilation. The coal wagons, being shunted by the "pug", bear the name of the mine owners: Robert Addie and Sons. The mine closed in the 1940's and the site is now covered by the motorway. [Courtesy of North Lanarkshire Heritage Centre]

Quarry. An open working or pit for granite, building stone, slate or other rock. The distinction between quarry and mine remains blurred in law but usage implies surface workings.

Pit. A place whence minerals are dug. The shaft of a mine. The pit head is the surface landing place. Apparatus for raising and lowering cages, trucks etc. is "pithead gear" and forms a distinctive feature of a coalfield. In common speech, "pit" meant any mine or colliery.

Opencast. (Mine) A coal or mineral deposit worked from the surface and open to daylight as in the Marampa Iron Ore site or as in the picture below from February 1944 of the visit of HM King & Queen to the opencast working at Wentworth in Yorkshire. Dad in donkey jacket and scarf is just visible to the left of the buffer beam of the locomotive. [Photo credit *Daily Sketch* circulated to staff by Sir Lindsay Parkinson & Co. and scanned from Family Collection]

Dook. In a Mining context, this word was unfamiliar to me, so I am once more indebted to David Bell and his volunteers at the National Mining Museum [q.v.] for the following guidance: "A mine or roadway driven to the dip (the dip was a layer of coal strata), usually the main road going to the dip." *Glossary of Scots Mining Terms, compiled by James Barrowman 1886* or "An underground roadway driven downhill, usually following the inclination of the strata" *British Standards Institution Glossary of Mining Terms, section 8: Winning & Working 1967.* In his email, David added: *"... one of our ex-miner volunteers told me that a dook in his day was any sloping tunnel."* This would make sense in the context of the extract below.

Adit. An access tunnel (usually nearly horizontal) leading to a main tunnel and frequently used (in lieu of a shaft) in the excavation of the latter or for exploration or drainage.

Coal Washer: This was the term used by Dad for the Coal Preparation Plants which were the area of specialisation of his father. The "coal washer" is where coal straight from the face may be crushed, washed free of impurities, screened or sorted or otherwise made ready for transport and/or sale. Maintenance of such plant is key to the smooth running of a mine, so John Crawford Yule's Mechanical Engineering skills would be of value

Splint coal: A hard bituminous coal with a dull lustre which burns with an intense heat – thus too hot for regular domestic use – and, as it does not cake or break up in a furnace., very useful to the iron and steel industry especially as its use eliminates the cost of coking.

Drift. A heading driven obliquely through a coal seam. A heading in a coalmine for exploration or ventilation. An inclined haulage road to the surface. Hence: a "Drift Mine" where access to the deposits is from the surface and no shaft is needed.

Brickette: From the French briquette: any small block of coal dust or any other combustible material which can be used as fuel. A useful way for a colliery to turn waste material into a product and a cheap variety of fuel.

Bing: Scots word meaning any heap but used especially for the large mounds of waste material from coal mines which are a distinctive feature of a coalfield [and the battlefield of Loos] and elsewhere might be [accurately] called a spoil heap or spoil tip.

Bings can be good for you

Waste material is not necessarily useless material. We have seen how the contents of the Banknock Colliery bing formed the basis for the successful Cannerton Brickworks but long before that, was a classic example of how discarded material should never be overlooked. In 1801, the Scots engineer and metallurgist David Mushet [1772 -1847] discovered that Black-band Ironstone, then tipped to one side as a useless form of coal, could be used economically to produce iron. This discovery, together with the ground-breaking discovery in the 1820s by James Beaumont Neilson [1792 -1865] that blast furnaces worked better using hearted air -he patented the Hot Blast Process in 1828- led to the remarkable expansion of the Scottish iron industry which was the basis of the country's 19th century prosperity.

Mining at Banknock

Whilst, as we have seen, Dad's home "village" of Uddingston was in the heart of the Lanarkshire "Coal and Steel" belt, Banknock and its adjacent industrial hamlets stood right on the northern tip of what was administratively the Stirlingshire Coalfield. Geologically speaking, it is a northern outlier of the of the Lanarkshire Coalfield formed by the downthrow of workable seams by two parallel E-W faults between Dennyloanhead and Coneypark. History records coal being mined in the westernmost of that string of hamlets, Coneypark, as early as the 17th century but it was the coming of the Forth & Clyde Canal in 1790 that boosted the economy and thereby demand for coal, and the emergent mines became linked to that waterway by wagonways. The course of one of these ran past the western boundary of the Browns' premises and by the time of Mum's Diary had become an unpaved track for motor access to the industrial premises across the railway. That site has relevance to this volume, as it originally was the Livingstone and Cannerton pits, sited to the north of Hollandbush and owned [along with Broomrigg and Knowehead at Dennyloanhead] by the Banknock Coal Company, of which Mum's maternal grandfather, William Brown, was manager. An oddity of the commerce was that coal from Bantón to the west of Banknock was conveyed eastwards along the canal passing the coal from Banknock which was going westwards!

Whilst Banknock – or what is probably now called Dennyloanhead – is mentioned by Guthrie Hutton [op.cit.] as a mining location right at the start of Scotland's Industrial Revolution, there never developed a size of colliery complex like Viewpark by Uddingston [see above] nor the Stirlingshire sites in nearby Kilsyth or Bannockburn. Nevertheless, the records show that in 1921, the pits employed over 400 underground workers and over 90 surface workers, so that these two pits alone were major local employers. Despite the Coneypark- Dennyloanhead axis never developing those huge colliery complexes, the variety and quality of the coal [especially the Splint Coal] won from the seams was such to keep coalmining profitable there into the 1930's, with some privately- owned pits still operating into the 1950's.

Banknock Rows

The picture below is not Banknock but is typical of Miners' Rows in Stirlingshire.
[Courtesy of the National Mining Museum Scotland Trust] See Illustrations 4

For an illustration of the accommodation provided by the Banknock Coal Company for its workers, we can turn to the Scottish Mining Website [q.v.] where we can find a copy of the Evidence given by Mr James Doherty and Mr John Barr of the Stirlingshire Miners' Union to the Royal Commission on Housing 1918. I was reminded of this quotation by the volunteers at the Scottish National Mining Museum *[anyone interested in the history of Mining in Scotland should really pay a visit to their site at Newtongrange -take the Borders Line from Edinburgh Waverley].*

"*Owners, Banknock Coal Company. These houses are of brick and consist of two rows of room and kitchen houses.*

Owing to pressure by County Health Authority great improvements have been carried out here recently, as there has been an epidemic of fever in the village. They are fair-sized room and kitchen houses, with the usual two box-beds in kitchen. The water supply is from street wells. The rent is 3s. 3d. per week.

There are now splendid water-closets, and a daily removal of refuse by bucket system.

There are good washhouses, but not enough, being in proportion of one for eight tenants.

The streets are in a deplorable condition but are in process of being repaired.

The walls are solid brick without lathing, and in consequence in wet weather the houses are very damp inside. Some houses are badly in need of repair owing to broken walls. There is no pavement in front, except what is formed by engine ashes, which makes streets very soft in wet weather."

Compared with Merry's Rows [see Introduction to Volume One] there has been some improvement here. However, Coalmining remained a hazardous occupation.

A hazardous occupation

A glimpse of just a few press reports from the *Scotsman* daily newspaper covering the Banknock pits alone at the time when Mum and Dad were young will show the hazardous nature of coalmining

From 29 May 1911:

Miner Killed – On Saturday, a miner named Robert Waugh, employed at Broomrigg Pit, No. 3 Banknock Collieries, was killed by a fall of stone.

From 4 August 1919

Fatal Accident at Denny – James Beattie, a labourer employed at Banknock Pits, has died in Denny Cottage Hospital from being run down and crushed by a railway waggon. Beattie was 68 years of age, and resided in Street Vale, [ADY Streetville] *Banknock. He was the father of Eddy Beattie, the well-known boxer.*

From 9 September 1927

Entombed Miners – Both Rescued Alive – A Dreadful Ordeal – The prolonged efforts to reach -the two men James M'Alpine, miner, Glasgow Road, Dennyloanhead, and James Docherty, miner, Banknock Terrace, Longcroft – who had been entombed in Broomrigg No. 2 Pit, Dennyloanhead, Stirlingshire, since Tuesday evening, were successful yesterday morning, and the men were got out alive.

From the above, one can see why those closest to Dad would eventually have been pleased that his "career progression" meant he was no longer employed underground.

The same paper [22 December 1916] reported a Fatal Accident Enquiry – the Scots equivalent of an "Inquest" under English Law – held in December 1916 concerning an accident to a 32-year old miner:

The case concerned the death of James M'Intyre Steel, coal-cutting machineman, 33 Anderson Terrace, Longcroft, who was drowned by an inrush of water in the Livingstone Pit, Banknock. The evidence showed that the roads were being driven forward towards an old working when the machine cut into the dook [see above for definition] *and there was a burst of water, which overwhelmed Steel, and caused the other men to run for their lives. The accident, it was stated, was due to the plans being incorrect, the officials having calculated that there was still 50 feet of coal between the cutting machine and the old working. The roads being driven were 28 feel out of alignment for the old workings.*

Some ten years later, one can envisage Dad's tutors emphasising the importance of accurate surveying underground, stressing that error could cause someone to die. Taking that on board early in his working life may have contributed to Dad's meticulous attention to detail – sometimes seen as fussiness by his colleagues – which was a feature of all he did at work.

Serious Students – Start Here

By 1923, at the age of seventeen, having held jobs of the traditional errand boy/office boy type, Dad was deemed ready to start a career in Engineering. Accordingly, we see him enrolled in the Continuation Classes run at Glasgow High School in association with the Royal Technical College which required him, as with thousands of young men after him, to study at "Night School" and then sit examinations. We do not know who paid the fees for these courses but his Certificates, now in the possession of the National Mining Museum, show that in June 1924 he obtained the **First Group Certificate** with a Pass [a mark in the range 55% to 59%] in Mathematics Stage 1 and a very creditable Second [60%-79%] in Engineering Drawing Stage 1. The year after, he gained the Second Group Certificate which records that he received 174 hours' instruction out of a possible 177. This suggests 58 x 3- hour sessions or at least 2 nights per week, of which he appears to have missed 1. For that we might well say: *Well done*! His examination results showed a Passes in Mathematics Stage 2 and Experimental Science Stage 2 with a Second in Engineering Drawing Stage 2. A glance at the Mathematics syllabus shows a very high correspondence between the topics and the contents of his textbook: *Mathematics for Technical Students – Junior Course* which suggest that its author S.N. Forrest MA BSc may well have been his course lecturer.

Having succeeded at the Basic level, Dad moved into the specialist realm at Royal Technical College Glasgow [now Strathclyde University]. The serious student of Mining Education will find the originals of the preserved certificates in the library of the National Mining Museum and this is what they contain.

The syllabus is printed on the reverse of his Certificates all of which are headed:

The Royal Technical College Glasgow
Evening Classes, Session 1926-27
Certificate of Merit

Each of the 3 certificates carries this on the reverses:

Excerpt from [*the splendidly Scottish! ADY*] Regulations regarding examinations

1. In each class there shall be a special examination at the end of the session, in addition to one or more ordinary class examinations during the session. No student shall be awarded a certificate of merit who does not acquit *himself* (ADY italics!) satisfactorily in the final examination.

2. No student shall be admitted to the final examination unless *he* (ADY italics!) has made at least three-fourths of the possible attendances, except under very special circumstances considered and allowed by the Board of Studies in each case.

3. There shall be two classes of certificate of merit – first class, awarded to students who obtain not less than 80 per cent of the marks assigned for the whole of the work of the class, including examinations, home exercises, and laboratory and drawing work; second class awarded to those who obtain 60 to 80 per cent. A list

shall be issued of students who are considered able to proceed to a higher course in the subject in which they have been examined.

This was what Dad studied with his final result in brackets alongside:

GEOLOGY Course I [Second]

Dynamical Geology. – Atmospheric weathering agents. The action of wind, rain, and frost. Underground waters. The denuding, transporting, and depositing actions of rivers, lakes, glaciers, and the sea. Earthquakes and slow movements of the earth's crust. Volcanic phenomena. Stratification. Concretions. Joints. Dip and strike. Folding and faulting of strata. Unconformity. *Elementary Mineralogy and petrology.* - The common rock forming minerals; their composition and chief physical properties. The classification and description of the common igneous, sedimentary and metamorphic rocks.

Stratigraphical Geology. - The principles of stratigraphy. The nature and origin of fossils. The succession of strata as developed in Britain, with special reference to the economic products of the strata of Scotland.

Dad's textbook: *Geology For Beginners;* Watts [See Sources]

GEOLOGICAL DRAWING [Second]

Interpretation of ordnance maps of different scales; contours; drawing sections to scale. Accurate colouring and interpretation of geological maps; method of drawing sections across those maps to illustrate various structural features present amongst stratified rocks, e.g., stratification, folding, faulting and unconformity. Intrusive igneous rocks. Accurate plotting of outcrops from given data. Determination of dip, strike, and depth of beds from given data.

MINING ENGINEERING and MINE SURVEYING Course I [First Class]

Instruction was given in the methods of making surface surveys by the chain. Construction of the miner's dial and its use. Surveying by the loose needle and Vernier. Methods of booking and plotting surveys. Setting-off of road underground, and connection of underground and surface surveys. Textbook: *Problems in LAND AND MINE SURVEYING; Davies* [See Sources]

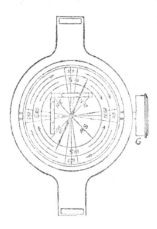

This sketch of a miner's dial [see syllabus immediately above] is reproduced from Davies (above) p237. The keen observer may think that East and West have become reversed from their compass positions but that is NOT the case for in this instrument the dial revolves about the needle and not as in a compass.

APPENDIX THREE *continued*

Mines & Mining Home and Away

Part 2 Away

Marampa – the Red Ore of Masaboin Hill.

Using the **DELCO** [unattributed] illustrations we can follow the path of the iron ore from mines to ship.

At the time of the Diaries [1930-37], the operations of **DELCO** at the Marampa site were

focussed on the winning of Haematite Red Ore which formed a cap of about 16 feet to the 600 ft high Masaboin Hill *[See various references in Vol 2]* The method of extracting the rock was to quarry the hillside so Dad was not working underground as in the Scottish coalmines but at an open- air site like the Yorkshire Opencast coalmines he was to encounter later though, unusually in a Mining operation, mineral had to be transported *down*. The Red Ore of Marampa was not massively bedded as, for instance, is the slate in North Wales so there was no blasting at a cliff needed to move rock. The DELCO illustrations, taken probably in 1935, show gangs of African labour loosening the ore bearing rock manually and loading trains of mine tubs. According to Mum's Talk, the African labour who worked on the hill: *"... received sixpence a day and 2 cups of rice."* Students of folk customs may be interested to note that she records: *"All the time they are working, they are singing in rhythm."*

Pictured above is the quarry face at No. 4 Haulage working the Red Ore cap on top of Masaboin Hill where Mum's Talk recorded: *"Monkeys swung from branch to branch"*.

The mine tubs in the illustration ran on a complex system which took them from the working level up on the hill down to the plain via several rope haulages – a "funicular railway" in effect. Pictured opposite is No. 6 haulage which shows the continuous rope system. The wire rope was probably driven by a steam engine at the lower level. Mum writes on 29 XI 1936 of travelling up one these haulages presumably by jumping on a truck such as shown here.

Down on the plain, there existed a complex system of tracks which seems, from the **DELCO** illustrations, to have been subject to many alterations as the mining of the cap of Masaboin Hill increased. Rope systems and small diesel locos propelled the trains of mine tubs through the washer and on to a loading bank where they were tipped into the bulk carrying waggons of the Iron Ore Railway which can be seen mid-left. The accompanying picture taken from the top of No. 6 Haulage gives an idea of the complexity already reached by the mid-thirties. [See also Illustrations Set 5]

The Red Ore train then travelled down the line to Pepel propelled by one of the Beyer Garratts [See Appendix Two] where it was bunkered to await shipping. [See opposite] As we have seen in previous illustrations, the ore trucks were not hoppers and so their cargo had to be tipped out. This involved a rather clunky operation but one which would be familiar to the engineers involved in its design as it was almost identical to the methods used for loading colliers at such ports as Goole in Yorkshire.

Tipping an ore truck at Pepel.

As we have seen, the Red Ore bade farewell to Africa at Pepel. A loading gantry stretched out to the deep- water channel and the ore travelled along another conveyor belt to be tipped into a freighter's hold as illustrated opposite. The name of the ship is not recorded.

Eventually the deposit of Red Ore was exhausted but there existed even more of the very fine-grained powder ore which required a great deal more processing before shipment. Thus, there grew up at Marampa a very large mining complex, - plant and accommodation and staff facilities - the size of which would have amazed Dad as a young surveyor in the bush in 1931. The channel at Pepel was deepened and the loading facility improved. The value of Sierra Leone's iron ore became even more obvious in the Second World War when UK lost access to the Swedish stock and in one wartime year, Marampa contributed over 1 million tons to the beleaguered home nation.

Coal and minerals are not mined for fun and there comes a time in the lifecycle of a mining project where the seams are exhausted, or the cost of extraction exceeds the income from sales. Sometime in 1970's, this happened to Marampa and mining ceased with the assets passing to government of a now-independent Sierra Leone. The site became a battle ground in the civil wars of the 1990's when much of the plant was destroyed. Some Red Ore mining was revived but the principal area of activity is now to the east round Tonkilili where the size of the deposits suggest that the tradition pioneered by DELCO and recorded by our Diarists will thrive for years to come.

APPENDIX FOUR

Kojonup – The Block *[See Volume 1]*

This was the comparison which enabled me to identify the parcel of land worked by Dad and Uncle Mailler. On the left, a transcription of Dad's Notes at the back of his Diary, on the right, a transcription of the press cutting from a year after they left, which was found and forwarded by Irene Doyle in Katanning. The name "David Mailer Yule" was the giveaway! Dad's description was pretty accurate, and it is good to see that clearing and the dam building were duly recorded.

From Dad's "*General Notes on Block*" *part* of the 12 pages of "Information General" at the back of the diary. Undated	*Sunday Times* - Perth WA - Sunday 27th March 1932 - page 9 The Selectors Guide - Tenders Returnable at Katanning - 2/4/1932 — 143/30
Position 12 miles South of Kojonup Area of block – roughly 1,600 acres. Boundary 7½ miles long. Block entirely in its virgin state i.e. all Bush country. Formation of land – undulating with granite outcrops, ironstone ridges and good (or bad) soil. One main creek with small tributaries all dry in summer. Our camp 12ft wide, 24ft long and 8ft high (lean-to roof) built of corrugated iron.	**Kojonup Location 7083** - being the whole of the Land comprised in Lease 11698/68 Standing in the name of **David Mailer Yule** Area 1693 Acres, 3 Roods Situated 9 miles south of Kojonup described as 650 acres - 1st class - good sandy to heavy loam 830 Acres - 2nd class - sandy and rubbly Balance - 3rd class 100 acres part cleared 1500 acres poison grubbed 2 dams of 1200cy 222 chains of finnier* fencing - half neighbours 132 chains of 6 wire fence Galvanised Iron Camp

*? "Finial" fencing i.e. fenceposts with a cap.

Notes on the Land Measures used above: [See also Appendix Five]
80 chains = 1 mile, so 354 chains of fencing is less than the 7 miles Dad recorded as boundary.
An acre is 4,840 sq. yards. A Rood is a quarter of an acre. A hectare is roughly 2.5 acres so 1,600 acres is about 640 Ha. About 40% of The Block was rated 1st class.

APPENDIX FIVE

Extras [or Sundries to Australian readers]

Alexander's buses

Both Diarists record catching the "Alexander's bus" and this company's blue buses were widely known all over Scotland from Glasgow to Inverness. Starting as Alexander's Motor Services in 1913, running between Falkirk and Bonnybridge, they expanded their service to cover Denny, then Kilsyth – which took them through Banknock – and ultimately to Glasgow. By the time of the Diaries, the firm had become W Alexander & Sons Ltd based in Camelon, Falkirk, with over 1,000 buses although by then, it had become part of the Scottish Motor Traction Company (SMT) group.

By no means an express service [as Mum noted on 6 XI 1936], the route of the Diaries was the Glasgow to Falkirk or Stirling via Kilsyth. From the bus stop opposite "Mr. Brown's shop" in Banknock, the blue bus – single or double decked – followed what is now the A803 through Kirkintilloch then coming into Glasgow via Bishopbriggs and Springburn, down the now-vanished Parliamentary Road to a terminus - now also subsumed into redevelopment – in Dundas Street, pictured above in a typical timeless scene from the 1960's. *[From an original photo by SJ Brown]*

Alexanders would also have played a part earlier in Mum's life, taking her to school in Kilsyth and supplying the open charabancs which took her with the family on group outings and with the Girls' Guildry to the excitement of the Annual Camp. The firm also expanded into the Coach Trip business, adopting the fondly remembered "Bluebird" brand in 1934 and running popular day trips from Falkirk in their comfortable fleet to such scenic destinations as the East Neuk of Fife, the Firth of Clyde resorts or the abbeys of the Border country.

At their peak, Alexanders were the largest bus company in Scotland and one of the largest in UK, but the march of time has taken away the "Bluebirds" and the blue service buses. However, the offshoot coachbuilding activities, which were transferred to a separate company in 1947, still thrive, at the time of writing, as part of Alexander Dennis.

Games

Most of the Diarists entries concerning sports, games or pastimes are about well- known examples that continue in popularity and are well documented elsewhere so these notes are about the less well- known games which appear in the entries – a shipboard and a "parlour game".

There is an obvious problem with traditional ball games on the deck of a ship [See Dad's entry for 29 IX 1931] so activities developed over many years of British seafaring where the ball was replaced by a puck or disc or a quoit. Of the former, there grew a wide variety based around the concept of striking a disc with a shaped cue towards a target and these

would seem to be what our Diarists are referring to in their mentions of "Deck Billiards" or "Deck Golf", games which might be loosely classed as "Shuffleboard". The age- old game of quoits is very suitable for a ship's deck as a rope ring is likely to stay where it pitches and not roll overboard. Using such a ring instead of a ball in a net game was an obvious development which gave rise to "Deck Tennis", probably the only game in which Dad reached the final of a competition [See 27 II 1930]. The game is played on a court roughly 40 to 50 feet (11 to 14 m) long and 15 to 20 feet (5 to 7 m) wide which may be played as either as singles or doubles [*as illustrated here in a Second World War shot from the IWM archives taken on board an RN aircraft carrier*]. The midcourt net is usually the height, or higher than that of a tennis net. The goal of the game is to serve by throwing the ring over the net into the court of the opponent who tries to catch it before it falls and throw it back immediately from the same position in which it was caught, with a point being scored when the server manages to land a quoit on the opponent's side of the court, the scoring system being either that of Lawn Tennis or Table Tennis.

The tradition of the Victorian "Parlour Game" was clearly alive and well in the Yule and Brown families and Mum records [3 XI 1936] playing a Word Game [she was good at them!] "Oh Dear" is a very simple children's round game where the first player will say, for example, "*I went to the shop to get me a carrot.*" The next player must quickly reply with a rhyming line beginning with "Oh Dear", in this example: "*Oh dear! They gave me a parrot*" would do. If the rhyming word is not acceptable to the other players - poor rhyme, made up word etc – or has been used before in the game, then that player is "out", and the next player has a try at rhyming. If the rhyme is good, it is that player's turn with the "I went to the shop ..." line. The game continues until a single winner remains. A clear strategy would be to use "orange" as a key word!

Lightships

Very simply - a lightship or lightvessel is a ship that acts as a lighthouse. They are used in waters that are too deep or otherwise unsuitable for lighthouse construction. The majority of English and Welsh lightvessels were maintained by Trinity House who painted them red, so they would be clearly visible in daylight and usually carried the station name in large white letters on the side of the hull with a system of balls and cones at the masthead for identification. The one pictured here by Alf van Beem [courtesy of Wikipedia Commons] will be very much like that which Dad noted on 1 II 1930.

The ships, not all of which could move under their own power, carried a crew whose principal task was the maintain the light and other warning devices but would also log passing ships and occasionally perform rescues. By the start of the 20th century, Trinity House lightvessels carried a crew of 11, of whom seven (a master and six ratings) would be on active duty at any one time. It was by no means an easy job and it would take 15 to 20 years of service to be promoted to master.

The majority of British lightvessels were decommissioned during the 1970s - 1980s and replaced with light floats or LANBY 's [Large Automatic Navigation BuoY] which cost about a tenth as much to maintain as a light vessel.

At the time of writing, eight light vessels remain in service in English and Welsh waters, all of which are unmanned and solar-powered. Some double as weather reporting stations, such as the Sandettie Light Vessel, north of Calais and at the east end of the Strait of Dover. Advances in underwater building technology made it possible to replace some vessels with automatic lighthouses. One such, on an accommodation platform on top of a single pillar arising from the sea bed, is the Royal Sovereign light whose distinctive T -shape on the horizon is often a focus of interest to tourists on the seafront at Eastbourne, East Sussex.

Bairds

The name "Bairds" crops up throughout this book and we are talking of a huge Scottish manufacturing firm - often described in the Victorian term as "ironmasters" - William Baird & Co., known – after the Scottish fashion - as "Bairds of Gartsherrie". Starting with coal and later ironstone mines in the 1820's, the company took its name from the eldest of eight brothers, though the driving force seems to have been James Baird [1802 -1876]. Innovative from the start, Bairds moved into the production of pig-iron at Gartsherrie [now part of Coatbridge] in the 1830's and became Scotland's major producer.

Units

An explanation of some of the units of Measurement which are mentioned throughout and may not be familiar to some readers.

Imperial measure	Metric Equivalent	Comment
Linear measure		
12inches = 1 foot	30.48 cms	1 inch ["] = 2.540 cms
3 feet= 1 yard	0.9144 metres	
22 yards=1 chain	20.17 metres	Chain of 100 links was a standard measuring & surveying tool thus making setting out a cricket pitch easy!
10 chains [220yards] = 1 furlong		Much used in Horse Racing
5.5 yards = 1 rod or pole or perch [Name varies throughout UK]		Standard width of building frontage = 16.5 feet
1760 yards or 8 furlongs =1 mile	1.609 kilometres	
Nautical		
6 feet = 1 fathom [A variable unit]		Depth of Scottish pit shafts was measured in fathoms
6080feet = Admiralty Nautical Mile	1852 metres	Current international definition
1 Nautical mile/hour = 1 knot	1.852 km/hr	Approximately 1.15 m.p.h.
Land or Square Measure		
10 square chains = 1 acre	Approx. 40% of 1 hectare	Area of a rectangle measuring 1 chain by 1 furlong. One quarter of an acre was known as a Rood
640 acres = 1 square mile	Approx. 259 ha.	
Currency		

The Diaries were written at a time when UK and Commonwealth & British Territories used the pounds, shillings and pence system with symbols £, s, d where 12d=1s and 20s=£1. Mum and Dad used the usual notation with the fore slash e.g. a sum of twelve pounds, ten shillings and sixpence is written £12/10/6. The penny was further subdivided into halves and quarters: halfpennies or ha'pence and farthings, much used in discount pricing. This gave rise to difficult calculations for such transactions as finding the cost of 5½ yards of material at 4s 11½d per yard [£1-7s-3¼d] so traders [perhaps Mrs. Solomons at Lunsar] carried a small pocket book called a "Ready Reckoner" and Accounts Departments had electromechanical calculators called comptometers.

  Coins in general circulation would be: "silver" – Half-crown [2s 6d], florin [2s], shilling, sixpence, threepence [rare]; "copper" – threepence [12-sided], penny, halfpenny, farthing [was legal tender until 1960]

SOURCES and FURTHER READING

So that I might bring the reader an authoritative voice on the background of the diarists and in explaining allusions in the entries, research for this book has covered many subject areas as both website and printed material was consulted. Where a source has been quoted directly or illustrative material reproduced, due permission and acknowledgment has been duly recorded elsewhere. The following is a list of those sources which I found helpful and which the reader may wish to consult if curiosity has been aroused. I have listed the edition used and its publisher but subsequent editions and reprints by other houses may exist. Please note that some titles listed are out of print, but copies remain in circulation and may be obtained second-hand.

PRINTED SOURCES

FAMILY HISTORY

Hanks P., Hodges F., Mills A.D. & Room A.; *The Oxford Names Companion*, OUP (2002)

Hennessey P.; *Having It So Good -Britain in the Fifties,* Penguin (2007)

Kynaston D.; *Austerity Britain 1946- 51*; Bloomsbury (2007)

Symes, Ruth A; *Tracing Your Ancestors through Letters and Personal Writings – a Guide for Family Historians;* Pen & Sword (2016)

SCOTLAND

Johnston J.B.; *Place-Names of Scotland;* Murray (1934 edition.)

Keay John & Keay Julia; *Collins Encyclopedia of Scotland*; Harper Collins (1994 edition)

Macleod I., Martin R. & Cairns P; *The Pocket Scots Dictionary*; Aberdeen Univ. (1988)

Magnusson M.; *Scotland -The Story of a Nation*; Harper Collins (2001 edition)

MINES and MINING

Hutton, Guthrie; *Lanarkshire's Mining Legacy*; Stenlake; (1997 – reprint 2012)

Hutton, Guthrie; *Mining from Kirkintilloch to Clackmannan & Stirling to Slamannan*; Stenlake (2000)

TRANSPORT

- On water

Banks, D.; *The Clyde Steamers*; The Albyn Press (1947)

Carter C.; *Cornish Shipwrecks – Vol 2: The North Coast;* David & Charles (1970)

Clark, A.; *Pleasures of the Firth – Two Hundred Years of the Clyde Steamers 1812 -2012*; Stenlake (2012)

Clark, A.; *Steamers to Arran*; Stenlake (2015)

Clark, A.; *Steamers to Rothesay and the Isle of Bute*; Stenlake (2015)

Cowden, J.E. & Duffy, J. O. C; *The Elder Dempster Fleet History 1852-1985*; Mallett & Bell (1986)

Deayton, A; *The Caledonian Steam Packet Company*; Amberley (2014)

Duckworth, C. & Langmuir G.; *West Highland Steamers*; Stephenson (3rd Edition 1967)

Hutton, Guthrie; *FORTH and CLYDE – The Comeback Canal;* Stenlake (1998)

Leach, Nicholas; *Cornwall's Lifeboat Heritage;* Twelveheads Press (2006 edition)

Paterson, Alan J.S.; *The Golden Years of the Clyde Steamers (1889-1914)*; David & Charles (1969)

Paterson, Alan J.S.; *The Victorian Summer of the Clyde Steamers (1864 -1888)*; David & Charles (1972)

Thomas, J.; *British Railways STEAMERS of the CLYDE*; Ian Allan (1948)

- On land

Brown, Stewart J; *Alexander's Buses;* Fleetline Books/Roadliner (1984)

Cormack I.L.; *Lanarkshire Tramways*; Scottish Tramway Museum Soc. (1970)

Engel, Matthew; *Eleven Minutes Late*; Macmillan (2009)

Ferguson N. & Stirling D.; *Caledonian in LMS Days*; Pendragon (2007)

Glen A. & Glen I. with Dunbar I.; *Caledonian Cavalcade*; Ian Allan Ltd. (1979)

Martin A.; *Belles & Whistles;* Profile Books (2014)

Nock O.S.; *Pocket Encyclopedia of British Locomotives*; Hamlyn (2018)

Nock O.S.; *Railways at the Zenith of Steam 1920-40*; Blandford Press (1970)

Stansfield, Gordon; *Stirlingshire & Clackmannanshire's Lost Railways;* Stenlake (2002)

Suggitt G.; *Lost Railways of Merseyside & Greater Manchester*; Countryside Books (2004)

Thomas J.; *Scottish Railway History in Pictures*; David & Charles (1967)

MILITARY HISTORY

Cooper S.; *After The Final Whistle*; The History Press; (2016 edn.)

Corrigan G.; *Mud, Blood and Poppycock*; Cassell (2004 edn.)

Corrigan G.; *Loos 1915 – The Unwanted Battle*; Spellmount (2006)

Hart, Peter.; *1918 A Very British Victory*, Weidenfeld & Nicholson (2008)

Lloyd N.; *Loos 1915*; Tempus (2006)

Royle T.; *The Flowers of the Forest*; Birlinn (2007 edn.)

SIERRA LEONE

Friends of the Sierra Leone Railway Museum; *The Mineral Railway of Sierra Leone;* published as Museum exhibition guide (2014)

Manson K. & Knight J. with Connolly S.; *Sierra Leone – the Bradt Travel Guide;* Bradt Travel Guides Ltd (3rd Edition 2018)

Sierra Leone Development Company Ltd.; *Iron Ore Mining in Sierra Leone*; Illustrated Company Brochure (1953)

REFERENCE WORKS and TEXT BOOKS

Davies, Daniel; *Problems in Land and Mine Surveying - Five Hundred and Fifty Questions and Answers (350 fully worked out;)* Charles Griffin & Co.; (2nd Edition 1921)

Forrest, S.N. *Mathematics for Technical Students -Junior Course*; Edward Arnold (1920)

Watts W W; *Geology for Beginners*. Macmillan (4th Edition 1926)

Whitelaw J. & Hearn, Col. Sir G.R.; *Surveying;* Crosby Lockwood (Eighth Edition 1929)

Sir William Arrol & Co. Ltd; *Bridges, Structural Steel Works and Mechanical Engineering Productions;* Published for private circulation 1909

ARCHIVED MATERIAL

Glasgow University Archives UGD164/4 Sierra Leone Development Co Ltd, 1927-1974

UNPUBLISHED SOURCES

Scott, Beverley; *Our Scott Family History.* Copies available on request.

Yule, Anne Copland; Scripts for Talks -*Sierra Leone; Robert Burns; The Middle Drawer*; plus sundry handwritten fragments.

Royal Technical College Glasgow: Examination Certificates for R S Yule. Now held in the Library, National Mining Museum Scotland, Lady Victoria Colliery, Newtongrange, Dalkeith EH22 4QN *[Best by Borders Railway: trains depart from Edinburgh Waverley every half hour. Alight at Newtongrange and use the direct pathway from the station to the museum.]*

INTERNET SOURCES

Any internet search on topics in this book will quickly reveal any number of sources, Wikipedia being the most obvious. Thus, no printed list can be exhaustive and those below are merely some of those the Author consulted when preparing this book. Note that websites can change over time. Those marked * are subscription sites.

FAMILY HISTORY

*Ancestry UK	www.ancestry.co.uk
*Find My Past	www.findmypast.co.uk
A Vision of Britain Through Time	www.visionofbritain.org.uk
*British Newspaper Archive	www.britishnewspaperarchive.co.uk
The National Archives	www.nationalarchives.gov.uk

SCOTLAND

*Scotland's People	www.scotlandspeople.gov.uk
Gazetteer for Scotland	www.scottish-places.info

MINES and MINING
The Scottish Mining Website   www.scottishmining.co.uk
National Mining Museum Scotland   www.nationalminingmuseum.com

TRANSPORT
Caledonian Railway Association   www.crassoc.org.uk
Scottish Built Ships   www.clydeships.co.uk
Scottish Tramway & Transport Soc   www.scottishtramwayandtransportsociety.co.uk
Transport Treasury   www.transporttreasury.com

MILITARY HISTORY
*Forces War Records   www.forces-war-records.co.uk

AUSTRALIA
Shire of Kojonup   www.kojonup.wa.gov.au
Shire of Katanning   www.katanning.wa.gov.au
National Archives of Australia   www.naa.gov.au
WA Genealogical Society   www.wags.org.au

SIERRA LEONE
www.sierra-leone.org   www.visitsierraleone.org/national-railway-museum

ACKNOWLEDGEMENTS

Whilst every effort has been made to establish the copyright holder of works quoted or reproduced in this book, the author apologises for any errors in attribution, omissions or oversights which will be corrected on written request.

The author would like to thank the following authors for permission to quote extracts or reproduce images from their work cited in the narrative and detailed under "Sources and Further Reading" as follows: Andrew Clark; Stephen Cooper; Matthew Engels; Nicholas Leach; Trevor Royle; Beverley Scott; Ruth A Symes.

Illustrative material which has been cited as "Family Collection" is the work of or was sourced from the private collections of the author and his family. Several images have been deemed to be in the Public Domain at the time of publishing, otherwise, the author would like to thank the following for permission to reprint the illustrations as credited:

Joan O'Halloran and the Kojonup Historical Society; Irene Ashby OBE and the Friends of Sierra Leone National Railway Museum; Glasgow University Archives; Falkirk Archives; EDLC Archives and Local Studies; Scottish Tramway & Transport Society; North Lanarkshire Heritage Centre; National Mining Museum Scotland Trust; Kezlan Images who hold the copyright for the W A C Smith Collection.

ENVOI

In affectionate memory of Mum and Dad

Lightning Source UK Ltd.
Milton Keynes UK
UKHW030626131222
413853UK00008B/292